BEETHOVEN'S ANVIL

BEETHOVEN'S ANVIL

Music in
Mind and Culture

WILLIAM L. BENZON

BASIC
BOOKS

A Member of the Perseus Books Group

Published by Basic Books,
A Member of the Perseus Books Group

Designed by Trish Wilkinson

Library of Congress Cataloging-in-Publication Data
Benzon, William.
    Beethoven's anvil : music in mind and culture / William L. Benzon.
        p.   cm.
    Includes bibliographical references and index.
    ISBN 0-465-01543-3
    1. Music—Psychological aspects. 2. Music—Social aspects.   I. Title.
ML3830.B35   2001
781'.11—dc21   2001037509

01 02 03 04 / 10 9 8 7 6 5 4 3 2 1

Dedicated to my fathers:

William Benzon
David Dysert
Richard Macksey
Chester Wickwire
David Hays

The Child is Father of the Man;
And I could wish my days to be
Bound each to each by natural piety.
        —William Wordsworth

CONTENTS

PREFACE:
SPECULATIVE ENGINEERING

I HAVE BEEN told that, one morning when I was very young, I listened to a certain record over and over, thereby driving a visiting uncle to distraction. While I do not remember this incident, I do remember the song itself. As I replay the tune in my inner ear the voice sounds like Burl Ives—it might even have been him, though I've never attempted to verify this—and the guitar sounds crisp.

The melody is simple and repetitive; the words are simple as well. I don't remember them all, and what I do remember doesn't feel quite like a connected sequence. Here they are, as I recall:

> *Fiddle-de-dee, Fiddle-de-dee*
> *The fly he married the bumblebee*
> *The fly said he, "Will you marry me*
> *And live with me, sweet bumblebee?"*
> *Fiddle-de-dee, Fiddle-de-dee*
> *The fly he married the bumblebee.*

That song fragment may well be my oldest memory—I've got a few ancient ones, none clearly placed in time, not with respect to one another, much less absolutely. This particular fragment is my mind's tether to history, my umbilical to the world.

That is the theme of this book: Music connects us to the world. Not so much the external world that was so problematic for Descartes and his spiritual descendants, but the social world—groups of two, five, twenty-five, five hundred, even billions of people—that comes into being through music. We sing and dance, therefore we are a community.

By any standard, such a theme is an ambitious one. In pursuit of it I discuss a wide variety of evidence and ideas—about music, the brain, emotion, ritual, motor behavior, cultural evolution, ecstasy, jazz, and more—in an attempt to put these into a uniform framework. It is thus perhaps inevitable that you will view this book as a synthesis, an attempt to show that the rope, the umbrella, and the log are but the tail, ears, and tusk of the elephant Music.

And yet, it is not that, not at all. For synthesis looks back over what we have learned and tells us what it means. While we have indeed learned a great deal, the story I tell is, in fact, as incomplete as it is ambitious. I have used empirical evidence wherever possible, but the evidence available scarcely covers the ground. There are gaping holes that I can only fill in with speculation.

For this reason, *Beethoven's Anvil* looks to the future, not to the past. It is a plan for intellectual journeys we have yet to take, not an account of voyages past. Even as you read what we have learned, it is only an indication of where we must go, and how we can go there. The synthesis I would like to offer cannot be written. It is better to read this book as the outline for conducting the research we need to get the evidence on which our successors can construct a more robust understanding.

This book is thus about building blocks. When I was a child I had an extensive pile of wooden building blocks: various sizes of squares and rectangles, with the rectangles in different length-to-width ratios, round rods that could serve as columns or as logs, triangles, arches, various relatively flat pieces, and so on. It was a miscellaneous collection, building blocks from various sets, but also odds and ends and scraps of wood my father gave me.

I loved building things with these blocks. I particularly remember building gasoline stations and oceangoing freighters. I surely must have built forts and castles, then rockets and spaceports. I certainly spent time building the tallest possible tower. In some cases the challenge was primarily imaginative: How do I make something like *this*?

In other cases the challenge was purely an engineering one: Just what is the *best* way to create that tall tower? No matter what I made, I used the same set of blocks.

Beethoven's Anvil is about the building blocks and design principles not so much of music but of the brains and societies that create that music. My argument is simply that these building blocks—mostly neural circuits and social structures—are necessary. I have no particular reason to believe that I've defined the complete set; in fact, I have some small reason to believe that the set is not yet complete, nor ever will be. The nervous system is plastic, taking the impress of its environment. As culture molds the human environment, so it molds the nervous system. Culture's possibilities may well be endless. Thus it seems quite possible that our descendants a century or two from now will have nervous systems that differ from ours in small but critical ways.

Thus I like to think of this book as an exercise in speculative engineering. Engineering is about design and construction: How does the nervous system design and construct music? The book is speculative because it must be. There is no other way to approach questions where our need and interest exceed our current evidence. The purpose of speculation is to clarify thought. If the speculation itself is clear and well-founded, it will achieve its end even if it is wrong, and many of my speculations must surely be wrong. If I then ask you to consider them, not knowing how to separate prescient speculations from mistaken ones, it is because I am confident that we have the means to sort these matters out empirically. My aim is to produce ideas that are interesting, significant, and clear enough to justify the hard work of investigation, both through empirical studies and through computer simulation.

The book's eleven chapters are organized in four parts. The first chapter is a section by itself and is a set of stories about musical experience: this is what I am trying to understand. I use the next three chapters to frame music as a means of coupling nervous systems together in precisely coordinated interaction. Here is where I lay out most of my basic building blocks, the conceptual equipment I use in the following two sections. Chapters 5, 6, and 7 focus on music in the brain, moving from emotion to rhythm and structure and finally to pleasure and ecstasy. The final four chapters look at music in culture, from its origins, as the means by which clever apes became proto-humans, through the interaction of European- and African-derived music in the United States during the twentieth century.

William L. Benzon

ACKNOWLEDGMENTS

IN WRITING THIS book I have incurred debts more various and convoluted than I know how to acknowledge. Walter Freeman has given generously of his time and energy in helping me understand neurodynamics. Valerius Geist has shared his insights into human origins and animal behavior, while Timothy Perper has been an invaluable guide through evolutionary biology. Charlie Keil offered advice on ethnomusicology and helped me sort through the origins of jazz, even as Jon Barlow contributed insight on both European classical and South Indian classical performance and theory. Albert Bregman gave advice on a tricky matter of acoustics and perception, while Manfred Clynes helped me understand his research on music. I thank Linnda Caporael, Arnie Cox, Richard Cureton, John Fentress, Ferdinand Knobloch, William McNeill, Jaak Panksepp, Aniruddh Patel, David Porush, Tom Rosen, and Lester Spence for their conversation and insight. In addition to their specific contributions, most of these thinkers read and commented on sections of the manuscript.

Norman Holland invited me to write, and then offered to publish, a paper that gave me an opportunity to think through my ideas about the self. Ramnad Raghavan generously invited me to watch him teach a class in *solkattu*.

Bill Doyle, Art Efron, Ellen Esrock, Al Flores, Richard Fritzson, Janet Hays, Bruce Jackson, Ade Knowles, Martha Mills, Howard Olah-Reiken, and David Porush gave me their friendship and support, as did the folks in the Classical, Jazz, MoBeef, and Kristen threads in *Salon*'s Table Talk.

MetaLogics, Inc. generously supported me in the early stages of this project, and for that I thank them. Through his catalytic energy and intellectual enthusiasm Howard Bloom created the milieu and relationships that made this book possible. Richard Curtis, my agent, supported me throughout this project and supplied perhaps the most important pair of words in the book. I thank my editor, William Frucht, for having the courage and imagination to undertake this book, and for his grace in helping me shape both the prose and the ideas. I couldn't have had a better editor. Michael Wilde wrangled the text with energy and aplomb while Kay Mariea calmly kept a steady hand on the tiller even as waves were washing over the deck.

Finally, I must acknowledge the men to whom I have dedicated *Beethoven's Anvil*. The late William Benzon is my father. Along with my mother, Elizabeth—to whom I once dedicated a high school paper—he gave me life and molded my mind and spirit. David Dysert taught me to play the trumpet; but he also taught me to make—and to love—music. Richard Macksey has guided my career ever since I studied under him at The Johns Hopkins University. Chester Wickwire, then Chaplain at Hopkins, set an example of courage and integrity that has remained with me for three decades. David Hays is the most original thinker with whom I have ever worked. I am honored to have been his student and colleague.

I

SOME VARIETIES OF MUSICAL EXPERIENCE

If a clod be washed away by the sea, Europe is the less, as well as if a promontory were, as well as if a manor of thy friend's or of thine own were: any man's death diminishes me, because I am involved in mankind, and therefore never send to know for whom the bell tolls; it tolls for thee.

—John Donne, *Devotions upon Emergent Occasions*, Number XVII

IF WE ARE going to undertake a study of music we need to begin with some sense of just what it is we are going to study. This chapter suggests the range of our subject by considering some stories about musical experiences. Those stories provide a context for questions, questions to be addressed in the rest of this book.

First, however, I would like to offer a new word and its definition: the verb *to music*, with *musicking* as its participle. The word was coined by Christopher Small, who defines it thus: "To music is to take part, in any capacity, in a musical performance, whether by performing, by listening, by rehearsing, or practicing, by providing material for performance (what is called composing), or by dancing."[1]

My use of this term should be transparent. I particularly like that it is a verb, allowing me to say, for example, "they musicked all night" in preference to "they made music all night" and that the term encompasses dance, an inclusion that will be particularly important when we consider the origins of music. For now, let us turn to our examples.

TEARS FOR JOHNNY

On May 21, 1992, Bette Midler was a guest on *The Tonight Show*. She had been on many times before; the show had, in fact, been important in launching her career, as it was for many performers. Yet this appearance was special: the penultimate show for Johnny Carson, the show's longtime host and star. He had decided to retire from television, and the shows that week in May were planned and publicized as a farewell to Johnny.

Carson, himself a skilled drummer, liked swing-era jazz and popular music. The band he maintained for *Tonight* was a fine swing band, better than television could accommodate. Midler was at home in that repertoire and was able to cajole Carson into singing a duet with her on a song she knew to be one of his favorites, Jimmy van Heusen's fine ballad "Here's That Rainy Day." Carson was certainly more proficient as a drummer than as a vocalist, but his difficulties in this performance were more emotional than technical. The strain on his face was that of a man holding back tears.

Then Midler sang "One for My Baby (And One for the Road)" by Johnny Mercer and Harold Arlen. Written for a 1943 Fred Astaire movie, it was covered in 1945 by Lena Horne. Frank Sinatra recorded it in 1959 on one of his finest albums, *Only the Lonely,* though it had been in his repertoire for several years. It was one of his beloved saloon songs, moody ballads testifying to the inevitability of deep personal loss. Framed as a 3 A.M. bar-closing solioquy, it was perfect for this occasion.

Now it was Midler's turn to veil her emotions. Her face glowed, eyes full open and brimming. Her voice too sounded of tears. As I watched and listened from Troy, New York, my throat was thick with tenderness, and perhaps I let out a sigh. Midler's music had reached me.

Millions were watching that show and many, perhaps almost all, were moved as I was—some more, some less, but all of us moved. How? How does music touch us so? What is it in the sound or the words that moves us? How does the performer's brain communicate with the heart, tongue, and ear? And why? Why do we transmute sorrow into the pleasure of song? Why does it feel so good to listen to sad music? Why do we sing at all?

Not all song affects us so. I've heard many songs without being so moved—I've even heard these two songs in other performances, good performances, but not ones that moved me to tears. What was special about these? Was there something in the sound that night not often present? I think the answer is yes, and will explain so at some length later in this book.

Yet there is no reason to think the answer lies *only* in the sound. Our experience is complex and so requires complex explanations. Any act or experience lies at the nexus of many causal threads, each one of which must be followed if we are to understand that experience. In this case I rather suspect that these particular performances were moving in part because both Carson and Midler themselves were moved. We could see them and thus more readily empathize with them. Yet in this world of recorded sound, we do not always see the performers. But we can still be moved.

Beyond that we must consider the nature of the occasion. It was the last week of Carson's career and thus the last time Midler could be his guest on *The Tonight Show*. The occasion was not ordinary for either of them; nor would it be for most of the viewing audience. Some had made Carson a part of their everyday lives. Others, like me, watched only occasionally. And undoubtedly a few viewers had never seen the program, or perhaps saw it only once a year or so, but tuned in for these final shows, which the network was promoting as an entertainment event much like the fabled final episode of *M*A*S*H*. Even those with no emotional investment in Carson and *The Tonight Show* could enter into the particular nature of this event and thereby make themselves more open to Midler's performance. The tears surely had as much to do with the occasion as with anything special in the sounds of the performance; they marked the departure of a beloved entertainer. Still, how was this sorrow transmuted into such pleasure without losing its sadness?

If we are to penetrate anywhere near to the heart of this mystery, we must realize just how strange and atypical this performance is in the range of human musical experience. All human cultures have music, but few have had musical performances such as these. For most of humankind's existence we have lived in relatively small bands where everyone knew everyone else. Only within the last ten thousand years or so have any of us lived in large-scale societies containing settlements so large that we had to interact with strangers on a daily basis. The formal performance is not the basic human experience of music, and recorded and televised music has been available only in the past century. Rather, our experience is of music among friends, or at least people whom we know and must deal with when the music is over.

When Bette Midler was singing to Johnny Carson, she was singing to someone she knew. Yet she didn't know most of the studio audience where *The Tonight Show* was performed, and while she certainly knew some in the broadcast audience, most were complete strangers to her and to one another as well. That we could all listen from our homes while negotiating the transit from waking to sleep is interesting, but is simply an elaboration of the basic situation of concertgoing—sharing music with strangers.

We will shortly consider these issues in more detail. For now, let us turn to another story.

RAHSAAN WORKS THE CROWD

Sadness and tenderness are certainly not the only emotions elicited by musical performance. Joy and exaltation demand our attention as well. Rahsaan Roland Kirk was the most reliably joyful performer I have ever seen. I first saw him at the Morgan State Jazz Festival in 1969. It was outdoors, and at night. Bright searchlights beamed onto the stage. As Rahsaan came out the light splintered from his black vinyl jumpsuit and from the complex textures created by the mantle of musical instruments he wore like liturgical vestments. He began by rapping to the audience as he walked onstage, "They can keep us off the radio, but they can't keep us outa the air!" He then took his band into the first number, "Volunteered Slavery," a raunchy blues proclaiming that "If you want to know what it is to be free/ you gotta spend all day in bed with me." Rahsaan did not have much of a singing voice, but he delivered the lyrics with force and vigor. He then took up his tenor sax and began to conjure a solo up out of the ground.

Rahsaan was a skilled and muscular saxophonist able to perform in a variety of styles from thirties swing to sixties freak-out. On this occasion he played straight-ahead all-out blues that achieved liftoff.[2] Rahsaan was playing a multiphonic riff on three horns at once, then simplified it to just the tenor sax, while his sidemen were riffing away. Rahsaan settled on one note and held it as the riffing grew louder. The drum figures became more complex, the piano more insistent, and, above all, Vernon Martin let loose a mighty thunder on the bass. As the swell crested Rahsaan began the concluding riff from the Beatles' tune "Hey Jude" on his tenor sax. The musical thickness cleared, Dick Griffen switched his trombone riff, and the audience let out a gasp. We rose to our feet, with some standing on their seats. People were clapping in time to the music and swaying back and forth together. Rahsaan had us and we were pleased to have him.

Who orchestrated this activity? The easy answer is, whoever organized the 1969 Morgan State Jazz Festival; but this isn't the question I'm asking. The true answer is that Rahsaan and his musicians orchestrated their performance. How did they do it? Part of the answer is traditional and banal: they practiced. Through careful rehearsal they've developed routines, signals, and an intuitive sense among themselves of how each shapes, moves, and reacts to musical flow. For all its rhetoric of spontaneity, jazz is a highly rehearsed music. The sequence of events in "Volunteered Slavery" might have been fully scripted before Rahsaan first played it with the group, though I doubt it. Or it may simply have happened that way in performance or rehearsal and worked so well that they made it their standard performance. The routine may reflect a self-organizing process typical of such musical collaboration. In either case, the performance rests on hours upon hours of rehearsal and practice by these musicians, individually and as a group.

Whatever happened among the musicians accounts for only part of the event orchestration, the part that happened onstage. Who organized the audience so that they knew when to gasp and rise to their feet? No one. That's the most interesting component of this orchestration.

Of course one follows certain conventions as a member of a concert audience. You sit in your seat; you don't talk during the performance; you applaud after a solo—this was a jazz concert, and applause after solos has been the convention for decades—and you applaud at the end of a number.

There are no conventions regarding gasping. As for clapping to the music and standing, there certainly were people in the audience for whom those were conventional responses, as is common in churches that favor enthusiastic song from the choir and parishioners. But this was not such a church; it was a jazz festival. Beyond that, no conventions govern standing on one's seat. That just happened in the enthusiasm of the moment. What is interesting, however, is that so many people got enthusiastic at the same time, a time that made musical sense. People rose to their feet and then to their chairs at a major shift in the music's energy—a behavior to be further discussed.

The distinguished historian William H. McNeill has recently argued in his book *Keeping Together in Time* that coordinated rhythmical activity is fundamental to life in society. By dancing together to music, by marching together in military drill, we bond with one another and become a group. In McNeill's view human society would not be possible without such activity. Music and dance are not mere luxuries consuming resources; they are every bit as fundamental as hunting or child rearing, for example, but fundamental in a different way.

MUSIC AND THE BODY

Leaving the performance as a whole for the moment, consider how musicians cross the threshold from an ordinary state of mind into performance mode. Roy Eldridge, swing trumpet star of the thirties and forties, made some remarks about what happened when he played his first solo of a show. He's talking about playing New York City's Paramount Theater with Gene Krupa's big band:

> When the stage stopped and we started to play, I'd fall to pieces. The first three or four bars of my first solo, I'd shake like a leaf, and you could hear it. Then this light would surround me, and it would seem as if there wasn't any band there, and I'd go right through and be all right. It was something I never understood.[3]

What do we make of this light that had nothing to do with stage lighting but was clearly created in the "inner eye" of Eldridge's brain? Is it a cousin to the light reported in near-death experiences? And what does he mean by going *through* the light—where does he get this sense of movement? It is as though Eldridge is moving from one mental space to another, with the transition marked by motor and visual symptoms.

Vladimir Horowitz, the classical pianist, tells a different story: "The moment that I feel that cutaway—the moment I am in uniform—it's like a horse before the races. You start to perspire. You feel already in you some electricity to do something."[4]

Horowitz, like Eldridge, is talking about a tangible physical state with definite sensations (electricity) and symptoms (perspiring). Something is going on in his brain and his blood to prepare him for performance. The fact that this transition is triggered by donning a "uniform" suggests that Horowitz has become conditioned to that uniform the way Pavlov's dogs were conditioned to bells and lights.

The jazz pianist Earl Hines also compares himself to a racehorse, but his horse is wearing blinders:

> I'm like a race horse. I've been taught by the old masters—put everything out of your mind except what you have to do. I've been through every sort of disturbance before I go on the stand, but I never get so upset that it makes the audience uneasy. . . . I always use the assistance

of the Man Upstairs before I go on. I ask for that and it gives me courage and strength and personality. It causes me to blank everything else out, and the mood comes right down on me no matter how I feel.[5]

Hines invokes a higher power in a manner reminiscent of the principal celebrants of a possession ritual calling on their divinity to descend and possess them. Is this higher power an inner animal in disguise?

We can glimpse the musical animal at full roar in Priscilla Presley's remarks on her husband's Las Vegas debut on July 31, 1969:

It was the energy, the energy that surrounded the stage, and the charisma that he [conveyed]—I don't think that I've ever felt that in any entertainer since. I mean, yes, other entertainers have a charisma, but Elvis exuded a maleness about him, a proudness that you only see in an animal. On the stage he'd have this look, you know prowling back and forth, pacing like a tiger, and you look and you say, "My God, is this the person that I—?" It was difficult to attach who he was to this person onstage. It was incredible.[6]

What Elvis undergoes is not a transition but a transformation. Hines and Horowitz thought of themselves as racehorses; Elvis is a tiger.

Perhaps this is mere metaphor, and fairly standard metaphor at that. We have animals within and the legacies we've inherited from the beasts of the fields include the hunt and the mating dance. Still, do musicians become different beings when they perform?

A bit of common wisdom among jazz listeners urges you not to go to the first or even second set of the evening, because the musicians won't really be "on" until later. Could this be because many musicians don't know how to make the transition described by Horowitz, Hines, and Eldridge, and executed so effectively by Presley? Or did they make the transition and just get better and better once they turned their "inner animals" on? Just how on were Horowitz, Hines, and Eldridge immediately after their transition? Did they get even better during the course of *their* performances? In any event, why should some musicians get better during a single performance? Why can't they be at their peak throughout? Why, for that matter, should some performances be better than others?

Consider the proceedings from the point of view of the audience. Here are some informal remarks the late David Hays made about performances by the New York City Ballet, an intimate aesthetic partner to music:

> At a typical performance of the City Ballet, a large part of the audience are naive. They are not familiar with the pieces being danced; many have never seen them before (the intake of breath that can be heard when the curtain rises on an effective stage set is evidence enough). They are not much expert in the art; the accounts that are published in newspapers and magazines are generally superficial, often in my judgment missing the essence of the work altogether. Audiences give ovations for performances that seem to me mediocre. Yet the difference in the crowd between entrance and exit is almost tangible. Watching the ballet [and listening to the music] has changed their mood in a favorable way.[7]

The performance as a whole moves the audience from one state of mind to another, more favorable, state. How do music and dance have such effects on people? How is it that something happening in the mind can so affect the body that people stand taller and walk more smoothly? These are the sorts of things we will consider when we examine the nature of musical pleasure and, correlatively, the nature of anxiety.

Thus the performers move from one state of mind to another when they perform, and members of the audience are transformed by the performance they witness. Nothing is mysterious about these phenomena, at least in the sense that they are common and familiar. But we don't know how they work, any more than we understand the more mysterious varieties of musical experience.

LEONARD BERNSTEIN BEYOND HIMSELF

Leonard Bernstein had one of the most diverse and spectacular musical careers in recent American history. As a conductor, composer, pianist, writer, and public intellectual he was beloved and hated; he was controversial; and always, he was impassioned. One of his great loves was teaching. He was well known for his efforts to bring classical music to children and made a series of highly acclaimed television programs about music. He also spent a great deal of time with students at Tanglewood, a retreat in the Berkshire mountains dedicated to training promising musicians and to presenting classical concerts. On one occasion Bernstein was talking to conducting students about how he had to learn to bring himself under control. As a young conductor he once got so wrapped up in conducting that he was afraid he was having a heart attack. So, he explained to the students, he had to learn how to restrain himself; he then spoke of ego loss:

> I don't know whether any of you have experienced that but it's what everyone in the world is always searching for. When it happens in conducting, it happens because you identify so completely with the composer, you've studied him so intently, that it's as though you've written the piece yourself. You completely forget who you are or where you are and you *write the piece right there*. You just make it up as though you never heard it before. Because you *become* that composer.
>
> I always know when such a thing has happened because it takes me so long to come back. It takes four or five minutes to know what city I'm in, who the orchestra is, who are the people making all that noise behind me, *who am I?* It's a very great experience and it doesn't happen often enough. Ideally it should happen every time, but it happens about as often in conducting as in any other department where you lose ego. Schopenhauer said that music was the only art in which this could happen and that art was the only area of life in which it could happen. Schopenhauer was wrong. It can happen in religious ecstasy or meditation. It can happen in orgasm when you are with someone you love.[8]

On another occasion Bernstein remarked:

Perhaps the fact of being myself a composer, who works very hard (and in various styles), gives me the advantageous opportunity to identify more closely with the Mozarts, Beethovens, Mahlers and Stravinskys of this world, so that I can at certain points (usually of intense solitary study) feel that I have *become* whoever is my alter ego that day or week. At least I can occasionally reach one or the other on our private "Hot Line," and with luck be given the solution to a problematic passage. Those are ecstatic times, those moments, and inform the entire *Gestalt* with new life. A new difficulty arises after giving such a "true" performance of what seems my own music, and then, suddenly, amidst applause and similar noises, having to become merely Leonard Bernstein again.[9]

What are we to make of these statements? I do not mean to cast doubt on them: I am willing to assume that Bernstein is reporting his experience as accurately as he can, and many people have reported similar experiences in various contexts. Yet the statements are a little strange. What does it mean to experience Mozart as though you were Mozart himself?

Consider a more tangible case. Imagine yourself in a room with several other people. In such a situation it is easy enough to imagine how that room would appear to someone else. In so doing you occupy or imaginatively recreate that person's current view of the physical world; in a limited way, you become them. What Bernstein seems to be saying is that, when preparing a score for performance, when actually performing the score, he comes to view that score as the composer did—he has an intentional attitude toward the score that is typical of someone writing the score, not of someone reading it. To project oneself imaginatively into another's shoes in physical space is easy, but how do you do that in an "intentional space" filled with musical scores?

One begins to wonder just what is a self, if Bernstein can lose track of his? The well-known phenomenon of sleepwalking shows that we can undertake fairly elaborate physical activities without conscious awareness or subsequent recollection. We have done something, our brain and body have executed a series of actions, but these actions are not accessible to our self, whatever that may be. Similarly, dreaming demonstrates that we can undertake elaborate, if chaotic, symbolic

activity without conscious intervention of this self, though we sometimes remember our dreams. The pathological phenomenon of multiple personalities shows that one brain can be home to multiple
selves. By continuing on in this way we might reach the conclusion
that what is so strange is not Bernstein's loss of self, but the very existence of such a thing. Whatever this self is, it is fragile and slips away
from attempts to define it.

This is only the beginning of the questions raised by Bernstein's accounts. One set of questions is cross-cultural: What states does the
musical mind take in other cultures? When Bernstein talks of "becoming" the composer he's conducting, that sounds like possession:
he becomes possessed by Mozart, Mahler, or Stravinsky. Spirit possession is certainly a feature of ritual practice in many cultures; a celebrant becomes possessed by the god or goddess and speaks with his or
her tongue. One would like to know whether the underlying neural
mechanisms are the same in the North American conductor and the
Yoruba priest. To the extent that they are the same, how is it that they
function in such different cultural contexts?

One can also wonder about self-loss and improvised music. Bernstein performed music written by others. What about the jazz musician who improvises a performance? In this case to talk of becoming
the composer doesn't make sense, for the performer is "composing"
the music that very moment; but the self can still be put aside. Thus
Ira Sullivan has said:

> I feel that I'm at my best when I can free myself completely from the
> effort of trying to put something out and feel more like I am the in-
> strument being played—like opening the channel to God, or whatever
> it is. I suddenly get the feeling that I'm standing next to myself, but
> I'm not thinking that this is me playing.[10]

Sullivan talks of standing next to himself, whereas Bernstein did not.
Did Bernstein just not talk about that aspect of the experience, or are
we dealing with different experiences? In any event, Sullivan is clearly
talking about a performance mode where his self is set aside. Like
Bernstein, he regards this performance mode as the best possible.

Whatever we're talking about here seems to have more to do with performance itself than with the difference between improvising and performing a score. Yet that difference too must be accounted for, as the processes of improvising and performing a score seem, at least superficially, to be very different activities.

Finally, one must point out that this ecstatic experience is not confined to an elite class of musical performers. Ordinary folks have them as well. Consider Karen, a thirty-seven-year-old businesswoman and mother with an interest in antiques, flea markets, and spiritualism. Here she is interviewed about her musical experiences:

> Q: Are there any times that you experience music in a particularly powerful way?
> A: The mood tapes. I've astral-projected with some of them, because of the visual effects it has played on my mind. I have gone with it, and I know I have. It's just like . . . like the mountain stream, or the backyard stream tapes. Nature. I don't visualize myself walking some place . . . I am there. I know I'm there.[11]

To be sure, the differences between Karen's experiences and those of Bernstein and Sullivan are important. Yet all betoken a radical alteration in a person's sense of self and where they are in the world at the musical moment.

Music allows us, for the duration, to radically reconceive and reconstruct our relationship with the world. If we are to understand how this is possible, we must consider how that relationship is constructed in the first place. Later on I will argue that the self at the center of this relationship is a construct largely driven by the demands of language, and that it is the linguistic nature of this self that allows it to be put aside by and for music.

KEATS, DIZZY, AND THE POPE

I too have been touched by similar experiences; this, above all, is why I find these various accounts to be credible. While not quite like Sullivan's or Bernstein's or Karen's, my experiences give me confidence that what they discuss is real. In so phrasing matters a distinction must be made between the experience itself and my judgment of its significance, which depends on broader knowledge. While my broader knowledge is based firmly in a Western scientific worldview, it also encompasses some of the aesthetic traditions that parallel and sometimes question that worldview.

I am not, of course, asking you to take my experiences at face value. Rather, I am asking you to judge the credibility of these various stories on the basis of your immediate experience and on your reading and conversations with family, friends, and acquaintances.

One touchstone experience took place during my senior year in high school, marching the left-guide position in my rank in the marching band. My responsibility was to help the right guide keep track of the other musicians in the rank, to see that they were in the proper position during maneuvers. During a street parade we were playing some march and had to execute a right turn. As we made the turn, I was watching the others in the rank and paid no attention to the music. When we finished the maneuver, I realized with some minor shock that I had been playing my part all the while. I was where I should have been in the music but obviously had not been consciously thinking about my playing. The music apparently played itself and my attention wasn't necessary.

This event, without being particularly dramatic or even delightful, is noteworthy simply because mind and body obviously continued to execute the music without any conscious intervention from "me." How could that have happened? I didn't know then, nor do I know now, but this one incident showed me that we can execute fairly complicated actions without attending to them—a skill we depend on when driving an automobile and conversing at the same time, for example.

The ecstasy Bernstein and Sullivan talk about is not simply a marching experience writ large, but there is a kinship. Later in my life, during my senior year in college, I had an experience that speaks to Bernstein's assertion that sometimes he feels as though he has recreated the work of the composer he is conducting. This incident did not involve music but rather the poetry of John Keats.[12] Late one night while working on a paper about Keats's poem "To—[Fanny Brawne]"

I was typing a sentence in which I asserted ". . . he died." As I typed *exactly* those words, vague ideas and feelings suddenly began to stir. I started leafing through my book of Keats's poetry and found one of his letters to Fanny Brawne. As I typed a passage from the letter into my manuscript I felt as though I were writing the letter myself. I then found my way to his "Ode on a Grecian Urn." My eyes locked onto the second stanza:

> *Heard melodies are sweet, but those unheard*
>   *Are sweeter; therefore, ye soft pipes, play on;*
> *Not to the sensual ear, but, more endear'd*
>   *Pipe to the spirit ditties of no tone:*
> *Fair youth, beneath the trees, thou canst not leave*
>   *Thy song, nor ever can those trees be bare;*
>   *Bold lover, never, never, canst thou kiss,*
> *Though winning near the goal—yet, do not grieve;*
>   *She cannot fade, though thou hast not thy bliss,*
>   *For ever wilt thou love, and she be fair!*

As I read those words my gaze seemed to be ahead of my comprehension and the comprehension seemed to flow from me into the text. While I read silently, I nonetheless read with rhythm. I felt an absolute and complete understanding of those words, as though I had written them myself, as though I had become, for a moment, John Keats.

"Becoming" John Keats for the seconds and minutes it takes to type a paragraph from a letter and a stanza from a poem is not, of course, the same thing as "becoming" Mahler for the hour or more it takes to conduct one of his symphonies, and even as my brain was enacting the role of Keats, I was also aware of who I was and what was happening to me. This experience is not the same as what Bernstein described, but it gives me confidence in his description. If *that* can happen to me while reading Keats, then surely *that other* can happen to a Leonard Bernstein at the top of his craft.

Let me offer one more touchstone experience. The late Dizzy Gillespie by his own admission didn't play his greatest but a few times in his life. In his autobiography, *To Be or Not To Bop*, Dizzy tells us:

Records you can listen to and tell the stature of a musician, but with many records, not one record. . . . Of course it's very seldom that you hear a guy who's best on records. But you can hear where his mind is going. Sometimes it gets on records and there's a masterpiece. I've never played my really best on records, and I've only played my best four or five times in my whole career. But I know records wasn't one of them—one of those times when everything was clicking.[13]

In the spring of 1972 I went to hear Dizzy Gillespie play a concert at Morgan State University in Baltimore. At the end of his solo in "Olinga" I had a definite sense that Dizzy was returning to himself, as though his "soul" had left his body during the solo and now was returning. While almost impossible to describe, my sense of this event is quite firm. Something in Dizzy's movement, as definite as it was subtle, betokened his return. Perhaps that concert was one of those four or five times "when everything was clicking."

About a decade after Dizzy's ecstasy I read an article on Pope John Paul II in the *New York Times Magazine* that began by describing a mass celebrated by the Pope and attended by President Sese Seko Mobutu of Zaire. After the Pope's final blessing, one of Mobutu's young aides turned, awestruck, to a senior official in his group and gasped, "I see him coming back into himself."[14] His phrase precisely describes how I had conceptualized what I saw in Dizzy Gillespie: it was the coming back, not the going out, that was remarkable.

Given these and other experiences, I am willing to believe the accounts given by Bernstein and Sullivan, and by many others as well. Musical ecstasy certainly is not just extreme joy or delight while making music; it is a separate experience—or perhaps a family of experiences—with a particular feel, a particular phenomenology. If we are to understand how music works in the mind and in society, then we must attend to the specifics of these and other experiences.

ROLL OVER DESCARTES

Such experiences, then, are at the heart of this book's exploration of music. This is not to say that I will neglect such traditional topics as rhythm, melody, harmony, and form. Rather, I will situate them within a discussion of music as lived and performed experience. Those traditional topics are important to the extent that they tell us something about what was happening between Carson and Midler as they sang "Here's That Rainy Day" to one another, about how Rahsaan's musicians negotiated the passage from the blues to the Beatles and how that, in turn, tipped the crowd into a new mode of response. The rhythm that interests us is that which allowed Bernstein to become Mozart, if only briefly and in his own mind. The melody that interests us is that which allowed Karen to find herself beside a mountain stream. The harmony that interests us is that which resonated between a Polish pope and a Zairean diplomatic aide.

To understand these examples, however, we must go back to basics. The types of experiences we have been examining are secondary in the modern Western intellectual tradition. To be sure, such experiences are discussed, but not with the passion, precision, and prestige granted to discussions of reason, of language and science, of justice and cognition. While this intellectual tradition has many roots, it is both conventional and convenient to think of it as beginning with the seventeenth-century French philosopher and mathematician René Descartes. Descartes's concern was with a lone individual trying to make sense of the world: Is it a dream or is it real?

On November 10, 1618, Descartes had dreams that he took as a divine sign to create a new system of scientific and mathematical thought. He thereupon set about working on physics and mathematics and, two decades later, began to publish his philosophy, which was concerned with the question of how we come to have valid knowledge of the world. Descartes is perhaps most widely known for the assertion on which he chose to ground his philosophical system. He was looking for an undoubtable truth, for to ground one's philosophy on doubtful assertions could only lead to folly. The assertion he settled on was, in the original French, *Je pense donc je suis*, which translates into Latin as *cogito ergo sum* and into English as "I think, therefore I am."[15]

Were I a philosopher and were this a philosophical treatise, I might well feel a similar obligation to start with an undoubtable truth. In that case I would probably choose to begin by asserting, "We sing and dance, therefore we are." I am not, however, a philosopher, nor is this book the exposition of a philosophical system. These speculations aspire to objective knowledge, not to first truth. But that statement captures the thrust of these speculations. What interests me is not how we come to know the world but how we cooperate with one another, how we are implicated in one another's lives. If we are to understand music, this must be our starting point.

In thus setting myself over against Descartes I join a long parade. In the early eighteenth century the Italian philosopher Giambattista Vico thought Descartes's views too heavily weighted by the needs of mathematics and the physical sciences and therefore not well suited to understanding human actions and history. He rejected Descartes's appeal to self-consciousness in favor of the notion that we can know only what we have made, expressed in the Latin phrase *verum factum*. As we did not make the natural world, Vico believed we cannot truly understand it. We have, however, made our own societies and history, and so these are the proper arenas for our understanding. To this end Vico worked out a theory of history laid out in his *Scienza nuova, The New Science*. His work found little favor in his time, but during the nineteenth century a number of thinkers read him with sympathy, including the French historian Jules Michelet. The Irish novelist James Joyce was the most important twentieth-century thinker to be influenced by Vico.[16]

However, Vico's critique was peripheral to the main currents of philosophical and scientific thought and so was ignored. In our own time the attack on Cartesian thinking has become vociferous. The most sustained assault comes from such postmodern theorists as Jacques Derrida and Michel Foucault, who reject the possibility of grounding knowledge in self-awareness. More immediately, we have Antonio Damasio's argument, in *Descartes' Error*, that the Cartesian split between mind and body is made untenable by modern neuroscience and that the separation of emotion from reason that follows from this split is mistaken. Reason is grounded in emotion and emotion is grounded in the body. Thus, Damasio argues, if we are to understand the brain, we must free our psychology of the Cartesian emphasis on reason.

In one way or another the postmoderns are obsessed with the possibilities and difficulties of interpersonal understanding. That is what is at the heart of the so-called science wars and the intellectual free-for-all that the study of literature has become. Since language, in the postmodern view, is but an arbitrary system of signs, we must inevitably misunderstand one another, systematically and relentlessly. If scientists cannot understand one another, then how can they do science? If blacks and whites cannot understand one another, then how can they do anything but fight? And if men and women can't understand one another, where did love go? In the words of Rodney King, can't we all get along? Not, it would seem, in a Cartesian world, one that starts with the isolated self in search of the external world.

It is not enough, however, simply to declare an end to the Cartesian regime. One must also provide a new starting point—something Damasio has begun with his emphasis on tying reason to emotion. Damasio has a neuroscience available to him that Descartes did not have. We will avail ourselves of it in the following pages.

Where Cartesians start with the lone individual, we think about two or more individuals interacting with one another. Where they are interested in reason and cognition, we think about emotion and expression. Where they are puzzled by perception, we are fascinated with action. Gather these themes together—a group of people acting together to express emotion—and we have Beethoven's anvil, the workshop in which human culture was first forged and which continues to sustain us as we evolve into the future. Musicking is the central activity in that workshop.

PART I

COLLECTIVE
DYNAMICS

II

MUSIC
AND COUPLING

I was pretty young when I realized that music involves more than playing an instrument, it's really about cohesiveness and sharing. All my life,
I've felt obliged to try and teach anyone who would listen. I've always
believed you don't truly know something yourself until you can take it
from your mind and put it in someone else's.

—Milt Hinton

THE THEME OF this chapter is simple: *Music is a medium through
which individual brains are coupled together in shared activity*. Obviously, music isn't the only such activity; dance, theater, and ritual also
come to mind. The notion of brains coupled together is, however,
odd. Normally we talk of people communicating or interacting,
knowing, of course, that this involves processes in their brains. But I
think there is much to be gained by thinking about this interaction as
a coupling *between* brains.

Let us begin with a concrete example of such coupling and then
work our way, by degrees, to a more abstract level of contemplation.

THE MAGIC OF THE BELL

This is a story about me and three other musicians. Led by Ade
Knowles, we were rehearsing a piece based on Ghanaian musical

principles. Each of us had a bell with two or three heads on it—the bells were of Ghanaian manufacture. Ade assigned three of us simple interlocking rhythms to play and then improvised over the interlocking parts. Once the music got going, melodies would emerge that no one was playing. The successive tones one heard as a melody came first from one bell, then another and another. No one person was playing that melody; it arose from cohesions in the shifting pattern of tones played by the ensemble. Depending on the patterns he played, Ade could direct the tonal stream perceived as the melody, but the tones he played weren't necessarily the melody tones. Rather, they served to direct the melodic cohesions from place to place.

Occasionally, something quite remarkable would happen. When we were really locked together in animated playing, we could hear relatively high-pitched tones that no one was playing. That is, while each bell had a pitch tendency (these bells were not precisely tuned), these particular high tones did not match the pitch tendency of any one bell. The tones were distinct, but not ones that any of us appeared to be playing.

These tones only appeared when we were in the state of relaxation conducive to intense playing—a groove, if you will—that I could certainly feel as a buzz in my body. Without the relaxation, no emergent tones and melodies. According to Ade, that's how it always is. The "magic" of the bell happens only when the musicians are in a groove. My friend Jon Barlow tells me that a similar phenomenon is familiar to people who gather together and chant long tones in unison. When the chanting is going well, and only then, the chanters hear distinct and relatively high-pitched tones that seem to be located near the room's ceiling.

I'm not certain how to explain these magic tones.[1] The literature on musical acoustics does talk of various types of subjective tones, but they are quite unlike the ones we heard.[2] If the bell tones are subjective, the same subjective mechanisms must have been operating in all four of us, for we each heard them. I suspect, however, that those tones were not subjective, and that they would register on a suitable recording.

I believe these tones resulted from an extra degree of precision brought about by shifting into a more animated mode of playing; in any case the phenomenon is irreducibly social. We each played our individual parts and we all heard everything. Those magic tones are only the most palpable token of the social nature of our music.

Ade, Druis, Fonda, and I created that music together. Some would say that we used the music to communicate with one another. I find that way of thinking very misleading, especially if communication is conceived in terms of what metaphor theorist Michael Reddy has called the *conduit metaphor*.[3] Reddy examines the language we use to talk about communicating with one another and concludes that we generally speak of thoughts or words as traveling through some imaginary conduit from one person to another. For example, when one person urges another to "Try to *get* your *thoughts across* better," that language is not unlike "Try to *get* the *sheep across* the bridge." The conduit metaphor in no way describes what Ade, Druis, Fonda, and I were doing when playing our respective bells. We weren't sending messages to one another, we were sharing in the creation of common sounds. We were coupled.

The purpose of this chapter and the next is to argue that coupled nervous systems in some sense function as a single system. If we insist on thinking of musical sounds as signals, we must think of them as signals *internal* to the social group—in this case, four musicians—rather than as signals passed *between* Cartesian individuals. If we also wish to insist on attending to the physical nature of this situation, then we can think of musical sounds as signals between brains, provided we do not think of those brains as implementing separate Cartesian individuals. Cartesian individuals do not make music.

COUPLING: INTERACTIONAL SYNCHRONY

For over three decades, William Condon and his colleagues have been studying the rhythmic structure of human speech communication.[4] They make films of people interacting and then do a frame-by-frame analysis of body motions and speech sounds. They have discovered two kinds of synchrony: self-synchrony and interactional synchrony. Self-synchrony is the relationship between a person's speech patterns and body movements: head, shoulders, arm and hand gestures, and so on. Interactional synchrony is the relationship between a listener's body and the speaker's voice.

That self-synchrony exists is not particularly surprising. After all, the same nervous system is doing both speaking and gesturing, and the cortical structures for speech and manipulation are close to one another. But Condon found a close synchrony between speakers and listeners as well. How do the *listener's* gestures become synchronized with the speaker's vocal patterns? To be sure, the synchrony isn't exact—the listener's body movements lag behind the speech patterns by forty-two milliseconds or less (roughly one frame of film at twenty-four frames per second), "like a car following a continuously rapidly curving road."[5] That is a small enough lag to make one entertain thoughts of mind reading.

It's not simply that gestures move to the same basic pulse as speech. That is easy enough to understand, at least superficially: the speaker needs only to detect the pulse's period and adopt it for herself—unconsciously, of course. Synchrony, both self- and interactional, involves more than this. Speech is hierarchical. Phonemes are organized into words, words into phrases, and phrases into statements (see figure 2.1).

In both self-synchrony and interactional synchrony this hierarchical structure is reflected in the synchronized movements. Larger gestures, perhaps of the whole arm, will track phrases while smaller gestures, such as finger movements, will track words or phonemes. Furthermore, infants exhibit near-adult competence at interactional synchrony within twenty minutes of birth. Since the human auditory system becomes active three or four months before birth, we may become entrained to speech patterns in utero.

Condon and others have also investigated interactional synchrony in children suffering from various pathologies, including dyslexia and autism. Here they find multiple entrainment. They have observed dyslexic children whose right side would entrain within the normal 42-millisecond period, while the left side would entrain with the same

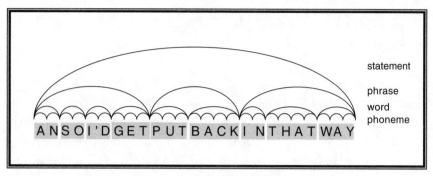

Figure 2.1   The hierarchical structure of speech and gesture.
SOURCE: Condon 1986, 60.

sound at a delay of 100 to 266 milliseconds. Autistic children were similar, except in their case the right side is delayed.

The ability to match one's movements to another's seems to be a condition of normal interaction with others. When this capacity is hampered, as it is in dyslexia and autism, communication is compromised. Synchrony creates a space of communicative interaction, a coupling between two brains in which each can affect the other's internal states.

Interactional synchrony is not conscious or deliberate—it is not something one thinks about; it just happens, at least for most of us. That interactional synchrony is working at birth implies that it is mediated by core brain structures that are phylogenetically old, for only these structures are operative at birth. The newest and largest brain structure, the cerebral cortex, is an uninsulated mass of nerves incapable of coherent processing at birth. Its fibers become insulated over the first several years of life.[6] That is to say, tightly synchronized interaction with others constitutes part of the *maturational environment for the cerebral cortex,* just as the sounds of adult speech penetrated the womb and thus became part of the maturational environment for those neural structures active at birth. Before we can see the external world and grasp objects, we hear sounds and are able to kick and wiggle in response.[7]

I first learned about Condon's work from the late David G. Hays, who thought Condon had made a key observation about the nature of human society.[8] Hays emphasized that, so far as we know, our closest primate relatives can neither synchronize with one another nor hold a steady beat. In his book on the origins of music, Leonard Williams observes:

> I have discussed the question of chimpanzee "dancing" with a number
> of circus trainers and they were all of the opinion that the chimpanzee
> has no real sense of time or rhythm. . . . Rudi Lenze insists that not
> one of the chimpanzees among the thirty animals he has trained, as an
> individual or in the group, has ever displayed a rhythmic ability that is
> remotely connected with keeping time to music (except by accident),
> or even to the strong beat of a drum.[9]

For all the time and effort that has been expended on the matter of apes and language, here we have a simple, largely overlooked behavior that humans exhibit easily and routinely from birth and that seems utterly beyond our primate relatives. This behavior, Hays believed, is what makes human society different from ape society.

This speculation is one of the fundamental ideas of this book. Accordingly, it deserves to be a named principle:

The Social Principle: human beings create a uniquely human social space when their nervous systems are coupled through interactional synchrony.

As a set of observations that is consistent with this principle, I offer Timothy Perper's work on human courtship behavior. After logging over two thousand hours observing human courtship in bars, church socials, and elsewhere, Perper concludes that courting behavior goes through a series of stages. Starting with the initial approach, courtship interaction moves from ordinary conversation to full-body synchronization where the couple are "looking at each other nearly continuously, touching each other regularly, talking face-to-face and moving in full-body synchrony with each other," which is generally as far as things go in public.[10]

Perper, though he knew of Condon's work, did not undertake the kind of video analysis that Condon did. In the absence of any evidence to the contrary, we must assume that couples were in fact conversationally synchronized from the beginning; that, in Condon's view, is simply how conversation goes. What Perper observed was an increase in the scope and complexity of synchronization as hands and arms and legs and ultimately the torsos of two individuals began to move in harmony.

Dance is an ideal medium for full-body synchronization and is routine in many courtships. But many cultures, including our own, have forms of dance in which whole groups of people move in synchrony. We are now in territory explored by the historian William H. McNeill in *Keeping Together in Time*, in which he coined the term *muscular bonding* to cover the large-group synchronized motor behavior typical of dance and military drill. "Moving together rhythmically for hours on end," McNeill argued,

> can be counted upon to strengthen emotional bonds among those who take part. . . . Far larger bands than any existing today among chimpanzees or other great apes could therefore come into being. . . . What we may think of as the human scale of primary community, comprising anything from several score to many hundreds of persons, thus emerged, thanks to the emotional solidarities aroused by keeping together in time.[11]

The combination of military drill and music yields marching bands, which are fixtures of many American communities.

Finally, neuroscientist Walter Freeman has argued that ritual music and dance trigger brain mechanisms that foster social bonding and so have been essential to creating the trust upon which all social interaction depends.[12]

COUPLING AND PARKINSON'S

It is worth considering here the therapeutic effects music sometimes has on people with Parkinson's disease. Parkinson's is caused by a deficiency of the neurotransmitter dopamine, and its various symptoms include unsteady, jerky movement or almost complete immobility. In his book *Awakenings* Oliver Sacks writes of music's effect on Miss D.:

> By far the best treatment of her crises was music, the effects of which were almost uncanny. One minute would see Miss D. compressed, clenched, and blocked, or jerking, ticcing, and jabbering—like a sort of human bomb; the next, with the sound of music from a wireless or a gramophone, the complete disappearance of all these obstructive-explosive phenomena and their replacement by a blissful ease and flow of movement as Miss D., suddenly freed of her automatisms, smilingly "conducted" the music, or rose and danced to it. It was necessary that the music be legato; staccato music . . . sometimes had a bizarre effect, causing Miss D. to jump and jerk with the beat—like a mechanical doll or marionette. [13]

Sacks reported that music had similar effects on all his Parkinson's patients. These effects would even happen when a person only imagined the music. One patient, a former music teacher, would be summoned out of immobility when a song spontaneously came to mind. When the song vanished, so did her mobility.

Another patient, also sensitive to music, had difficulty walking alone but could walk if someone walked with her. She explained that this was very like music. When walking with another, "I partake of other people, as I partake of the music. Whether it is others, in their own natural movement, or the movement of music itself, the feeling of movement, of living movement, is communicated to me. And not just movement, but existence itself." [14]

By unconsciously entraining herself to the movement of others, by coupling her nervous system to theirs, it was as though this woman could "borrow" the form of their movement to knit her otherwise conflicted and jumbled motor impulses into a coherent form. That music has the same effect gives us a clue to its power and elemental nature—a clue we will explore more explicitly when we examine the relationship between imitation and rhythm in the origins of music.

PHYLOGENY AND
THE NERVOUS SYSTEM

We now confront the nervous system directly. To do so we need to know some basic neuroanatomy. Fortunately most of my argument depends primarily on general properties of neural tissue and on the general pattern of organization rather than on detailed and exact patterns of connection and influence between tens or hundreds of neural centers.

Much of what we need to know can be summarized by Paul MacLean's well-known metaphor of the *triune* brain.[15] The idea is simple: the mammalian brain consists of a brain, within a brain, within a brain. Each such "brain" has sensory inputs from and motor outputs to the world, and each has some capacity for central integration. While MacLean's idea has been criticized because neither anatomy nor function are as clearly segregated as he implies, the concept remains useful because it reminds us that the human brain is heir to 500 million years of vertebrate evolution.[16]

The *reptilian* brain has structures like those of reptile brains and is the innermost of these structures, like the heart within the artichoke. (Technically, this likeness is homology: the structures in the human brain are developmentally the same as those in the reptile brain.) Wrapped around this reptilian brain is the *paleomammalian* brain— our inheritance from primitive mammals—while the *neomammalian* brain is at the surface. This terminology reflects the fact that brains are not remade anew over the long course of evolution; rather, older structures remain in place and active while newer structures are added on.[17]

What makes this aspect of neuroanatomy so interesting for us is that, as David Bowsher argued in 1973, the nervous system has evolved so that the more primitive structures can activate the newer structures, but not vice versa.[18] Newer structures do send impulses to the older ones, but those impulses seem largely inhibitory—they can turn the older ones off but cannot turn them on. The older structures, however, have a strong determining influence on the newer ones. This distinction will be important in our study of music, for music provides an indirect way for the phylogenetically newer structures to regulate the activity of the older structures.

The older, more central structures are necessarily concerned with the basic tasks of living—from regulating metabolism, physical growth, and repair, through the four Fs: feeding, fighting, fleeing, and sex. The newer, more peripheral structures support more sophisticated perception and analysis of sensory input and, concomitantly, more flexible motor control. Thus mammals in general have more sophisticated olfactory, auditory, and visual systems than reptiles, are more efficient at locomotion, and have more differentiated control over the facial muscles.[19] Primates, in turn, possess color and stereoptic vision and differentiated control of the digits, allowing for manipulation.

Most discussions of the neural underpinnings of behavioral differences between man and ape concentrate on these highly differentiated, phylogenetically recent structures. Crudely put, these are the structures that most differentiate us from them. While the critical importance of these newer structures is not in dispute, we cannot give them all of our attention. As I observed above, these structures are nonfunctional at birth, yet human infants are capable of interactional synchrony, a behavior apparently impossible in apes. If we are to explain that behavior, we must therefore consider ancient structures, because those are the only ones active at birth. First, however, we must consider the general flow of information between the nervous systems of two people engaged in closely coupled interaction.

ACTING IN TWO ENVIRONMENTS

Consider figure 2.2, which depicts the brain's functional relationship to its environment.

The point of this sketch is simple: the central nervous system (CNS), consisting of the brain and the spinal cord, functions in two domains external to it, the internal milieu and the external world. The CNS monitors the external world through various sensory systems and uses the skeletal muscles to move the body and thereby act in and

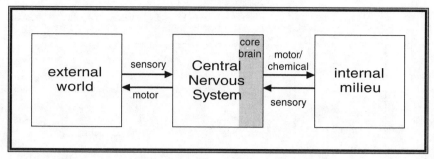

Figure 2.2   The central nervous system in two environments.

on that external domain. The CNS also monitors the body's internal milieu (including tracking concentration of various chemicals in the body) and affects that domain by controlling the endocrine and exocrine glands and the smooth muscles of the gut, blood vessels, and heart. The organism's survival, of course, depends on the integrity of its internal milieu, and as noted previously, the structures involved in regulating this environment are ancient.

We can express these functional relationships in the following principle:

Two Environments: the central nervous system operates in two environments, the external world and the internal milieu, and it regulates the relationship between the external world and the interior milieu *on behalf of* that milieu.

If we examine the evolution of the nervous system, we see that by far the greatest growth and elaboration has been in the structures and systems for observing and acting in the external world. The interior milieu of a human being is pretty much the same as that of a rat, but their capacities for perception and action are quite different. Consequently, most of the differences between a rat's brain and a human's have to do with externally directed activities.

Now consider figure 2.3, where we see that Ginger, a person whose nervous system we are examining, is contemplating some arbitrary person in the external world whom we call Fred. Ginger has some

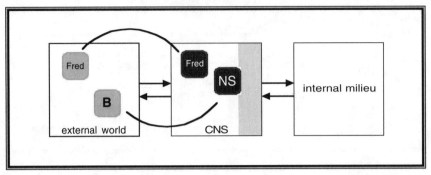

Figure 2.3   Ginger and Fred in the world.

neural representation of Fred in her CNS—notice the line indicating that relationship. (While the neural representation of other people will be complex, our immediate purposes do not require such complexity; a rounded square will suffice.)

Look at B, representing Ginger's body. What is her body doing in the external world on an even footing with Fred? The answer is quite straightforward. Imagine that you are looking at your leg. That leg is in the external world just as Fred is. You are examining that leg through your visual system just as you examine Fred. If you notice a cut on your leg, you examine it by touching it. When you put a bandage on your cut, you are using your motor system to act on your leg as though it were an external object just like Fred. You are your body, but the division of the nervous system directed toward the external world is quite capable of treating your body as an object on a footing with other objects. The neural self (NS) in the CNS is the neural representation of that body. [20]

The diagram's limitation is that it doesn't adequately depict the privileged relationship between oneself and one's nervous system. I have indicated one aspect of that privilege by nudging the neural self against the shading representing CNS structures regulating the internal milieu. There is more to it than that, of course. You can move your muscles but not someone else's. You can see only some parts of your body (unless you have a mirror) while all parts of other people's bodies are visible; and you can see through your eyes, hear through your ears, and so on, but not through the eyes and ears of others.

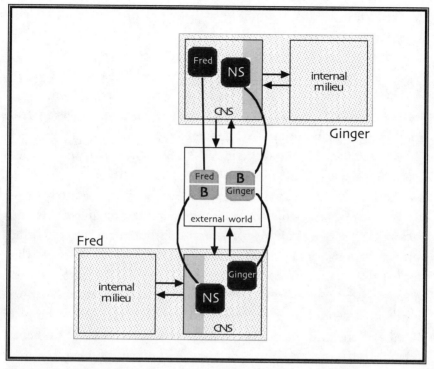

Figure 2.4   Ginger and Fred dancing together.

Thus the neural self is linked to the rest of the nervous system, and to the body, in a distinctly different way from representations of others. While this difference is important, it is irrelevant to the point made here, that in a certain way and to a certain extent, our bodies exist in the external environment of the nervous system and so can be perceived through the same externally directed sensory systems we use to perceive others.

This puts Fred's body and Ginger's body on the same footing, as it were, allowing them to serve as the coupling between their respective nervous systems. Imagine that Ginger and Fred are dancing together, perhaps as a prelude to the kind of mutual grooming so beloved of chimpanzees. Each has his and her own body, CNS, and interior milieu, and each has the appropriate representations of both bodies. For this reason, the two objects in the external world are labeled to reflect how they are regarded by the two people. Thus the Ginger object in the external world (at the middle of the diagram) is simply body (B) to Ginger and is represented within Ginger's CNS by the neural self (NS). From Fred's point of view, however, Ginger is a completely independent person and so appears as Ginger and is represented within Fred's CNS as such. And so it goes with the Fred object as well.

As the dance proceeds, Fred sees his hands encircle Ginger's waist, out there—though not far—at the same place in the world where her waist is moving. His kinesthetic sense notes the movements of his hands and fingers, while his haptic sense picks up the texture of Ginger's gown. He regulates his actions through the intricate interplay of his body and hers, while she reciprocates, albeit in high heels and backward. The object of this particular reciprocal interplay is to bring about a consonance between his interior milieu and hers—could this be courtship? This activity would be impossible if one's CNS did not, to some extent, represent one's own body in the same terms as those of others. To interact in a common space, that space must be perceived and one must be perceived in it on the same footing as others.

Fred and Ginger's dance, of course, follows the rhythms and phrases of some piece of music. Music structures the mental and cultural space wherein Fred and Ginger weave their dance, and marks the rhythms of their coupling.

THE CONTROL OF BEHAVIOR: FROM THE RETICULAR FORMATION TO THE LIMBIC SYSTEM

Where do we find the neural structures responsible for interactional synchrony? In the case of Fred and Ginger, we most likely find them throughout the brain. For the moment, however, let's return to Condon's work with infants and ask just how they synchronize with speaking adults.

As far as I know, this has not actually been determined, but we can make a reasonable guess. While speech itself requires structures that are widely distributed in the brain, the infant isn't speaking. She's just moving her body in synchrony with the rhythm of mother's speech.

The fact that infants can synchronize rules out the cortex as the source of the rhythm, for the cortex is not mature at birth. We are thus left with subcortical structures, and of those the oldest, those of the *reticular formation* (RF) deep in the brain's core, is the likeliest source of rhythm in newborns, for several reasons.

In the first place the reticular formation is known to be involved in maintaining muscle tone and generating pulses for rhythmic activities such as walking and breathing. But that is not enough. Whatever structures are involved also need access to auditory input. The reticular formation has such access. In fact, it receives input from all sense modalities and from the viscera as well. The RF is thus positioned to receive rhythmic input through hearing and to send rhythmic output to the muscles.

While classical descriptions of the RF have focused on its role in mediating sleep and arousal, more recent discussions have argued for a broader role. Thus Vanderwolf and Robinson have argued that the RF plays a general role in the control of adaptive behavior through its ability to influence the cortex. More recently, Damasio has argued that the RF and closely associated structures play a critical role in "managing body states and representing current body states. Those activities are not incidental to the brain stem's well-established activation role: *they may be the reason why such an activation role has been maintained evolutionarily and why it is primarily operated from that region.*"[21]

These views are reminiscent of a very elegant model proposed by William Kilmer and Warren McCulloch in the late 1960s. Noting that "no animal can, for instance, fight, go to sleep, run away, and make love all at once," Kilmer and McCulloch went on to list fifteen "mutually incompatible modes of vertebrate behavior." Their exact number and identity is not important. What is important is that, at all times, an animal must be in one and only one of these modes. Kilmer and McCulloch hypothesized that it was the RF that determined which mode the animal was committed to at any moment. Given that the RF has extensive afferent (incoming) connections from the rest of the brain and also has extensive efferent (outgoing) connections to the rest of the brain, it is in a position to determine the current modal requirements and effect commitment to a mode. Perhaps establishing interactional synchrony is the RF's way of establishing a mode for interpersonal communication and interaction.

While, in the Kilmer-McCulloch model, the RF commits a vertebrate to a general mode of behavior, it does not determine just what the animal will do while in that mode. That requires more specific awareness of the external situation and of the animal's capabilities than the RF has. In Walter Freeman's view, this is a job for a set of structures collectively known as the limbic system. The structures making up the limbic system are located in the reptilian and old mammalian parts of the brain. The limbic system does not include the neocortex, the mass of tissue that has mushroomed and covered the brain.[22]

The various structures of the limbic system integrate information from all sensory modalities, both visceral and somatic, and generate motor output. The limbic system is known to be heavily involved in emotion and the regulation of social interaction. It also plays a central role in generating signals that prime the sensory systems, "making it easier to capture expected or desired stimuli."[23] We are always anticipating the immediate future, and a mismatch between what we anticipate and what actually appears requires close scrutiny. It could be an unanticipated treat, it could be a threat, or it could just be something different but of no particular consequence. This expectation game is an important aspect of our emotional response to the world; it is also an important aspect of our response to music.[24] Thus we would expect limbic structures to play an important role in our musical experience, a matter on which (as I will discuss in chapter 5) we are now getting direct evidence from brain imaging studies.

Behavioral control is thus organized at two levels: a lower level that determines the general sphere of activity, and a higher level that determines just what is done within that sphere. Both control systems have broad networks of connections with the full range of sensory and motor systems, and they are intimately involved with our emotions.

Yet something is very peculiar about our emotional circuitry. It is both inside and outside the brain, public as well as private. This is the psychic "space" in which music is made.

EMOTION INSIDE OUT

In his 1996 article "Emotion: An Evolutionary By-Product of the Neural Regulation of the Autonomic Nervous Systems," Stephen Porges has argued that there are three phylogenetic stages of neural regulation of the organism's inner state.[25] Porges is particularly interested in the regulation of heart rate, since that is a major factor in the body's capacity to expend energy. The most primitive stage of regulation is common to all vertebrates and is found in the structures of the parasympathetic nervous system. This system acts to lower the metabolic rate and to conserve oxygen resources, such as might be necessary in diving or in feigning death (a common protective strategy among primitive animals). More advanced vertebrates develop a sympathetic system, which is capable of mobilizing visceral activity for high-energy fight or flight responses. This system is particularly important for land-dwelling animals since they must support their entire body weight during locomotion and so expend more energy than water dwellers.

The third stage emerges only in mammals, which have more varied and flexible facial muscles and a nervous system to control those muscles.[26] This, Porges says, allows our social behavior to follow "a strategy that focuses initially on communication via facial expression and vocalizations. This strategy has low metabolic demand and, if appropriately interpreted, results in contingent social interactions via verbal-facial mechanisms." In other words, heart rate, and the various bodily states associated with it, are in mammals socially controlled—to some extent—through facial expression.

While music certainly does affect heart and respiration rates—even third-trimester fetuses show changes in heart rate in response to music—it also has more specific effects, more like facial expression. We will postpone that particular discussion until chapter 5 and here focus on the interesting role of facial expression in the ecology of interacting brains.

The modern study of this subject goes back to Charles Darwin's *The Expression of the Emotions in Man and Animals;* Paul Ekman and Carroll Izard have been its most vigorous contemporary students.[27]

They have argued that feedback from one's own facial expression is an important influence on one's emotional state. If you feel yourself smiling, for instance, you actually feel happier. This feedback seems to provide a means by which cortical brain centers can find out what the lower centers have been signaling through the motor system.

Figure 2.5 shows a sketch of this relationship.

At the left the skeletal muscles are shown as a box at the very surface of the body to make the point that these are visible from the external world, while the inner milieu, of course, is not. A variety of subcortical centers are involved in monitoring and acting in the interior milieu. These centers connect to the cortex via channels that are *internal* to the CNS, but they also have connections that are *external* to the CNS. When these systems modulate the skeletal muscles, especially the facial muscles, in an emotionally expressive way, cortical centers concerned with the state of the body are able to sense the state of the muscles and thus identify the expressive "message" that subcortical structures are signaling to the external world.

Since those same facial expressions are visible to other people, the face is a *tertium quid* between the inner milieu and the public space of the external world. The body in effect faces in two directions: toward the neocortical brain centers that sense facial expression, and toward the external world. This gives us another principle:

Facing Principle: as a vehicle for expressing emotion, the body presents the inner experience of individuals *both* to the external world and to higher brain centers.

The Facing Principle is, of course, closely related to the Two Environments principle. The body constitutes one of those environments (the interior milieu) and it exists in the other environment as both an object of perception and a vehicle for action.

The peculiar position of the body in the ecology of mind figures in another line of thought about emotion that goes back to William James and Carl Lange. This theory concerns the relation between body state and some emotion-inducing fact or situation. In James's formulation,

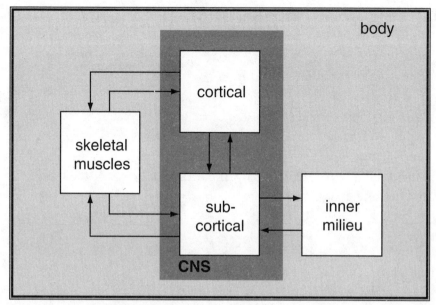

Figure 2.5   Emotional expression.

"bodily changes follow directly the perception of the exciting fact, and . . . our feeling of the same changes as they occur IS *the emotion."*[28]

These strands of thinking come together in Antonio Damasio's 1994 book *Descartes' Error*. Damasio's theory of emotion includes assessment of the body state through direct sensing of the internal milieu and through somesthetic and kinesthetic sensing of one's muscles and joints. This dual mode of sensing couples individuals together even as it also links subcortical and cortical systems within individuals. This is the arena where music and dance forge a group of individuals into a community sharing a common culture—a culture that is, first of all, a means of sharing and coordinating emotions. Let us return to Condon.

Condon, as we have seen, found that children with a variety of pathologies did not exhibit normal interactional synchrony: they could not manage the precise mutual timing of gestures that most of us manage unconsciously. Autism is one of these pathologies. Autistics are very poor in social interaction; they do not seem to recognize other people as living beings with intentions, feelings, and thoughts.

One investigator, Simon Baron-Cohen, described them as "mind-blind" in that they do not pick up, interpret, and respond to the cues—especially the direction of one's gaze—by which we signal our interests and intentions.[29] Autistics seem incapable of establishing an interpersonal coupling.

I would like to suggest that the capacity for interactional synchrony is the most basic form of interactional coupling and that without it, many if not most cues about the inner state of others are invisible. Musicking, by its use of neural structures at all levels in the brain, facilitates interactional coupling.

WALLIN'S HYPOTHESIS

Given this background we are now ready to consider an idea proposed by Nils Wallin. He opens his book *Biomusicology* by asserting that there is a "morphodynamic isomorphism between the tonal flow of music and its neurophysiological substrates."[30] The crucial idea lies in the forbidding words "morphodynamic isomorphism." The sound pattern of a musical performance has a form; pitches follow one another in a certain pattern, they are higher or lower, softer or louder, and so forth as the piece unfolds. That pattern of change is the morphodynamics of the music. We can also speak of the morphodynamics of what happens in the nervous system of either a performer playing music or someone listening to it. Wallin is saying that these two patterns, one realized in sound, the other in the electrochemical processes of the human nervous system, have the same form: musical flow equals neural flow.

Unfortunately, Wallin's mathematical language implies more precision than the current state of our understanding can deliver. Yet a study by Aniruddh D. Patel and Evan Balaban, entitled "Temporal Patterns of Human Cortical Activity Reflect Tone Sequence Structure," tracked neuromagnetic activity in the cortex using 148 sensors distributed over the scalp. Patel and Balaban found that "temporal patterns of activity recorded over particular brain regions track the pitch contour of tone sequences, with the accuracy of tracking increasing as tone sequences become more predictable in structure."[31] That is, brain neurodynamics tracks musiclike sequences more accurately than nonmusiclike sequences. Further, coordination between widely spread sites was highest for tone sequences that were musiclike.

Gratifying as it is, this result is hardly enough to validate Wallin's hypothesis. We need more such work using real music.[32] That neurodynamics does a poor job of tracking random tone sequences, however, indicates that brain neurodynamics does not automatically follow any arbitrary sound but only sound with certain properties.

Wallin's idea implies that when two people are making music together, and really listening to what each is doing, they are sharing in the same pattern of neural activity. If a third is listening to them, then three folks are partaking of the same pattern. If the whole village is listening and dancing, then the whole village is enacting a single pattern of musical activity, even though they are physically distinct individuals with distinct nervous systems. What makes this sonic communion possible is that all these physically distinct nervous systems are cut from the same mold, and all are attuned to the same pattern of sound.

Obviously the motor system and auditory system are adapted to one another. The motor system is good at producing sounds and gestures that the ears can perceive, and they in turn are good at perceiving the sonic effects of motor action. While these systems are quite different, they both operate in time, and so sound can function as a *tertium quid* between them. We would expect motor dynamics and auditory dynamics to exhibit the same patterns.

It is not entirely up to the genes to bring about this fortunate result, though the innate capacity to move one's body in synchrony with another's voice is obviously a critical starting point. Beyond this we know, for example, that neonates can readily discriminate a wide range of vocal sounds. By six months or so this range has begun to narrow down to the range of sounds characteristic of the language the infant hears spoken. The infant discriminates among these sounds very well but will ignore distinctions among sounds that are not used in what will become the infant's native language. A Japanese newborn, for instance, can discriminate between *r* and *l,* but typically loses this ability in a few months. Similarly, infant babbling starts with a wide range of sounds, then narrows down to just those sounds the infant needs to speak her native language. Thus infants "tune" their vocal and auditory systems to their linguistic environment.[33]

The sounds that mediate this tuning exist, of course, in the public arena. Rhythmic sound thus functions as a medium through which the intentional structures of different brains become coupled together. The fidelity of this coupling depends both on the capacity of the transmitting medium—air—to maintain the structure of the musical waveform and on the capacity of the coupled nervous systems.

Wallin's notion, however, is not adequate, for it implies that one need only listen to music, any music whatever, and one's neural dynamics will automatically become entrained to the musical dynamics. This is not true. While music certainly travels across cultures more easily than language does, it remains culture-specific. Sounds that are music in one culture may be noise in another and, as such, incapable of mediating secure coupling. In polycultural societies, such as the United States or India, different subgroups may differentiate themselves through their music—an issue we will examine in the last chapter.

Thus I propose a weaker version of Wallin's hypothesis:

Wallin's Hypothesis: for individuals sharing a common musical culture, there is a strong and systematic similarity between the tonal flow of music and its neurophysiological substrates that allows a tight coupling between the brains of those individuals. While participating in the music those individuals constitute a community of sympathy.

This formulation allows for differences between cultures and within a given musical culture. Some people will prefer one culturally accepted repertoire over another.

OF MEMES AND MUSIC

Imagine that every community has some process or set of processes (let's not worry about their exact nature) that proposes arrangements of sound for use as music. The acceptance of any one proposal depends on whether or not various groups within the community as a whole use the arrangement to mediate their synchronized interaction. A song, for example (an arrangement of sound), won't enter the repertoire unless lots of people sing and dance to it. Or a riff (an arrangement of sound) won't become part of jazz practice unless lots of musicians (performing alone or in groups) use it. One can find multiple examples.

If we adopt a term proposed by Richard Dawkins in *The Selfish Gene*, we are now talking about cultural evolution on a Darwinian model: the term is *meme*, by which Dawkins means the cultural equivalent of the biological *gene*.[34] The aforementioned arrangements of sound are memes, while the community is the environment of evolutionary adaptiveness in which those memes either survive or die out.

Memes physically exist in that communal emotional expressive space that is both internal and external to individuals. A meme's ability to survive depends on whether or not it meets the emotional and expressive needs of the individuals in some group. Thus we have another hypothesis:

Memetic Survival: a meme will survive only if it meets the coupling needs of groups in some community.

Thus stated, the hypothesis is completely general and not confined to music. Dawkins clearly had such generality in mind when he first wrote about memes, and those who study cultural evolution are certainly focused on the general case. At the moment, however, I am interested only in the cultural evolution of music.[35]

This leads to one final idea, which will be explored in chapter 8: a bunch of clever apes became protohumans when they "discovered" the social process of musicking. In this process the human body *as a whole* becomes a vehicle for interpersonal coupling. In ordinary mode the human body is just a primate body, something to move the mouth to a place where the hands can shovel food in, and so on. In this mode, of course, we have the expressive moves and gestures discussed earlier; but these are just specialized functions of this or that part of the body—facial expression, posture. In musicking mode the body operates as a whole to couple individual nervous systems into a synchronous social group.

This formulation leads us to expect that much if not all of music's neural substrate will be found in structures that evolved to serve other behaviors. In a recent review of the neural literature on music and the nervous system, Harvard's Jude Tramo asserts, "There is no 'music center' in the brain, no grossly identifiable brain structure that works solely during music cognition. All of the structures that participate in the processing of music contribute to other forms of cognition as well."[36] While Tramo does allow the possibility of musically "unique connections," the thrust is clear: brains make music by using old structures and systems in a new way. When our clever apes began to dance, they did not need new neural structures. They had only to discover a new, collective way of using the structures they already had.

III

FIREFLIES:
DYNAMICS AND
BRAIN STATES

Physicists and philosophers won't know anything
until they learn to dance.

——Friedrich Nietzsche

PHYSICISTS DO UNDERSTAND one element of dance—simple
repetitive rhythm. This understanding has been applied to many biological systems,[1] including that of male fireflies in Southeast Asia.
These fireflies gather in large groups on riverbanks, flashing on and
off in unison to signal their availability to females. When they begin
gathering around sunset, their flashings are uncoordinated. But as
dusk darkens into night, regions of synchronized flashing emerge and
spread until whole trees are cloaked in fireflies flashing in synchrony.[2]

There is no reason to believe that this activity is directed in the
way that a conductor directs an orchestra. No lead firefly sets the
pace of the others. The flashing simply emerges; it is self-organized.
Each firefly flashes on his own, influenced by the activities of his
neighbors. This activity has been analyzed as a system of coupled oscillators, a phenomenon first noticed by the seventeenth-century
Dutch physicist Christian Huygens, who invented the pendulum

clock—the pendulum being a prime example of an oscillator. One day Huygens saw that the pendulums of two clocks on the same wall were swinging in perfect synchrony. He disturbed one of them so that the synchrony dissolved, but it returned within half an hour. After a bit of experimentation he concluded that the clocks were affected by the vibrations each transmitted to the wall behind them. These vibrations led them to synchronize their periods and thereby minimize their collective energy expenditure.

Any phenomenon common to systems as different as pendulum clocks and fireflies must be very general. No one to my knowledge has attempted to model human interactional synchrony in this way, but it is a plausible first guess that such synchrony involves coupled oscillation between two individuals. This notion has, however, been used in the analysis of simple motor behaviors, so that is where we go next.[3]

COUPLING AND
EQUIVALENCE: FINGERS, YOURS AND MINE

During the early 1980s Scott Kelso began to study the dynamics of motor behavior. His experimental setup was quite simple. Subjects were asked to move their index fingers horizontally back and forth in time with a metronome. Each finger thus functioned as an oscillator. They were asked to do this in two ways: moving both fingers in the same direction (in phase), and moving them in opposite directions (antiphase). For some unknown reason, these are the only two stable patterns. The coupling function that links the two motions cannot, for example, have one finger a quarter or a third of a cycle behind the other. They move *together* or in *opposition*, but nowhere in between.

Kelso's metronome started out beating 1.25 cycles per second and the tempo was gradually increased. When it became sufficiently rapid, those who were moving their fingers in opposite directions spontaneously switched to moving them in the same direction. Yet subjects who started by moving their fingers in phase never made the reverse switch. Thus at a higher tempo the coupling has only one mode: move the fingers in the same direction.

Kelso offers no explanation as to just why things are this way: these are simply the observed characteristics of the system. What is interesting, though, is that a rather different human system displays the same dynamic characteristics.

R. C. Schmidt has given two people the task of coordinating the swinging motions of a leg while sitting within sight of one another. As the tempo of the metronome increased, there came a point when pairs who had started moving their legs in opposite directions spontaneously began moving their legs in the same direction. Again, however, the opposite transition did not occur. Thus each system only allows parallel motion or opposite motion, and each has two different dynamic regimes depending on the tempo: a low-tempo regime where coordination can be either in phase or antiphase, and an up-tempo regime where coordination must be in phase.[4]

That this should be the case may seem obvious or even trivial. Isn't this kind of thing ubiquitous in music? Consider, for example, someone playing Franz Liszt's piano reduction of Beethoven's *Fifth Symphony.* Here we have one person playing music that was written for a whole orchestra. To be sure, many players in the orchestra play the same part (e.g., the violas), and the piano reduction does not capture everything in Beethoven's score; but the principle holds true. Music that was written to be performed through the synchronized actions of several independent musicians can also be performed by a single musician. Similarly, one can hear Bach's *The Art of Fugue* performed by a lone keyboardist or by various ensembles—Bach never specified the instrumentation in the score.

Or consider African and Afro-Cuban polyrhythmic percussion playing such as the bell music described in chapter 2. In such music the tonal streams one hears as single musical lines are often composed of sounds created by different musicians. Yet a modern jazz drummer such as Elvin Jones can play a different rhythm with each limb and thereby create the illusion of several different percussionists playing simultaneously. Here too several oscillators in one musician can produce the same music as oscillators distributed over several musicians.

That one or more players commonly create similar sounds in music, however, should hardly be seen as trivial. Indeed, it is precisely because many forms of music can readily be played by one or many that music is so fundamental to human society. You might say that music is the "zero" case of human interaction, where every actor knows everything and can, in theory, play every role.

Why autonomous individuals, coupled together in rhythmic interaction, should display the same dynamics as two hands of a single individual is not obvious. After all, the two hands are directed by the same nervous system, while autonomous individuals by definition are not. This suggests that even in the single individual the coupling mechanism is quite abstract: it is not specific to particular motor systems (i.e., the fingers or the legs) or even to the motor system at all, for two people who do not share the same motor system can easily couple their behavior. The coupling clearly has as much to do with how we perceive the motions of our bodies as with how we control the muscles and joints.[5]

The fact that coupling between two people displays the same dynamics as coupling within one person recalls Condon's observation that interactional synchrony and self-synchrony have the same structure. We should also note that the dynamicist's "abstract" coupling mechanism is acting in that zone of psychological space where one's own body is on an equal footing with the bodies of others. Rhythmic structures occurring in that zone can be executed equally well by one or several individuals.

This observation is important enough that it deserves to be a named principle:

Equivalence: the rhythmic behavior displayed by the coupling between two or more oscillating components of one body has the same dynamics as that displayed by the coupling between oscillating components of two or more different bodies.

This makes me wonder about situations where one simply loses the distinction between oneself and another, as Leonard Bernstein would lose all sense of himself as a separate individual when conducting. As a conductor he intends to produce the music that is actually executed by the musicians under his baton. Is there a sense of self defined primarily through rhythm—that is, the relation between the rhythms of one's motor system and the rhythms one senses through vision, hearing, and touch? Is the intersubjectivity that is so problematic in the Cartesian worldview a simple and basic property of people who music together?

Yet however significant this equivalence may be, we have so far only discussed simple oscillation. This is, of course, the necessary foundation for all music, at least up until recent experiments with arhythmic music, but it is not sufficient. Musical rhythm is organized on several levels, with the basic pulse only one of them. The pulse may be divided into smaller units, and several pulses are typically grouped together into a repeating group of pulses. (This will be discussed in considerable detail in chapter 6.)

We have already seen this hierarchical organization of time in Condon's work; others have been interested as well. In 1976 Mari Reiss Jones published a provocative discussion of temporal structure in attention, perception, and memory. She began with the observation that we live in a world replete with rhythm—though she didn't stress that much of this rhythm is created by other people.[6] In such a world a nervous system would do well to have its own intrinsic rhythms and to interact with the world by entraining its rhythms to the world's rhythms, thus allowing it to track that world, to anticipate its moves, to live in it and act upon it. We interact with the world, Jones wrote, through a structure of "hierarchically nested time zones." We don't regard time as a simple succession of atomic instants. Rather, our minds operate simultaneously on several timescales, with shorter intervals nested within longer ones. We are creatures of rhythm.

THE BRAIN AS A PHYSICAL SYSTEM

Our nervous system is a physical system that consists of parts of various kinds and sizes. These parts are variously arranged, and they interact in a wide variety of processes. Our nervous system is able to regulate our behavior by virtue of its parts and processes. We can understand this regulative role only if we consider the physical nature of the nervous system. We must think of the nervous system as a kind of thing in the external world, a part of the world it must somehow "represent."

With this thought we enter the territory explored by the great John von Neumann in his classic study *The Computer and the Brain*.[7] Von Neumann begins by asserting that computing machines are of two broad types, "analog" and "digital" (quotes in original text), and then writes:

> In an analog machine each number is represented by a suitable physical quantity, whose value . . . is equal to the number in question. This quantity may be the angle by which a certain disk has rotated, or the strength of a certain current, or the amount of a certain (relative) voltage, etc. To enable the machine to compute . . . it is necessary to provide organs (or components) that can perform on these representative quantities the basic operations of mathematics.

In an analog computation scheme the physical dynamics of the computer *directly implements* the computation, whatever it is.

By contrast, "In a digital machine each number is represented in the same way as in conventional writing or printing, i.e., as a sequence of decimal digits." One effect of this is that the physical dynamics of the computer are effectively divorced from the course of computation itself. The course of computation—the algorithm—can be abstractly represented and realized by various kinds of devices, including "electromechanical relays, vacuum tubes, crystal diodes, ferromagnetic cores, and transistors." Regardless of how the physical device works, the algorithm remains the same.

This is a very useful and powerful property and is one of the reasons digital computers have all but eliminated analog computers—though there is now considerable interest in analog circuits inspired by neural models.[8] In thinking about the brain, however, von Neumann speculated that "processes which go through the nervous system may . . . change their character from digital to analog, and back to digital, etc., repeatedly," a view with which I am sympathetic.[9] In particular, I believe the fundamental processes to be analog, with digital processes emerging only with the evolution of language.

Coupling between brains is an analog process, and Wallin's principle would seem to require that the neural dynamics of music be an analog representation of musical sound. Sound waves exhibit rhythmic behavior, as does neurodynamics. To the extent that neurodynamics is analogous to sound waves, music provides an analog coupling between one brain and another.

This immediately raises the specter of reductionism, a ghost I will largely sidestep in this book.[10] The literature on this subject is vast. Note, however, that by insisting on treating the brain as a physical system, I evade the mistake of reducing human social interaction to the mere sum of the processes in individual humans. As I will argue a bit later, the fact of coupling means that we cannot treat social interaction as a simple sum of individual psychological processes. When brains couple they create a system whose properties cannot be deduced from the properties of its individual parts.

FROM BRAIN STATES
TO INTENTIONALITY

Given that we are committed to thinking about the brain as a physical system, we need to adopt a general way of thinking about physical systems. We must consider the system's states: What are they, how many are there, and how do you get from one state to another?[11] We describe the state of a volume of gas, for example, by giving the position, direction of motion, and velocity of each molecule at a given moment. Since the number of molecules is likely to be large, the specification of the exact state of the substance could be quite complex. For most purposes, however, this is more detail than we need. So we work with average values, expressed as temperature and pressure. These are far from complete descriptions, but they let us mark the gas's transition to liquid and solid states and back again.

How many states a nervous system could have is not at all obvious, although the number is clearly very large. Let us assume the neuron as the fundamental unit. The human neocortex has been estimated to have approximately 2.74×10^{10} neurons (i.e., 27,400,000,000). Assume that at any moment each neuron is either on or off, where on means that it is generating an output impulse and off means that it is not. In this case the number of possible states of the neocortex would be 2 (the number of states each element can have) raised to the 27,400,000,000th power (the number of elements in the system).

As large as that number is, it must be too low. We probably want to know the state of each synapse—a juncture where neurons meet—rather than that of each neuron. Each cortical neuron has between 1,000 and 10,000 synapses, giving us between 2.74×10^{13} and 2.74×10^{14} synapses. So now we are raising 2 to some power between the 27,400,000,000,000th and the 274,000,000,000,000th. Yet as large as this resulting number is, it is surely too low, for each synapse has more than two possible states. The brain is a complex electrochemical machine with over 100 different neuroactive chemicals. As synapses are subject to the influence of several of these chemicals at a time, we probably want to know the concentration of each chemical, at each synapse, for each neuron in the cortex. Taking these into account will make the number of possible states even larger.[12] Moreover, the neocortex is not the entire nervous system. The cerebellum, a large subcortical structure, probably has ten times as many neurons as the neocortex. Clearly the nervous system can assume an enormous number of different states.

Actually, the number of possible states is smaller than this analysis implies. We assumed that the states of our basic units are independent of one another, but this is not true. Neurons are connected in complex and far-ranging networks and circuits. Whether we assume the neuron or the synapse as the basic unit, neural connectivity implies considerable dependency between the units. A neuron will affect the states of neurons to which it is connected; the state of one synapse will affect the states of neighboring synapses.

Still, the nervous system has such a very large number of elements that the number of possible states it can assume remains very very large.

In the most commonly believed account of the nervous system's ability to learn and adapt, that ability depends on constructing dependencies between elements. Back in 1949 the Canadian psychologist Donald Hebb speculated, "When an axon of cell A . . . excite[s] cell B and repeatedly or persistently takes part in firing it, some growth process or metabolic change takes place in one or both cells so that A's efficiency as one of the cells firing B is increased."[13] Thus as the nervous system learns about the world, the number of distinctly different states it can assume decreases. But the transitions between the remaining states track transitions between world states more and more accurately. The state dependencies that are introduced into the nervous system as it moves through the world reflect the system's involvement in the world.

It is as though the nervous system's state space were a block of marble sculpted into a likeness of the world through interaction with it. We do in fact see something like this during the maturation of the nervous system. Very early in life the neurons in the cerebral cortex develop a large number of dendrites—small branches that terminate in synapses. Then, as the nervous system continues to mature, always interacting with the world, synapses that are not reinforced die off, and perhaps even dendrites and neurons as well.[14] Thus the dependencies that become wired in to the nervous system reflect patterns of dependencies between states in the external world. Many of those external states are created by the rhythmic actions of one's fellows. The remaining synapses continue to be subject to the kind of learning Hebb described.

To use a word that Walter Freeman adopted from the medieval philosopher and divine St. Thomas Aquinas, these dependencies reflect the nervous system's *intentionality*. The basic requirement for intentional action is that the nervous system have its own means of generating a large state space that it can then "offer" to the world through interaction. That state space is, in effect, the system's "well" of potential intention, upon which it draws in learning the world. Given this well, Freeman explains perception thus:

> A stimulus excites the sensory receptors, so that they send a message to the brain. That input triggers a reaction in the brain, by which the

brain constructs a pattern of neural activity. The sensory activity that triggered the construction is then washed away, leaving only the construct. That pattern does not "represent" the stimulus. It constitutes the meaning of the stimulus for the person receiving it.[15]

Freeman is one of the pioneers in applying work in chaos, complex systems, and nonlinear dynamics to the study of the nervous system. This body of work arose in the physical sciences toward the end of the nineteenth and beginning of the twentieth centuries, but did not flower until it became possible to study such systems through computer simulation. One key point of this work is that, under certain conditions, physical systems exhibit self-organizing properties. For such order to emerge the system must have a very large number of parts as well as an abundant source of external energy.

As a simple example, consider a pan of water on top of a stove. You turn on the burner and initially the water remains still. As it heats up, however, currents begin flowing in a rolling pattern between the top and bottom of the water volume. Where did they come from? As they certainly are not imposed from the outside, they must arise within the water itself as the externally generated heat flows from the bottom of the pan to the top. When the difference between the top and bottom temperatures passes a critical point, minute fluctuations in the motions of individual molecules can become coordinated and amplified into large-scale convection currents.[16]

That is a particularly simple example. Its more complicated brethren—the weather is a notorious example—can be readily multiplied. Freeman, of course, is not directly interested in such examples, but rather in the underlying principles that explain how a physical system can organize itself. If you consider the nervous system as a physical system, then you need principles of self-organization to explain how the nervous system functions. Without such principles the nervous system is merely a passive reflex of the environment. Yet animals move about the world with autonomy and purpose. They cannot get those properties from the environment.

COMPUTATION AND
TIMING IN A NERVOUS SYSTEM

Intentionality is inherently temporal; it expects the world to meet it at the proper time. Without "pressure" from streams of sensory input, the delicate timing of neural processes begins to degrade.[17] Whether one is talking about the operations of a digital computer or the brain, timing is critical. The right signal must be at the right place at the right time in order for the process to proceed. A conventional digital computer has only one processing stream, but the brain has tens or hundreds of streams operating in parallel and tuned to the rhythms of the external world. Without sensory input supporting these many processes, they will no longer converge and synchronize as they should.

In digital computers timing is regulated by a clock that is otherwise external to the computational circuitry. The brain is very different. We know that the body and brain have oscillators that function on various timescales, from the circadian "clocks" regulating sleep and waking to spinal and core brain circuits generating pulses that time walking. But it is not clear whether an overall "clock" times all of the brain's activities. Much of the timing seems to depend on the local interaction of the various neural centers.

Music, more than any other human activity, is an exercise in timing. Perhaps it serves as a means of coordinating the temporal activities of widely distributed brain regions—for we know that music is processed in an extensive set of neural centers. We also know that music can be quite precise in its timing. Working from master tapes, Manfred Clynes examined the timings of Brahms's *Haydn Variations Op. 56B,* as conducted by Arturo Toscanini in 1935, 1938, and 1948. The overall timings were 16 minutes 44 seconds (1935), 16 minutes 50.6 seconds (1938), and 16 minutes 50.3 seconds (1948). The 1938 and 1948 performances differ by only 0.3 seconds, which works out to about 1 part in 2,000 for the total performance. The difference between the 1935 and 1938 performances, the greatest difference in the set, is only 6.6 seconds, about 7 parts per 1,000. Timings of the individual variations (nine, plus the original theme) generally agreed within 1 second, demonstrating a remarkable overall consistency in timing.[18]

More recently, Xiaodan Leng and Gordon L. Shaw studied cases of mental rehearsals in which musicians and dancers merely imagined their performances. The timing of different rehearsals generally varied by less than 1.5 percent for performances up to eight or nine minutes long. Leng and Shaw contrast this with a study in which twelve people were asked to estimate durations. The subjects showed an average error of 28 percent when estimating a ten-second interval.[19]

Variability in mental rehearsals of music is considerably less than that of response times for single cortical neurons, which is about 10 percent. Why musical rehearsal should be so consistent when basic neuronal processes seem so loose is not clear. Apparently, the activity of billions of neurons is timed more precisely than that of just one.

Leng and Shaw are interested in a general theory of higher brain functions, including such activities as mathematics, chess, and music, taking place over periods of minutes "without necessarily requiring sensory input." They suggest that such activities do require very precise timing among organized groups of neurons widely scattered in the cortex, and that the structure of the cortex is such that it has a wide variety of spatiotemporal patterns inherent in it.

Let's return to Mari Reiss Jones's suggestion that we operate in the world by entraining the endogenous rhythms of the nervous system to the rhythms of the world. Leng and Shaw's proposals are in that spirit. Just as Jones suggested that we interact with the world through a structure of "hierarchically nested time zones," Leng and Shaw argue that the cortex functions on a variety of different timescales, from milliseconds to tens and hundreds of seconds. Music assumes particular importance, for it is the purest case of a sensorimotor activity with a rich temporal structure.

We might also recall David Hays's observation, reported in the first chapter, that people seemed to be favorably transformed attending the ballet. Perhaps seeing the performances and hearing the music give the nervous system a spatial-temporal tune-up by providing a richly patterned and precisely timed input stimulus. One takes leave of the mundane world and enters a magic realm that is exquisitely attuned to the inherent patterns of one's nervous system.

Mainstream cognitive science has been largely unconcerned with the timing of neural events. Cognitive scientists tend to believe that what is important about the mind is the information it processes, and that information by definition is independent of any particular physical realization. In theory, mental processing could be executed as easily by a digital computer as by a brain. This worldview assigns the details of timing to the implementing medium—neural wetware or silicon hardware—and does not consider them intrinsic to mental processes. Thus it is not surprising that conventional cognitive science has little to say about music, and what it does say tends to focus on harmony and melody, not on the brute physicality of rhythm.

COLLECTIVE STATES IN COUPLED BRAINS

Let us expand our description of the brain to encompass social systems of two or more people. When thinking about the dynamics of individual brains, we are thinking about how complex brain states evolve from one to another. Social dynamics is about the evolution of states of the collective neural tissue. As far as I know, no one has yet considered this issue, and it remains unmapped territory. We're going to have to make things up out of whole cloth.

As an extreme case, imagine that we are dealing with a pair of individuals, Frick and Frack, such that each brain has the same number of possible states, Q. These two people are in different locations and completely unaware of each other. Thus there is no dependency between what happens in these two brains; they are completely decoupled. If Frick is in state number 23,587, Frack could be in any one of Q states and the reverse is true as well. Since Frick can be in any one of Q states, it follows that we have Q^2 (i.e., $Q \infty Q$) possible states for the pair.

Once Frick and Frack start interacting, however, dependencies develop between their respective brains; their actions constrain one another. The number of possible states for the pair is no longer Q^2. I don't have a general strategy for how to estimate the number of states possible to the ensemble; nonetheless, I would like to consider an extreme case, where one person is attempting to *imitate* the other exactly—a scene, for example, that was brilliantly realized in the Marx Brothers' classic film *Duck Soup*. In that case, I suggest, the number of states possible to the ensemble approaches the number possible to one member of the ensemble acting alone. We can say that this interaction has the maximum possible *coupling strength*. Less demanding interactions will have weaker coupling.

This is not to say that during imitation, Frick and Frack have the *same* brain states; that is meaningless, for there is no way to compare the states of two brains. As Freeman has noted, brains are unique, reflecting unique histories.[20] Rather, the demands of imitation force the two brains to depend on one another so that the state space available while performing that task approaches that of a single, unconstrained human brain.

Imitation has been extremely important in recent cultural theorizing; it is at the heart of memetics and of Merlin Donald's influential book *Origin of the Modern Mind*. One might object that, however closely two individuals match their physical motions, their minds are free to wander—to which one may respond that their minds aren't *that* free: it takes quite a bit of concentration to imitate someone. In any event, this analysis is quite informal.

The same argument holds for a group of three or more people. If they are completely decoupled, the number of possible states in the ensemble is Q^n, where n is the number of people in the group. To the extent that all members of the group are doing the same thing, the number of possible states will—as in the case of Frick and Frack—approach Q, the number of states possible for an individual brain. What, now, do we make of an orchestra of musicians performing Beethoven's *Fifth Symphony?* Given that this composition can also be realized by a single musician performing Lizst's piano reduction, it would seem that the number of states in the orchestra must approach the number possible to one individual.

The musicians in the symphony orchestra, however, are not imitating one another. Yes, the musicians playing the same part are doing the same thing, but the piece as a whole is scored for some twenty-plus highly interdependent parts. Thus we have a new principle:

Ensemble State Collapse: the size of the collective neural state space of a musicking ensemble approaches that of a typical member of the ensemble.

This is closely related to the Equivalence principle described earlier. That principle was about the physical continuity of the coupled system: one neuromuscular system or several? This one is about the size of a system's state space.

If this seems counterintuitive, remember that everyone in the ensemble *hears* all of the parts. They differ in what they are doing, but what they are doing is constrained to the sounds they are hearing. The major components of the brain dynamics of each musicking individual will be entrained to the music itself. The differences, of course, will reflect the different motor dynamics required of each person to make his and her contribution to the music. In order for the individual part to fit in, each musician must actively track and intend the full musical texture. In his book *African Rhythm and African Sensibility*, John Miller Chernoff notes that even the most skilled African drummers often find it difficult, or at least strange, to play against a multipart rhythm when even one of the interlocking parts is missing. They need the whole gestalt.[21]

Let us now once again consider Ginger and Fred. These two principles—Equivalence and State Collapse—tell us in what sense they are one. By Equivalence, it makes no difference who moves which leg, and thus we can attribute intentionality to the group (in this case, a pair) as a whole. By State Collapse, Ginger and Fred's collective intentionality has the same scope of action that each has individually.

In the previous chapter we depicted Fred and Ginger in some interaction. Assume the term *persona* to mean the representation of an individual distributed across all individuals in the society. Thus Fred's persona in figure 2.4 consists of his representation of himself and Ginger's representation of him. Ginger's persona consists of her representation of herself and Fred's representation of her.

The notion of persona extends to groups of an arbitrary size as shown in figure 3.1.

Here we see five individuals, A, B, C, D, and E, each represented by a square. Each has some neural image of the others. These images are represented by small circles within each individual. Each also has some representation of him- or herself, indicated by a circle labeled with the Greek letter epsilon (for *ego*). Additionally, all the images of person A have been connected with a set of lines labeled *persona A*, and the same has been done with person D. Note that *personas A* and *D* are linked to the ego nodes in their respective individuals. (Each person in the group has a persona, of course, but to prevent clutter the connections for B, C, and E were not drawn.)

Persona corresponds to what Erik Erikson thought of as a person's identity; it is one's position in the social system.[22] It is important that the individual's sense of self, represented by the ego node, be consistent with other people's sense of him or her, and that these various other senses be mutually coherent. Much of social interaction is about achieving coherence among the neurally distributed components of a single identity.

In figure 3.2 our same five individuals are enacting two different *statuses*. Each individual has a neural representation of each status but is only identified with one of them—notice where the epsilon is for each individual. Individuals A and D have status 1, while B, C, and E have status 2. A social status is simply one's position in the social system.[23] Where that system is organized by kinship, as it is in the preliterate world, one's status is given by the kinship system: you are someone's daughter, someone else's cousin, someone else's mother-in-law, and so forth. A *role*, by contrast, is the social "script" you use to enact your status in a particular situation. The script you enact with your mother is different from that which you enact with your husband or your husband's sister or the son of your husband's sister. These require different roles.

The individuals in figure 3.2 might, for example, be children of the same parents, with status 1 being daughters and status 2 being sons. We could in fact think of one's kinship status as a specialized aspect of one's persona, an aspect one shares with all other individuals of the

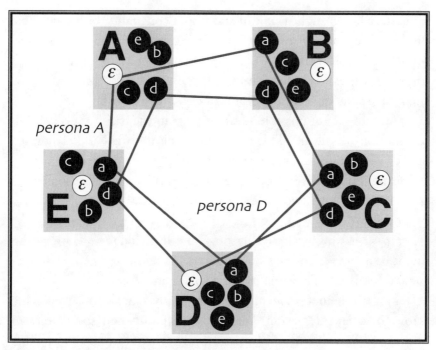

Figure 3.1   Social identity.

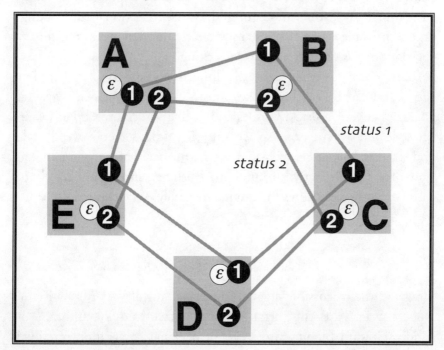

Figure 3.2   Five individuals and two statuses.

same status. We might think of status as a constraint on the persona, but better perhaps to consider it the core of the persona, which determines the basic features of one's interactions with others. One's unique features and capacities are then "attached" to that core. As such, the status exists in the brains of everyone in the culture.

In fact, the set of possible statuses exists in the brain of every adult member of the culture. This set of statuses is affirmed and elaborated in the culture's stories and rituals; it forms the core of social life.

Yet the individuals in figure 3.2 might also be players in some musical ensemble with two different parts. With that in mind, consider figure 3.3.

Status 2 is now occupied by only one individual, C. This group might be a mother and her sons, a foreman and his crew, or a conductor and her band. The situations are analogous.

Taking a role in a performing group clearly is analogous to playing a role in social interaction. Yet people play out their social roles in mundane life, while musical roles are strictly confined to musicking. Moreover, while social roles place constraints on behavior—dictating such things as posture, mode of address, conversational turn taking, and permissible actions—these roles clearly do not constrain ordinary social groups as severely as does musicking.

This severe constraint, the distilling of social life to its simplest forms and moves, is what makes music special. But it is the general analogy between musicking roles and ordinary social roles that relates the style and structure of a society's music to that society's overall style and structure—matters we will examine further. The general ebb and flow of social life between mundane existence and highly ritualized music making constitutes the unique social life of *Homo sapiens*.

THE "GLOBAL BRAIN,"
BIG BRAINS, AND MEMES

Thus far, the discussion suggests the metaphor of society as a brain. Robert Wright uses this metaphor in his recent study of cultural evolution. Howard Bloom, after years of personal observation of crowd

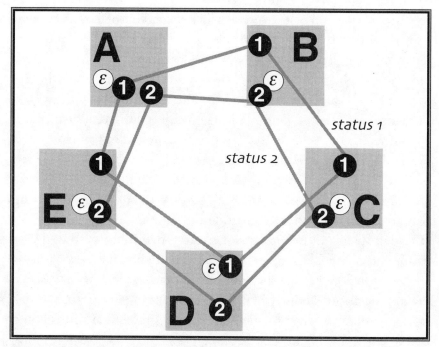

Figure 3.3   Mother and sons, conductor and band.

behavior in relation to popular music, has built a book around it.[24] The point of this metaphor is that societies have an organic wholeness that is more than the sum of their individual members. This is but a version of an older metaphor, society as a body, which has entered our everyday speech in phrases such as *head of state* and *body politic*.

As I believe a society really is greater than the sum of its individuals, I agree with the impulse behind this metaphor. Yet I have never found it useful. In suggesting a kind of ethereal, glowing cloud hovering over the land, the society-as-brain metaphor concretizes the notion of wholeness without giving us a means of actually thinking about it. The notion of neural coupling, however, suggests one way of thinking about that wholeness in concrete terms. This coupling is physically real, as Condon's videotapes and Schmidt's two-person experiments have shown. If the general reasoning here is valid, then appropriate EEG investigation of interacting individuals should produce further evidence of such coupling.

Further, we need a finer-grained understanding of how couplings happen in society, those involving two or three people, half a dozen, ten or thirteen, fifty, a hundred, three thousand people at a time. How long does a given coupling last—five minutes, an hour, ten hours? What music, dance, or ritual mediates the coupling? How many performances are onetime only, and how many occur weekly (such as a church service), seasonally (holidays), annually, and so forth? We have bits and pieces of this information for many of the world's societies, but very little systematic information with accurate counts of people and time spans. We are thus largely ignorant about the fluctuating patterns of interpersonal conjunction that sustain our cultural life.[25]

Rather than continue to lament research that hasn't been done, let us turn to Susan Blackmore's recent speculation about why humans have such big brains. She suggests that "imitation requires three skills: making decisions about what to imitate, complex transformations from one point of view to another, and the production of matching bodily actions. . . . Being good at imitation," therefore, "requires a big brain."[26] She may be correct on both counts, but I would cast her notion somewhat differently.

Blackmore is a leading theorist of orthodox memetics, a position I rejected in the previous chapter. As such, she assumes that we need large brains to contain all those memes, which are large, complex mental objects. Since I believe memes—such as music—reside in the external world, I must put something else inside the head. That something else is the neural machinery for imitation and, above all, for coupled interaction.

Blackmore thinks of this machinery as a collection of memes, while I consider it machinery for mediating coupled interaction. In our interpretation, the critical consideration comes from the principle of Ensemble State Collapse—that is, the principle that the size of the collective neural state space of a musicking ensemble approaches that of a typical member of the ensemble. It follows that the typical member of a musicking ensemble must have a brain large enough to generate such a state space. That is why our brains are so large and possess such a structure. Of course, this is all just grand assertion on my part, as it is on Blackmore's part. While I would like to say that the truth of the matter can only be determined through experimentation, that is not an adequate formulation. I certainly cannot, offhand, think of one experiment or even a small handful of them that would settle the matter. While each of these views implies different research programs, this is certainly not something answerable within the confines of this book.

MUSICKING AND
GROUP INTENTIONALITY

Let us abandon this flight of theoretical fancy and conclude this chapter the way it began, with a bit of solid empirical work. You may be familiar with the synchronized clapping that routinely rewards a successful performance—music, drama, the circus, and so on—in Eastern European communities, but which is less common in Western Europe and North America. Néda and colleagues have investigated this phenomenon, recording applause for a number of performances in Romania and Hungary.[27] The applause would start out randomly then quickly become strongly synchronized. Synchronized clapping would continue for a short while then disintegrate into random clapping, from which synchronized clapping would reemerge, and so forth.

Analysis of the recordings revealed two things:

1. The average noise level was greater during the random clapping than during the synchronized clapping.
2. During random clapping individuals clapped at roughly twice the frequency they used during synchronized clapping.

Clearly the greater volume during random clapping came because individuals were clapping faster; but during this phase, the time between individual claps varied more than when people clapped at the lower rate. That variability made it impossible for the group to synchronize at the higher rate—a result that has emerged in a number of studies of groups of globally coupled oscillators.

Néda concluded that audience members were caught in a conflict. On the one hand, they can express one value by clapping as rapidly as possible, thereby making the loudest noise. If, however, they wish to express another value by synchronizing their clapping, then they have to clap more slowly, thereby lowering the volume. It is impossible simultaneously to maximize these two aims. The group deals with this conflict by switching back and forth between two different expressive regimes.

We would, of course, like to know what these two values are. The investigators assume that the loudness of the clapping reflects the audience members' enthusiasm for the performance, while synchronous clapping expresses group solidarity. This seems reasonable enough. For our purposes, however, what is significant is the mechanism by which these two values, whatever they are, were expressed by the group. That mechanism is clearly self-organizing. No one leads audiences in this behavior. It just happens.

Freeman has techniques for identifying and studying intentionality in the brains of individual animals. Néda and colleagues have demonstrated a method for studying *group intentionality* in this very simple case—one that is grounded, however, in coupled behavior. If we are to understand musicking we need techniques that work in more complicated cases, such as the Rahsaan Roland Kirk performance described in the first chapter, or the bell magic, or the jam session we turn to next. The important point is simply that group intentionality is amenable to empirical study.

IV

MUSICAL CONSCIOUSNESS AND PLEASURE

Music gives us ontological messages which non-musical criticism is unable to contradict, though it may laugh at our foolishness in minding them.

—William James, *The Varieties of Religious Experience*

A COUPLE I know threw a big party to celebrate their new house and her pregnancy. As he is deep into the Hoboken folk music scene, about a dozen guitars were there, and some other musicians were there as well: a flautist, a few pianists, a woman who brought a dozen or so shakers that folks could play, a soprano saxophonist, and me, on flügelhorn and clave. We played one or two songs as old as dirt, but also lots of Beatles, Van Morrison, Bob Dylan—very sixties.

The front room on the ground floor served as the music room. The music would start and stop, musicians of all levels of ability came and went, and the boundary between players and others was wonderfully fluid. The music was ragged and rambling and occasionally confused, and the rhythm would get lost every now and then. From an evolutionary point of view it was just a bunch of apes hanging out and grooming one another while munching on some choice leaves and termites.

Yet one moment, at least, was unlike anything exhibited by bands of apes. Around one thirty or two in the morning we were jamming on Bob Dylan's "Knocking on Heaven's Door." I took a flügelhorn solo early in this long jam and when I was done, went to the bottom register of the horn and started a simple repetitive swelling figure that I played more or less continuously to the end. The soprano sax played harmony to my line, and I to his, and sometimes did a little obbligato, and a guitar solo floated up here, a piano solo there; vocal choruses and refrains happened as needed. At some point I decided to see how much I could drive this train by leaning on my simple line and bearing down. A half minute or so later, four or five or six voices chimed in on the refrain at the same time. A lump came to my throat. There we were, knocking on heaven's door.

How did those people decide to come in on the refrain? The performance was not rehearsed, and it was not modeled after a well-known recording that all might have heard. It just happened, almost as if the performance had organized itself.

To be sure, the situation was constrained. The group was playing a particular song in a particular key at a particular tempo. These factors certainly put limits on how people could participate in the performance, but even then a great deal of room was given for individual discretion. People still had to decide that, yes, they wanted to take an active role, they wanted to join in on the refrain, and they wanted to do it *now*.

One might guess that my decision to bear down on my particular line had something to do with this. Perhaps it did, but I was only one of ten or so musicians. Maybe the key impetus was something one of the others did, but what and which one? Moreover, if my decision was the critical one, why did I make it? The best I can offer is that it seemed a good thing to do at the time. Since music making has occupied me for most of my life, this decision reflected the accumulated effects of that experience. This applies to everyone else involved in that performance.

What happened is irreducibly grounded in the dynamics of group interaction, which reflect the cumulative histories of the group members. Those histories, of course, trail off into our individual lives and the imprint those lives have left on our brains. Yet for some tens of minutes our brains were coupled together in a self-organizing musical configuration.

To the extent that such self-organized musicking was pleasurable, individual musickers are motivated to repeat it. Musical elements that repeat from one performance to the next are the memes discussed in chapter 2. In this particular case, Dylan's tune is itself a meme, for it has been the basis of many performances by many groups. "Knocking on Heaven's Door" may be nothing more than a historical curiosity 100 years from now, or people might still be performing it. Some tunes have been the basis of hundreds of thousands of performances over centuries, such as the Gregorian chants used in the Roman Catholic liturgy, or "Greensleeves," which is not quite so old. These tunes persist because they give pleasure. To understand that pleasure we must understand the mind.

NEURAL WEATHER: THE MUSICAL MIND

Thus far we have considered the states of the brain, intentionality, coupling, and timing, all while examining the nervous system as a physical system. We can no longer avoid the mind-body problem. I want to approach the problem in the manner of Gilbert Ryle's *The Concept of Mind*. Rather than wonder how the mysterious and ineffable mind can connect with the mysterious but concrete brain, I propose a definition:

Mind: the *dynamics* of the entire brain, perhaps even the entire nervous system, including the peripheral nervous system, constitutes the mind.

The thrust of this definition is to locate mind, not in any particular neural structure or set of structures, but in the joint product of all current neural activity. As such the mind is, as Ryle argues, a bodily process; in the words of Stephen Kosslyn and Olivier Koenig, "*the mind is what the brain does*."[1] Whether a neuron is firing at its maximum rate or idling along and generating only an occasional spike, it is participating in the mind. This assertion is not meant to imply that no localization of function exists in the brain; surely it does. But the mind and the brain are not the same thing, though they are as intimately related as the dancer to the dance. That the dancer is segmented into head, neck, trunk, and limbs does not mean that the dance can be segmented in the same way. Likewise, we should not think of the functional specialization of brain regions as implying a similar specialization of the mind. It is not at all clear that the mind has "parts" in any meaningful sense.

If the functional proclivities of a patch of neural tissue are not relevant for a current activity, those neurons will not be firing very often, but they will still generate some output. The only neuron that does not generate any output is a dead one. Neurons firing at low intensity one moment may well be recruited to more intense activity the next. As Freeman has said, a low level of activity is still a means of participating in the evolving mental state.[2]

Thus in this view, the mind is like the weather. The same environment can have very different kinds of weather. And while we find it natural to talk of weather systems as configurations of geography, temperature, humidity, air pressure, and so on, no overall mechanism regulates the weather. The weather is the result of many processes operating on different temporal and spatial scales.

At the global level and on a scale of millennia we have the long-term patterns governing the ebb and flow of glaciers that, in one commonly accepted theory, is a function of wobble and tilt in the earth's spin axis and the shape of the earth's orbit. At the global level and operating annually we have the succession of seasons, which is caused by the orientation of the earth with respect to the sun as it moves through the year. We can continue on, considering smaller and smaller scales until we consider the wind whipping between the twin towers of the World Trade Center or the breeze coming in through your open window and blowing the papers off your desk.

Weather is regular enough that one can predict general patterns at scales of hours, days, and months, but not so regular that making such predictions is easy and routinely reliable. Above all, no central mechanism governs the weather—it just happens.

The flow of information on the Internet is much the same. Individual computer users can choose to send messages, send or download files, surf the web, and so forth. These decisions send packets of bits flowing through the Internet. The specific paths taken by these packets, however, are determined by routers and gateways that are widely distributed. No command center regulates overall message traffic on the Internet. The global state of Internet traffic at any given time is the net effect of independent decisions by many thousands of human and electronic agents.

So it is with the brain. The overall state is not explicitly controlled, at least not at a high degree of precision. Rather, that overall state reflects activities at various levels within the whole system. At the smallest level we have the individual neurons. Neurons are living cells and, as such, act to maintain their existence. Individual neurons in turn are grouped into functional units at several levels, with many neurons connected to others at distances ranging from fractions of a millimeter to several centimeters or more. Many of these functional units are coupled into systems that explicitly control something else—whether it be another system within the nervous system, or something external to it, either elsewhere in the body (e.g., the muscles or the viscera) or in the external world. Yet no component of the brain regulates all of this activity in detail. The overall activity just happens. That overall activity is what I am calling the mind.

Some of the activity may be conscious, some unconscious. Some activity may, in principle, always be outside the reach of consciousness— and the "contents" of consciousness certainly vary from moment to moment. No matter; it all contributes to the global state of the nervous system, to the mind. Nor should we think of this division between conscious and unconscious activity as two "parts" of the mind: it simply denotes two different kinds of activity. Just where these are located in the brain is likely to shift from moment to moment.

As a practical matter, many *microscopically* different states of mind are *macroscopically* the same. This is true of weather as well. The weather near my apartment as I type this varies from one fraction of a second to the next. The positions, velocities, and directions of air molecules are constantly changing. Each individual change, no matter how small, constitutes a change in the microscopic state of the system. For almost all practical purposes, however, the macroscopic state of the weather is the same from minute to minute, if not hour to hour. Thus the current temperature is about 52°F, it is sunny, there are no clouds in the sky, and the wind is calm. The number of microscopic states that fit that macroscopic description is quite large, but we can consider them the same.

So it is with states of mind. For some purposes ordinary wakefulness and dream sleep are perfectly good characterizations of states of mind. We will later examine work by J. Allen Hobson aimed at explaining such states. Bette Midler's heartfelt song and Leonard Bernstein's ego loss are also macroscopic states of mind. Each is like a macroscopic state of weather, cool and sunny, hot with thunderstorms, and so on. Each of these macroscopic states encompasses untold different microscopic ones. The range of things flitting through one's mind in ordinary wakefulness is frankly mind-boggling, but no less so than what can happen during dreams. Similarly, Bernstein can be as lost in a Mozart symphony as in a Stravinsky ballet. Macroscopically the states are the same; microscopically they are not.

Whereas macroscopic states of wakefulness and dreaming recur regularly through the day and seem to be largely under the influence of a particular set of brain mechanisms deep in the core of the brain (concentrated in the reticular formation), we have no reason to believe that Bernstein's ego loss or Midler's song is under the strong influence of any particular neural mechanism. It just happens.

MIRACLES OF RARE DEVICE

In such self-organizing dynamical systems, small microscale fluctuations under the right conditions can become amplified into new macroscale states—a characteristic that has entered the pop intellectual lore as a rather misleading tale about a butterfly in China precipitating a major thunderstorm over North America.[3] At the right time in the right place, a sharp sound can trigger an avalanche. Compared

to the energy released by the cascading snow, the energy in the trigger-
ing sound is almost negligible. A musical improvisation that was
heading in one direction can change direction completely because one
note came out differently than the player had expected. The example
is real enough—all skilled and experienced improvisers know the phenomenon, some even cultivate it—though we do not actually know
whether this is an example of self-organizing dynamics. It is certainly
a promising candidate.

So too are Midler's and Bernstein's altered states of consciousness.
Somewhere in the brain a small fluctuation takes hold and becomes
amplified to the point where it takes over global brain dynamics. This
is not something you can will to happen—at least not directly—but if
you put yourself in the right frame of mind and do the right things,
then the magic may happen.

I believe that some undetermined set of musical states are of this kind
and that establishing them will require careful work in all the world's
musical cultures. Consider tears while musicking. Of course neither
Carson nor Midler was full-out crying. She had to continue singing and
he had to maintain his composure; but their eyes teared up, and that is
not something they willed. The willed aspect of singing is organized in
the cerebral cortex and involves a cascade of neural structures at the core
of the telencephalon and elsewhere. That is to say, the *internal dynamics*
of certain regions in the cortex have a strong determining effect on the
dynamics of subcortical structures. We don't know exactly where crying
is organized, but it is probably in the brain's core.[4]

We have no reason to believe, however—and this is a point I will
later consider in more detail—that any neural structure regulates the
interaction between the willed and unwilled aspect of this kind of
musical performance. Such interaction is regulated by the whole
brain. In other words, there is no region within the brain whose *internal dynamics* routinely has this exact determining effect on global dynamics. Somehow, when coupled to sounds patterned in certain
ways—patterned to fit the brain's rhythms like a key fits its lock—the
brain can coordinate patterns of activation that are otherwise uncoordinated, if not actually in conflict.

Such serendipitous coordination is indigenous to the expressive arts and has various manifestations. Bernstein's ego loss is rather a different one. The following passage, one of the most famous in twentieth-century literature, presents still another variation on this theme. The narrator of Marcel Proust's *Remembrance of Things Past* is recounting the magical effects of tea and some small morsels from a *petite madeleine*.

> No sooner had the warm liquid, and the crumbs with it, touched my palate than a shudder ran through my whole body . . . at once the vicissitudes of life had become indifferent to me, its disasters innocuous, its brevity illusory—this new sensation having had on me the effect which love has of filling me with a precious essence; or rather this essence was not in me, it was myself. I had ceased now to feel mediocre, accidental, mortal.

The narrator goes on to drink a second and a third mouthful of tea and, no more magic ensuing, decides that "the object of my quest, the truth, lies not in the cup but in myself." And so

> I decide to attempt to make it reappear. I retrace my thoughts to the moment at which I drank the first spoonful of tea. I find again the same state, illuminated by no fresh light. I compel my mind to make one further effort, to follow and recapture once again the fleeting sensation. And that nothing may interrupt it in its course I shut out every obstacle, every extraneous idea, I stop my ears and inhibit all attention to the sounds which come from the next room. And then . . .

And so on to no avail. That particular magic did not return.

The narrator, Marcel, tried to regain that magic by retracing his thoughts, by attempting to recreate his state of mind when the magic happened. He couldn't directly will another occurrence of the magic, but he could attempt to get it back by repeating what he had done before in hopes that the magic would reassemble itself. Alas, the magic failed to cooperate, the brain dynamics could not be recreated. The magic itself is spontaneous, it is not willed, like raising one's arm. Nor is it like being overcome by emotion, which is not willed but does reflect the determining effects of particular neural regions. Such spontaneous states are beyond the determining capacity of any particular center or systemic organization of them.

Musicking, however, differs from Marcel's reverie in that it is typically a group experience. Bernstein is standing on a podium conducting an orchestra as his consciousness is awash in the music.[5] In one obvious sense we must think of his ego loss as happening in his head; but the nervous system in his head—and neck and trunk and pelvis and limbs—is tightly coupled with the nervous systems of the musicians in the orchestra. Thus in another sense Bernstein's ego loss is enabled and supported by the musicking group. The same is true of the tears Bette shed for Johnny. She was singing directly to him, in front of a studio audience, with a pianist accompanying her. However important it is that we understand events inside individual heads, we must also understand how the neural processes in these heads are affected by coupling.

CONSCIOUSNESS AND
SUBJECTIVE EXPERIENCE

Given a conception of mind, we need to think about consciousness. How do we distinguish between the conscious and unconscious mind? Having identified the mind with global brain dynamics, logically we should identify consciousness with some aspect or component of those dynamics, the rest being unconscious.

The study of consciousness has undergone a renaissance in psychology and the neurosciences, and the literature is large and growing. This is certainly no place to review that literature, but I do prefer certain lines of thought over others. I feel an affinity for the ideas of Walter Freeman, Gerald Edelman and Giulio Tononi, and the somewhat older work of William Powers.[6]

While Powers's conception, like that of the others, is embedded in a fairly technical and sophisticated model, his is the most general treatment. His idea is derived from Norbert Wiener's conception of adaptive control, which Wiener illustrated by asking that we consider what we do when driving on an icy road:

> Our entire conduct of driving depends on a knowledge of the slipperiness of the road surface, that is, on a knowledge of the performance characteristics of the system car-road. If we wait to find this out by ordinary performance of the system, we shall discover ourselves in a skid before we know it. We thus give to the steering wheel a succession of small, fast impulses, not enough to throw the car into a major skid but quite enough to report to our kinesthetic sense whether the car is in danger of skidding, and we regulate our method of steering accordingly.[7]

That quick jiggle of the steering wheel is, in Powers's model, consciousness. His discussion centers on learning. Powers imagines, on the one hand, a perceptual and behavioral system that has certain (unstated) characteristics.[8] There will be times and situations where the system doesn't have routines that will produce the desired food, shelter, sex, and so forth. In those cases the system needs to learn a new routine: it must *reorganize*, to use Powers's term. He suggests that the reorganizing system has the power to inject "an arbitrary test stimulus" (in Wiener's example, the jiggle of the steering wheel) into the behaving system and to sense the effects of that stimulus on the system. Then the system can use that information to guide reorganization more effectively. *Consciousness* then, in Powers's view, is the effect of superimposing this test stimulus on behavior.[9]

Neither Freeman nor Edelman and Tononi have an overall behavioral and reorganizational model comparable to that of Powers. That makes it difficult to compare their concepts directly with his. Yet it seems that, on a gross level, their views are consistent. There are two issues on which all three agree: consciousness is associated with learning, and consciousness does not occur at any one place or set of places in the brain. Consciousness is not a "sketchpad" in the brain comparable to the short-term memory of a digital computer. Consciousness is a process, and one that is physically mobile—Edelman and Tononi are particularly insistent on this point. In this view, then, the unconscious mind is the complement of the conscious mind. If consciousness is mobile, so is unconsciousness. Neither is a fixed set of rooms and passages in some mental house.

Having considered the mind as neural weather, imagine now what it feels like to be a sunny day in midsummer at the seashore. The temperature is 85°F, a few clouds are in the sky, and a 5 mph breeze is blowing in from the sea. Contrast that feeling with that of snowstorm in zero-degree weather in a mountain range. What does it feel like when the snowstorm finally dissipates and the sun comes out and melts the topmost layer of snow? For that matter, what does it feel like when the sunny day at the shore gives way to a thunderstorm?

Subjective experience, by definition, is directly available only to the subject. Someone can tell us about his or her experience but we cannot climb inside the person's mind and reconnoiter it for ourselves. (Even if we could, would the experience be that person's or would it be ours?) What we *can* do is observe a person's body and ask them what they felt at this or that moment. We then correlate our objective observations with their subjective reports and attempt to draw conclusions about the neural and bodily processes that *feel like that.*

The essential privacy of subjective experience is the ineradicable truth of Cartesianism. We cannot know how it feels to be another.

CONSCIOUSNESS AND RITUAL

Subjectivity is an aspect of neurodynamics, and neurodynamics is open to the world through sensory organs and the motor system. When people are coupled with one another through musicking, each steers his or her own raft of subjectivity in the collective sea of neurodynamics. The motions of each raft are transmitted to the others through the sea, as Huygens's clocks transmitted vibrations to one another through the walls. These subjectivities thus adjust themselves one to the other, for they all are components of the same process.

Reconsider, then, the musicking with which we opened this chapter. We were at a party where lots of musicians were jamming. Near the

end of a jam on "Knocking on Heaven's Door," several people spontaneously joined in on the refrain. This wasn't planned ahead of time,
nor did those singers discuss it among themselves while the rest of us
were playing.

I mentioned a deliberate intent to "drive" the group by playing a
simple line and "bearing down." That decision was a conscious one
(though not as clear and differentiated as it may seem when I spell it
out in words) and resulted in a certain shift in my consciousness. Bearing down is something I often do when playing: it involves attending
to and adjusting the tension in my trunk musculature; the only effect
on the music is a certain intensity and emotional tone. In this case I
was playing a simple melodic line, but I will also bear down while playing the most complex lines. In that situation, fingers and tongue may
be spitting out tens of notes per second, but they're on their own; *I'm*
still attending to muscles in my abdomen, shoulders, back, and but-
tocks. Those are the muscles that most strongly affect the overall air-
flow, and that's what I care about when I'm bearing down.

And that, by our conception of consciousness, is where my nervous
system is reorganizing and making minute adjustments. I have no in-
trospective awareness of precisely what neural areas are reorganizing,
but no doubt we are dealing with circuitry involving both emotional
expression and voluntary control of large muscles. Yet even while attending to these muscles, I am always listening to the sound of the
whole group. I bear down *just so* in order that the sound I hear may
also be *just so*—but my sound is only a part of the group's, and at this
particular point, a subordinate part.

This means that my nervous system's *reorganizational* activity is responsive to the sound made by each and every person in the musicking group. I am attuning my motor and emotive system to the sound
that is the joint activity of this group, and each person is in turn doing
the same thing. Each player, merely by being a conscious musician, is
making minute adjustments to his or her nervous system in response
to the sounds that all are creating.

We are now in territory explored by Walter Freeman in a recent essay on music and social bonding.[10] Freeman is interested in those rituals in which a core group of celebrants move from one status in

society to another, as from child to adult or single to married. In such rituals, as individuals are conveyed from one social status to another—recall our discussion in the previous chapter—they require changes in the collective neural tissue. Funerals, for example, are in this class. As the bodies of the dead are conveyed to a final resting place, the living must disengage from their attachments to those who are no longer among them. In this case, an entire persona (see, e.g., figure 3.1) must be disengaged from active use in the collective neural tissue. Conversely, when a child is born, the group must undertake a ritual that recognizes and thereby creates a new persona in the collective neural tissue.

In all of these situations the bonds between individuals must be altered in fundamental ways that require considerable neural reorganizing. Freeman suggests that such rituals involve a neuropeptide called oxytocin. He asserts that oxytocin "appears to act by dissolving preexisting learning by loosening the synaptic connections in which prior knowledge is held. This opens an opportunity for learning new knowledge. The meltdown does not instill knowledge. It clears the path for the acquisition of new understanding through behavioral actions that are shared with others." As the oxytocinated individuals move to the rhythms of well-established ritual, their synaptic connections are restructured in patterns guided and influenced by the events in the ritual. Obviously, the microdynamics of each individual will be unique, but they will be shaped by rhythmic patterns common to all. These rituals provide a space in which individuals can mold themselves to one another as the infant molds her actions to those of her mother.

Such ritual would likely have benefits on less extreme occasions than those requiring the restructuring of social relations—think of our little jam session. Social life is difficult and taxing. Hostilities build up. Such ritual may well help take the edge off of growing tensions, reconciling individuals to one another and allowing them to "reset" their relationships on more favorable terms.

Thus we have another core hypothesis:

Freeman's Hypothesis: by attending to one another through musicking, performers attune their nervous systems to one another, restructuring their representations of others. This results in more harmonious interactions within the group.

Each individual consciousness may be an island of Cartesian subjectivity, but in the close coupling of musicking, those subjectivities are intimately and delicately conditioned and regulated by one another.

Perhaps such rituals play a role in helping to establish and maintain the subjective continuity of the neural self. By entering into a wide variety of emotional states (with their various neurochemical substrates) in a socially controlled situation, individuals in a community ritual create an *equal access zone* in mental space where each can experience and contemplate extremes of joy and anger, tenderness and hate, and know that all these feelings have a place in their shared world.[11]

THE PLEASURES OF
MUSIC: INNER MOTION

The most important aspect of our subjective musical experience no doubt is pleasure. Why is it a pleasure to make, dance, and listen to music? I am as curious about ordinary musical pleasure as about altered musical states. Music can be quite compelling and pleasurable even if you don't enter into some heightened state of awareness and self-loss.

If you had read or heard about pleasure centers in the brain, you might suggest that music stimulates one or more of those centers. This is presumably what Stephen Pinker had in mind when he asserted that "Music appears to be a pure pleasure technology, a cocktail of recreational drugs that we ingest through the ear to stimulate a mass of pleasure circuits at once" in his book *How the Mind Works*.[12] The reasoning is obvious:

1. The brain has pleasure circuits.
2. Music is pleasurable.
3. Therefore music stimulates the brain's pleasure circuits.

Problems arise, however, when we start searching for the pleasure circuits that music stimulates.

The first so-called pleasure centers were discovered quite by accident in the mid-1950s by James Olds and Peter Milner.[13] Crudely put, they found small areas in the core of the rat's brain that seemed to give the rat pleasure when they were electrically stimulated. Yet the formulation "give the rat pleasure" presumes a nonexistent intimacy with the rat's subjective state. What the researchers observed is that if a rat could stimulate one of these areas simply by pressing a bar, it would do so time after time for hours. This behavior was taken to indicate that the stimulation is pleasurable; we couldn't, of course, ask the rats whether they were experiencing pleasure. Some surgeons even implanted such electrodes into patients suffering from epilepsy, in the hope that they could afford their patients some relief. The result, suggests Freeman, does not sound much like the delirious pleasure Pinker suggested:

> In different places they reported feeling pleasure, sometimes sexual, but mostly rather bland. Some other patients, who were afflicted with chronic pain, reported that they got temporary relief from their suffering. They were given the opportunity to go home with a battery and a switch, so that they could treat their own pain by stimulating themselves and adjusting their own dosage of electric current.
>
> But no one wanted to keep the wires. Some doctors feared that a black market might grow, with pleasure addicts going to third world countries to get implanted with wires and stimulators. That didn't happen, because whatever the pleasure is, it doesn't last, and it isn't happiness.[14]

These so-called pleasure centers are involved in regulating appetitive behaviors such as eating and drinking. Karl Pribram has argued that self-stimulation has the effect of tricking the animal into thinking it has satisfied one of these desires. Pribram thus suggests that "the self-stimulation process would be something like repeatedly adjusting and returning to its original location the setting device on a home thermostat in a room that is already warm. The furnace turns on briefly, only to go off again as the setting is returned to its baseline." The pleasure is thus not some generalized pleasure, but the virtual satisfaction of a virtual need.

More recently Jaak Panksepp has noted that self-stimulating animals "did not have the behaviorally settled outward appearance of animals consuming conventional rewards. Self stimulating animals look excessively excited, even crazed, when they work for this kind of stimulation." They look like they are exploring and investigating, not basking in the enjoyment of needs well-satisfied. Panksepp believes these neural centers are components of an exploratory system.

If these "classical" pleasure centers aren't really pleasure centers, maybe we need to look elsewhere. Panksepp, for example, looks to the homeostatic systems that directly regulate the body's energy balance by attending to such things as thirst, hunger, and temperature. Perhaps the centers regulating these variables yield pleasure when the variable reaches the desired level. Thus Panksepp asserts that "most of our feelings of sensory pleasure arise from the various stimuli that signal the return of bodily imbalances toward an optimal level of functioning." Yet what does that have to do with music? Are we to believe that music provides virtual satisfaction for virtual thirst?

The notion of so-called pleasure circuits begins to unravel as soon as one examines it. Just what these circuits are and how and why music might affect them isn't clear. Still, to deny out of hand the existence of specific pleasure circuits accessible to music could be premature. Perhaps we will discover them; who knows? I would like to suggest, however, a different way to think about pleasure. The pleasure circuits view asserts the existence of centers that monitor certain variables. When the variable assumes the desired value—for example, when you've consumed enough water or when you are no longer cold—the center detects that desired result and signals "We've got it." That signal is experienced as pleasure.

There is, however, another kind of pleasure. John Jerome was interested in the pleasures of athletic excellence and informally proposed what he calls the Sweet Spot Theory of Performance.[15] By sweet spot he means that spot on a baseball bat, tennis racket, or golf club that affords the squarest contact with the ball, transfers energy to it most efficiently, and thereby minimizes jarring transmitted back to the hands. That spot, Jerome assures us, is not fable but mechanical fact.

Generalizing from this principle, he argues that the superior athlete "is the one who in effect reaches the sweet spot of the arc for each segment of his or her skeleton as he or she goes through the athletic motion." The pleasure of sport—at any rate, the pleasure that derives from the activity itself, rather than from beating someone else in competition—is simply the subjective feeling of smooth fluid physical motion in which one's motive force exactly matches and counters any resistance.

The pleasure of music, I submit, is like that. Musicians certainly know the kind of physical pleasure Jerome talks about, as do dancers. Yet so do those who only listen.

Jerome is focused on the smoothly functioning athletic body. Muscles, however, cannot contract and flex in the right way unless the nervous system controls them just so. The smooth motion is in the body, but the pleasure is in the nervous system. Even if a listener does not move his body, his or her nervous system does have to follow the sound. In other words, a great deal of the pleasure we take from music lies in the overall dynamic character of the activity itself: it is a property of the neural weather. Some weather feels better than other weather. This is not a matter of some brain center detecting some property in the neural weather and signaling good or bad; rather, our pleasure reflects the overall state of the brain. You don't need to detect this state because this state is you—it is your mind.

We are now in familiar territory. The idea that music is linked to motion is an old one, explored by Charles Keil in his essay "Motion and Feeling through Music" and validated by studies that show activity in motor areas of the brain when people are listening to music.[16] Musical pleasure is an example of *flow*, a term coined by the psychologist Mihaly Csikszentmihalyi.[17] Flow is not special either to music or athletic performance, but is a capacity inherent in the nervous system and can happen during a wide range of activities. In Csikszentmihalyi's model, flow is a function of the conditions of task performance. Where one's skill exceeds the demands of a task by a considerable margin, the task is boring. Where task demands exceed one's skill by a considerable margin, the task provokes anxiety—which we'll examine in more detail in the following section. One feels flow only when the task demands are just a little beyond one's current skill. In that situation one must be fully alert and attentive in order to perform the task and, if this is accomplished, then it is possible to perform the task well. Thus flow represents a style of action, not some specific set of activities.

The idea of musical pleasure as flow does not preclude the possibility that music stimulates specific pleasure centers. Any such centers activated through music will contribute to that music's pleasure. Musical pleasure, however, does not depend on such centers. In general I expect that music is pleasurable in proportion to its capacity for exercising the inherent properties of the brain, especially the rhythmic properties. Thus,

Pleasure as Coherence: musical pleasure is the subjective awareness of overall neural flow where that flow is well-timed and coherent.

Further, this musical flow is not under the control of any particular brain system but rather reflects the joint interaction of all active neural systems, at all levels of interaction. The pleasure center view would have us believe that musical flow is regulated by those specific pleasure centers. If musical pleasure is not localized in a few centers, it follows that musical flow is not regulated by those centers. We have mutual adjustment and interaction here and there, indeed everywhere, but no omniscient master dictating the terms of the neural dance. Music's pleasures have no master.

ANXIETY AND DEFENSE

Pleasure, of course, has its opposite in pain. As we have already seen, the nervous system doesn't have neural centers specifically for pleasure, nor does it have anything that can be called a pleasure system. By contrast, the nervous system certainly does have pain receptors, a pain system, and pain centers, though the exact workings of this system are mysterious. The basic purpose of the pain system is to warn the organism about (possible) physical damage, which is detected by receptors in the skin.[18] The neurology of pain is thus quite different from that of pleasure, its nominal opposite.

I believe that the functional opposite of pleasure is not pain but anxiety. Just as pleasure is the subjective experience of neural weather that functions coherently, so anxiety is the *subjective experience of incoherent neural weather*. In Csikszentmihalyi's formulation of flow, anxiety is the neural weather that occurs when you try to perform a task that is far too difficult. You simply have not mastered the necessary mental or physical routines. You fumble and fidget, lose track of where you are, and can't think of what to do next. This is all quite uncomfortable; you feel anxious.

The literature on the neurobiology of anxiety is extensive and varied. The materials I have examined are not about some center or centers that detect or create anxiety. Rather, that literature is about fear, traumatic experience, conflict, the anticipation of harm or danger, the centers involved in such anticipation, and the biochemical and physical consequences of anxiety.[19] Without disputing any of this, the net result of these various causal forces and factors nevertheless is badly timed and incoherent neural flow. Thus Michael Posner and Marcus Raichle assert, "Adults who report themselves as able to focus and shift attention also say they are less prone to depression and anxiety than those who report themselves as less able to control their attention."[20] From this I infer a problem with neurodynamics: a conflicted brain will not be able to shift smoothly from one state to another.[21] Moreover, Jeffrey Gray has linked anxiety to *mismatches* between expectations and actuality as detected in limbic structures.[22]

Thus, parallel to our concept of musical pleasure, we have:

Anxiety as Incoherence: anxiety is the subjective awareness of overall neural flow where that flow is poorly timed and incoherent.

What does this really mean? Here is an analogy Norbert Wiener used in some speculations on psychopathology in *Cybernetics:* traffic jams. Wiener wasn't so much interested in the flow of cars over roads as in the flow of electrical signals through complex communications networks. In both cases, however, an overload of traffic leads to breakdowns.[23]

One thing anxiety and traffic jams have in common is that both are symptoms. Traffic jams can have various causes—construction, an accident, a sobriety checkpoint, outflow from a sporting event, and so on. Similarly, anxiety has many varied causes. Some anxieties may reflect inner conflict of the sort best worked out in psychotherapy; others may reflect phobias that can be handled through some kind of behavioral therapy. Csikszentmihalyi talks of task difficulty as a cause of anxiety. Other anxiety results from rational assessments of genuinely threatening situations.

To anticipate chapter 8, imagine a band of protohumans somewhere on the African steppe. Things in this particular group are getting pretty edgy, for whatever reasons—independently of any other causal forces, social life certainly produces stress. Somehow, the group members begin stomping their feet in the same rhythm and start to vocalize wildly, each singing his or her own line yet all somehow managing to blend together in a fine raucous mix. They do this for an hour or so, and the anxiety gradually dissipates as the rhythmic actions recruit more and more neural circuits into the flow, dissolving the neural traffic jams. Whatever the root causes, the symptom has been alleviated.

Such things need not be confined to long ago and far away. When, as mentioned in the first chapter, Hays remarked that people seem more relaxed after the ballet than before, most likely he observed the effects of anxiety reduction. Reports that brain wave activity appears more coherent while subjects are listening to music seems consistent with this conception—though the investigators who reported this have not, as far as I know, attempted to assess anxiety levels in their subjects.[24] Finally, we know that music alleviates the symptoms of separation anxiety in young chicks, who cry less when they hear music.[25]

Should further investigation confirm that music does indeed relieve anxiety, we will find ourselves in classic psychoanalytic territory, with musicking functioning as a defense mechanism.[26] A group's anxiety may have multiple causes: a lion attack narrowly defended, unusually hot weather; or perhaps water is scarce, an infant has died, or two adults have been fighting. The net result is stress and anxiety all around. The longer the group engages in musicking, the more neurons get recruited to patterns of coherent flowing activity. Musicking can thus function as a behavioral technique for alleviating anxiety while leaving the ultimate causes of the anxiety untouched.

That is what makes musical activity a defense mechanism in the psychoanalytic sense. As long as musicking alleviates symptoms without leading individuals or the group to ignore fatal problems, it is a good thing and it will be repeated, though it may take the group a while to develop reliable routines. The symptomatic relief may even increase the group's capacity to deal with challenges—that is, it may be adaptive.

The possibility that music relieves anxiety need not imply that it always does so or that we make music only for this purpose. Pleasure is its own reward. Return to the traffic analogy. We might think of our ordinary state of mind as being akin to congested traffic: not as bad as a complete jam, but not flowing freely either.

Thus we have two different reasons to make music, each a function of neurodynamics: to create pleasure and to dissipate anxiety. The question is how we distinguish between them.

BEYOND KNOWLEDGE OF DEATH

Intelligence allows humans to anticipate the future, to imagine what might happen in this or that circumstance, to imagine what we might do, and thus to prepare for things in advance. This surely is useful and adaptive, but it has disconcerting side effects.

What do we do about possible events over which we can assert little control, if any? What if we have seen a calamitous storm or an earthquake or a fire devastate our group, injuring thousands, destroying our animals, our dwellings? The group knows, from experience passed down through generations, that we can neither predict such things nor do much to prepare for them. While the scope of these potential disasters draws our attention to them, our vulnerability can turn such attention into a dangerous distraction, diverting us from beneficial activities.

One disaster we may be sure will occur, though we cannot anticipate just when. Our intelligence allows us to know that we will die, and the rituals through which we mark death are among the most important and intense we perform.[27] I suggest that without such rituals, death threatens to become a psychological trap for the living. Periodic participation in ritual musicking reduces one's sense of isolation and attaches one to the group, as Freeman has noted, making one's individual fate a matter of less concern. When we lose a parent, spouse, or close friend, ritual helps us mourn the loss and strengthen our ties to the living—it helps us, literally, get the deceased out of our (nervous) system.

Yet the same ritual that gives us comfort in the group has its dark side. If we are immortal in the group, why fear death? And if we no longer fear death, why not wage bloody war on those not in the group? The last century witnessed violence on a grand scale perpetuated by people who gathered in large groups, marched to military music, and sought meaning and belonging in war.

The difference between using music and being used by it therefore seems a subtle one. The price for relief from death anxiety can be high, but we should not think that music's pleasure is merely the obverse of anxiety. Even when we have dealt with our anxiety through other means, we find purpose in musicking. Perhaps only then can music's pleasure set us free.

PART II

MUSIC
AND THE MIND

BLUES IN
THE NIGHT:
EMOTION IN MUSIC

Our inmost yearning, our deep desire for harmony—harmony in an extra-musical, transcendental sense—feels affirmed, confirmed and calmed by music, and in this sense music seems to me a message—a lofty ethical message—that brings good tidings to the ethical part of our being from the mysteries of the world of sound.

—Bruno Walter

A NUMBER OF years ago I was playing trumpet with a rhythm and blues band in a bar in downtown Albany, New York. It was two in the morning and we were exhausted at the end of a five-hour gig. My chops were shot.

We decided to play one more tune, "Stormy Monday." Normally I didn't solo on that tune; however, it is a slow blues, and I dearly love a slow blues. So despite my exhaustion, I decided to take a chorus—one cycle through the tune. I started playing simple figures in the lower-middle register and then elaborated on those figures and moved to the upper register. I hit my climax at the penultimate bar of the chorus, as anticipated, and was ready to stop playing. But the rhythm section wasn't playing concluding riffs; they clearly expected me to play another chorus. If I'd had any sense I'd have ignored them and stopped. My lips were crying out in pain; if I played much more my lip muscles would surely fail.

I didn't like the idea of following a good chorus with a mediocre one. I couldn't remain in the trumpet's difficult upper register, nor could I drop back to the middle register and then build back up—the two most obvious options for constructing another chorus. In a split-split second I decided Oh, what the hell, and did a Sonny Rollins, dropping to the middle register, growling and flutter tonguing to make the nastiest, bluesiest sound I could. Another power had entered my playing. Captain cat went on the prowl and the music went into overdrive. Solid.

As the band stood around after the gig, several people came up to me and chatted, touching me on the forearm on their way out. But it wasn't me they wanted to touch. It was the power that emerged during that second chorus.

This other power did not possess me as fully as Leonard Bernstein seems to have been possessed by composers of music he conducted. I was at least residually aware of who, what, and where I was; but I was focused on the music to an unusual degree, and my playing had an unaccustomed edge and force.

A PERFORMER PREPARES

While this account makes it seem like I was doing a lot of thinking and calculating while playing, I wasn't. For one thing, there was no time; the whole solo couldn't have lasted more than a minute and a half. The thinking was mostly a matter of a few quick intuitive judgments and was done in (imagined) music and images more than in words or verbal symbols. The mental process resembled that used in riding a bicycle or carrying on a conversation more than that used in playing chess. On a bicycle, if you see a pothole, you don't need to explore and weigh alternatives; you just avoid it and continue pedaling. In conversation you say what you think; you don't make self-conscious decisions about each word and phrase.

So it was with that solo. I followed an improvisatory strategy I'd used thousands of times before: start simple and build from there.

The details, particular notes and riffs (melodic fragments) simply fell into place without any specific effort. The decision to attempt a second chorus consisted of a brief moment of panic, followed by an image. I remembered a concert where Sonny Rollins, the great tenor saxophone player, ended a solo to great effect by going to his bottom register and playing with strength, force, and *cajones*. The flash of that image was, in effect, both my decision to continue playing and my strategy for how to do it. Once I started that second chorus I had a definite sense that another force had entered my playing.

I have no idea how common such momentary inspiration is among performers. Musicians don't talk about such things among themselves, and journalists don't ask. These moments certainly do not happen to me on a regular basis. Whatever their frequency, however, they are not unique to music. Constantin Stanislavski, the great director and acting teacher, discusses this in *An Actor Prepares*. The book takes the form of an imaginary dialogue between a distinguished director and his students. At one point the director suggests that "you are playing the scene in the last act of *Hamlet* where you throw yourself with your sword on your friend Paul here, who enacts the role of the King, and suddenly you are overwhelmed for the first time in your life with a lust for blood." The director goes on to ask whether or not "it would be wise for an actor to give himself up to such spontaneous emotions as that" and to assert that:

> [T]hese direct, powerful and vivid emotions do not make their appearance on the stage in the way you think. They do not last over long periods or even for a single act. They flash out in short episodes, individual moments. In that form they are highly welcome. We can only hope that they will appear often, and help to sharpen the sincerity of our emotions, which is one of the most valuable elements in creative work. The unexpected quality of these spontaneous eruptions of feeling is an irresistible and moving force.[1]

That is what we must understand, those "spontaneous eruptions of feeling." Whether in music or theater, these eruptions enliven and unite performer and audience in a single encompassing consciousness.

ACTION IN TWO
ENVIRONMENTS, AGAIN

Something happens to performers, then, at rare moments—something they did not plan or will. When similar things happen in ordinary life we use expressions such as "he was overcome with grief," or "she was possessed by rage." As George Lakoff and Mark Johnson have noted, our commonsense view of the self easily accommodates the notion of multiple inner agents, often at odds with one another, acting on our behalf.[2] One task we face is to go beyond this commonsense view to suggest the neural mechanisms that underlie this experience. The other task is to account for the difference between what happens in ordinary life and what happens in performance. Both subjects stretch beyond this chapter, but we can get started on them. I want to begin with the first of these tasks.

It is not hard to find a multiplicity of agencies in the brain. Much of brain science is devoted to figuring out which neural centers control what bodily functions and actions, and how these centers are linked together. Some centers regulate internal processes such as heartbeat, respiration, and digestion. Other neural centers ride herd over complex behaviors such as grooming, nursing, exploration, fighting, foraging, and mating. To suggest similar lists of motor activity (e.g., locomotion, manipulation) and sensation (e.g., smell, vision) is easy enough. Neural centers are everywhere, for everything, too many for us to deal with in any detail.

For now it is sufficient to recall that the brain acts in two environments, the inner and the external. If, following Damasio, we think of our emotional life as being grounded in the neural regulation of body state, then it follows that spontaneous eruptions of feeling reflect the activity of those parts of the brain concerned with monitoring our bodily state *and* with communicating that state to others. The latter is crucial. We are social creatures, we depend on our fellows. When we express emotion we are signaling something about our interior milieu. We assume that others will pick up the signal and respond accordingly. Similarly, when we pick up on the emotions of another, our nervous system will bring about changes in our interior milieu. Our heart rate will increase or decrease, as will our respiration rate, and various hormones will be dispatched in the bloodstream to perform various tasks. Thus emotional communication is a means for mutual regulation of body states.

We express emotion through body posture and gesture, facial expressions, and vocal cries.[3] We move. Muscles in appropriate configurations extend or contract and a cry is uttered, the shoulders slump, and so forth. This is different from using the muscles in instrumental activity such as walking or running, throwing a ball, or cutting down a tree. This is also different from purely symbolic acts, such as giving directions to a stranger or writing a letter to the editor, which call on motor systems to shape the signs and symbols. The skeletal muscles are the final common path of all these actions, expressive, instrumental, or symbolic.

Given this multiple functionality it is not surprising that the skeletal muscles are not commanded by a single brain structure but are subject to multiple controls. The so-called extrapyramidal system is phylogenetically old, while the so-called pyramidal system is newer, appearing only in mammals. The pyramidal system is under strong neocortical control and seems to be especially important in fine control of the digits. The extrapyramidal system controls innate patterns for locomotion, fighting, mating, and so forth. The pyramidal system is concerned primarily with voluntary activity, while the extrapyramidal system is concerned both with involuntary and voluntary activity.[4]

The expression of inner state would be mediated by extrapyramidal control of the skeletal muscles. Those same muscles, however, are also subject to voluntary control through *both* the pyramidal and extrapyramidal systems. Just as the nervous system operates in both the inner and external environments, so the skeletal muscles serve both expressive and instrumental purposes.

DUAL CONTROL OF THE MUSCLES

Recall Bette Midler's performance for Johnny Carson's farewell. Instead of thinking about how that performance affected us, we might wonder what it was like for her. I recall that her eyes were teared; this suggests that she may have been skating on the edge of an impulse to cry.

I have had similar experiences while performing on my horn. Tears would well up in my eyes and I could feel a lump in my throat. If I gave in to the impulse I would be unable to continue playing. But if I tried to suppress it completely, the magic would be gone and my playing would become ordinary. I learned to bear down in my chest and abdomen "just so" and skate on the edge. The feeling didn't disappear, but I could continue playing my instrument.

We've all had similar experiences quite independently of music. Imagine you are in some public place and you receive bad news, perhaps about the death of a loved one. You are stricken with grief and feel a strong impulse to cry. At the same time you feel a contrary impulse to remain reserved in public, to suppress the sobbing and the tears. Later, you are called on to deliver a eulogy at the funeral. Once again you are torn. To speak intelligibly you must remain in control of your vocal apparatus. But you are speaking of your dead friend—and also so moved by a grief that wants to commandeer the same muscles in the service of crying out.

This is not an unusual situation, nor is grief the only occasion for such conflict. Laughter, anger, and physical pain can also generate impulses we struggle to suppress. What are the parties to this conflict? They must be inside us, in the nervous system, but where?

The impulse to cry or laugh or shout in anger arises in subcortical structures and acts on the muscles of the trunk, respiratory system, vocal system, and face through one set of pathways. The impulse to block such expression arises in cortical structures and acts on the same muscles through different, though often physically contiguous, pathways.[5]

Similarly, when I felt some other force enter my playing of "Stormy Monday," I was feeling the effect of strong subcortical impulses. Up to then my musical actions were primarily regulated by cortical circuits, long trained through years of practice. But at that point subcortical mechanisms added their expressive powers to the control signals reaching my muscles.

Why and how those subcortical mechanisms went into action just at that moment, I am not prepared to speculate. General exhaustion played a role, though that is hardly an explanation. For now we will have to rest content with knowing that the explanation we seek concerns the interaction of two distinct systems of neural circuitry, one phylogenetically old and concerned with emotion and motivation, the other phylogenetically new and concerned with fine motor control and planning.

MANFRED CLYNES AND ESSENTIC FORM

Some of the most remarkable work on emotional expression and its realization in music has been done by Manfred Clynes, a concert pianist, psychologist, and inventor. He has discovered precise temporal forms that embody emotion in touch and that can also be expressed in sound. Clynes calls these *essentic* forms. The essentic forms are remarkably similar across individuals and across a range of cultures (American, Balinese, Japanese, Mexican, e.g.), which suggests that they are biological rather than arbitrary cultural conventions. We are born with these expressive forms, we don't have to learn them. We do, of course, have to learn the musical devices that express them.

The peculiar experimental setup Clynes used to discover these forms is worth our attention. His subjects are seated in a straight-back chair with the arms free and with the middle finger on one hand—right or left, depending on handedness—touching a pad on an instrument he calls a sentograph. The finger remains in contact with the pad throughout the experiment. When a subject hears a cue she expresses an emotion by bearing down on the pad in a single expressive gesture in which her whole trunk moves, though only her finger touches the pad.

The cues are given with a tape recording. First is the name of an emotion, such as love or anger. Following the name the subject hears a series of soft clicks. Each time she hears a click she is to express the named emotion by pressing on the pad. It is important that the subject not be able to predict when the clicks will occur; therefore these are spaced at quasi-random intervals. Each click is thus a small surprise, and each expressive act must be deliberate.

The sentograph has sensors that measure the pressure the subject exerts on the pad both vertically and horizontally. The subject does thirty to fifty expressive acts for each emotion. The data from the different acts are averaged together to eliminate minor fluctuations. The averaged data can then be plotted to reveal the temporal patterns of pressure characteristic for each emotion.

In this way Clynes discovered distinct expressive forms for a number of emotions. Love, grief, reverence, anger, hate, joy, and sex have received the most extensive investigation, though Clynes has found forms for courage, hope, and what he calls "being apreene" (the feeling associated with intellectual insight). These expressive forms are on the order of one to six seconds long (see figure 5.1).[6]

While the decision to express an essentic form is voluntary, the exact shape of the form is not under voluntary control. The essentic form is preprogrammed and once initiated takes its course automatically.

More is involved, though, than a motor pattern. Clynes also examined oxygen consumption, respiration rate, and heart rate during the essentic expression. The basic finding is simply that processes varied significantly from baseline values (no emotion) and from one emotion to another. This is a clear indication that we are dealing with more than simple motor processes. These variables are indicators of energy processing, and that is regulated by subcortical brain mechanisms. If one is using more energy, then the heart will pump faster and the lungs will breathe more rapidly, both of which facilitate the consumption of oxygen (and the removal of waste). That is what Clynes observed for anger, joy, sex, and hate, suggesting that the body is preparing to use energy at a high rate. For grief, love, and reverence these levels dropped below the baseline, indicating that the body is preparing to conserve energy. Furthermore, Clynes and others have found that essentic forms correlate with both blood biochemistry and brain state.[7] They are thus the motor component of *an overall behavioral state* that includes visceral state and brain state as well. Clynes calls such states *sentic* states.

It would be a mistake to imagine that one can experience an emotion and then decide to communicate it by generating the appropriate essentic form, as though the emotion and the essentic expression were separable. They are not. To be sure, we can choose to suppress emotional expression through firm self-control—but that is quite different

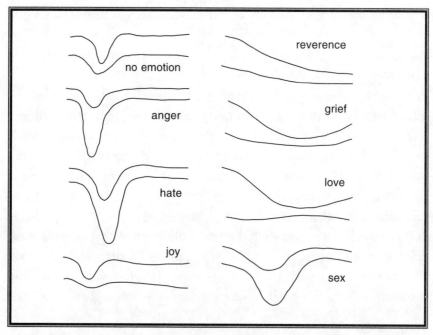

Figure 5.1 Essentic Forms: Each form is represented by the trace of the two sentograph transducers, vertical pressure on the top and horizontal (i.e., forward–backward) pressure on bottom. Time flows from left to right.

from not generating the expression at all. The latter is not physically possible. When the appropriate subcortical mechanisms organize some emotional state, they will modulate the skeletal muscles with the appropriate essentic form. Whether one's body freely expresses that form depends on the neocortical motor systems: they may allow the expression or try in varying degrees to suppress it.

In any event, much of our interaction with our fellows is about motivational and emotional states, which in turn are intimately linked to the state of the viscera: heart rate, whether we are breathing rapidly or slowly, what hormones are circulating in the bloodstream, and so on. Essentic forms thus convey information about visceral states. Information about the visceral state of one's fellows in turn will affect one's own visceral state. Thus essentic expression is one means by which individuals in a group sense and respond to—and thereby regulate—one another's visceral state.

One of the most striking aspects of Clynes's experimental paradigm is that it elicits emotion in the *absence* of any emotion-provoking situation. Clynes reports that initially subjects will fantasize situations appropriate to the emotion they are supposed to express, but after awhile such fantasies are unnecessary. The emotion exists in and of itself, free of any connection to fantasy. This is important to our understanding of music: it suggests that we can express and communicate emotion directly, unmotivated by any real or fantasized context. While the words of a son or the actions of an opera may provide a context to motivate specific feelings, purely instrumental music lacks such extramusical context.

If Clynes is correct, it should be possible to embody essentic forms directly in musical sound and thereby generate feeling directly in all who hear the music. Perhaps this is what the great violinist Yehudi Menuhin was thinking when he wrote,

> There are some artists so completely at one with the music that the emotion stems from the work and not from any outside stimulus. This can happen when playing alone, or when reading a composition. The performer's job is to translate what he sees in a composition, the ideal image of the score, into the sound. There is a wonderful chain of events that happens and reinforces the performance when everything is smooth and working well, when the act of interpretation creates its own momentum and the imagination is enriched by the very palette that one is using.[8]

Recall again Midler singing farewell to Carson. We have no difficulty imagining both artists being influenced by the extramusical context—Carson leaving *The Tonight Show* forever. People in both the studio and broadcast audience may also have been so influenced. Clynes's work suggests another mechanism at work. Regardless of precisely what caused Midler to sing the way she did, once she felt the sadness it would appear in her singing as the essentic form for grief, perhaps mixed with that for love, shaping the nuances of her melodic line. The audience then feels the emotion directly, the essentic key turning in the affective lock, without necessarily having to know or care about the nature of the occasion. There is no reason why both mechanisms can't be active, direct essentic propagation of feeling and response to Carson's leaving the program.

The question, of course, is whether essentic forms can be directly embodied in music, thus providing us with another example of Wallin's principle, one that Wallin himself has considered.[9] Clynes clearly believes they can be. There is nothing particularly odd about this possibility. After all, we operate our voice and other musical instruments with our muscles. The patterns of pressure that Clynes measured with his sentograph could surely be imparted to vocal and instrumental musical sound.

We do not have much evidence on this matter, but we have some. Donald Hodges played a tape of sonic versions of the essentic forms and found that his subjects were able to identify anger, joy, reverence, and, to a lesser degree, grief; the forms for love and sex were poorly recognized. Clynes has reported the forms for grief and love in two different renditions of a Bach prelude. In a different study Clynes collaborated with Nigel Nettheim to show how the essentic form for grief could be embodied in twenty-eight different melodic fragments.[10]

In all of his work, Clynes emphasizes the precision of the expressive forms, and that precision appears to come from the subcortical expressive systems, those not under willful control. Clynes has performed an experiment that bears this out.[11] He traced a graphic representation of an essentic form onto the face of an oscilloscope. The subject was then asked to guide the oscilloscope beam in tracing the essentic form by pressing on a pressure-sensitive pad whose output drove the beam. This proved difficult. Occasionally, however, the beam would suddenly lock on to the essentic form. Invariably it would turn out that the subject had closed his eyes and was generating the essentic form without reference to those traced on the oscilloscope. The involuntary mechanisms had become activated and were modulating the subject's motions.

How then can musicians activate these sentic systems? Clynes offers no explanation, nor can I. One line of speculation is that the musician imagines emotionally appropriate scenes, and those scenes in turn evoke the emotion.[12] If we want to follow this line we must understand how imaginary events can trigger real emotion. We know that such things happen and that actors often use such techniques.

A different possibility, however, builds on the fact that the motor system has several independent sources of control. Here I suggest that skilled musicians—including actors and dancers—may be able to create good voluntary *approximations* of essentic forms. Part of the physical skill involved in musical performance is learning such approximations. If the approximation is good enough, it may entrain the subcortical mechanism responsible for essentic forms. Once again we have coupled oscillation—in this case, coupling between cortical and subcortical dynamics.

The voluntary and involuntary systems are connected to the same muscles. If the voluntary motor control system moves the muscles in a pattern that is sufficiently close to some essentic form, motor feedback to the involuntary system might trigger it into generating the essentic form. That could in turn generate feedback that activates other involuntary systems. Thus the motor system, through the medium of music, may provide an indirect means for the will to influence involuntary, affective systems.

SOCIETY IN MUSIC

Think for a moment about Clynes's core list of sentic states; it is easy to imagine real-life contexts for grief, love, sex, anger, and hate. The common expression *jump for joy* suggests the general domain of joy. Reverence may seem more obscure, at least to those who don't believe in divine powers. The late David Hays once remarked, however, that reverence is what the infant feels for its primary caregivers. This in turn would suggest that the arm-outstretched beseeching gesture people use when addressing their divinities may be descended from the raised arms that signal the infant's desire to be picked up. In any event these are not abstract, context-free gestures. They constitute a medium of social interaction.

There is a tradition of music commentary dating back to the nineteenth century, in which writers and critics discuss music using social and emotional metaphors. Within this tradition, for example, it became commonplace to think of the first subject (or theme) in a sonata form as masculine in character and the second subject as feminine. The development of those subjects, then, becomes an interaction between male and female principles, or forces, or virtual individuals.[13] My friend Jon Barlow has told me how, in his student days, he was having difficulty getting a handle on Mozart's piano sonatas. He brought the matter up with his teacher, the late John Kirkpatrick of Cornell, who told him to think of the sonata's subjects as characters in a drama. In playing the sonata, Barlow would, in effect, be enacting various roles in a play.

This is not the language of music theory, which talks of themes, chords, rhythm, cadences, repetition, development, variation, pitch classes, and so on. Yet if music makes crucial use of neural circuitry that evolved for the communication of inner feeling states, what could be more natural than to think about music in terms of such states?

Let us consider an example of such metaphoric criticism. E. T. A. Hoffmann was one of the earliest practitioners of the style and his review of Beethoven's *Fifth Symphony* is a good example of it. Describing a passage in the first movement (starting at measure 168), Hoffmann says:

> They are sounds which purge the breast of a presentiment of the colossal—a presentiment which had wrung it and alarmed it. Like a friendly form that moves through the clouds shining and illuminating the deep night, a theme now enters which had only been suggested by the horn passage in E-flat major at m. 59 in the first part of the movement.

In likening a theme to "a friendly form" Hoffmann seems to be imputing agency to it. The theme is more than a particular set of pitches, deployed in a certain rhythm, and implying a certain harmony: it is a force with the power to "purge the breast of a presentiment of the colossal."

Describing a passage in the third movement, Hoffmann writes:

The restless yearning which the theme carried with it is now heightened to a fear which tightly constricts the breast permitting only fragmentary, disconnected sounds to escape; the G-major chord seems to lead to the close, but then the basses sustain the A-flat pedal note pianissimo for fifteen measures . . . [a passage of extended technical description] Why the master allowed the dissonant C of the kettledrum to continue to the end is explained by the character he was striving to give to the whole work. The dull, hollow strokes, having the effect of a strange, frightening voice by their dissonance, arouse the terror of the extraordinary, of the fear of spirits.

Here we have a theme capable of carrying a "restless yearning" that becomes transformed into a fear "which tightly constricts the breast." Is Hoffmann here speaking of something that happened in his body when listening to this passage, or something that happens only in some virtual body?[14]

Hoffmann's essay contains many similar passages in which he mixes the metaphorical and technical. We could say, of course, that Hoffmann is mistaken in talking about the piece itself when surely he can only be talking about his response to it, but this is secondary to his talking about the music in this way at all.

Such talk would not be surprising to Ferdinand Knobloch, a psychologist who writes that, in his youth, he had dreams in which the actions of the characters "were accompanied by closely synchronized music."[15] He began systematically to listen to music while sleeping lightly and noted that "sometimes I identified with the leading forces and took part in a forceful activity, but much more often I felt that the force was coming from outside." Knobloch concluded that music somehow carries "the drives, impulses, tendencies and attitudes directed to other people and sometimes received from them . . . listening to music engages one in human interaction."

Knobloch is not the only contemporary thinker who sees drama in music. Another psychologist, L. Henry Shaffer, suggests that "music can convey an abstract narrative . . . and the gestures of musical expression [may be seen] . . . corresponding to the emotional gestures of an implicit protagonist who witnesses or participates in the event."[16] Such thinking also figures in recent philosophical writing. In a recent article entitled "Music as Drama" Fred Everett Maus analyzes the opening of Beethoven's *F minor quartet, Op. 95.* He asserts that the opening two bars offer "a loud, aggressive, abrupt outburst" followed by a contrasting outburst in measures three to five. As he pointedly remarks, these are not the standard terms of musical analysis.[17] Following the lead of these thinkers I note that the opening of Chopin's *Scherzo No. 3 in C sharp minor, Op. 39,* seems to be a conversation between two imaginary agents, one forceful and imperious, perhaps male, and the other relaxed, expectant, reflective (perhaps female), but then growing animated.

Such examples show that music routinely has a level of structure and intention that standard music theory completely misses with its talk of rhythm, harmony, melody, and so forth. Think about trying to understand the artistry of Shakespeare, for example. Surely versification is an essential component of his artistry. If you would understand his plays, though, you must come to grips with his characters—their motives and actions. Verse is but the medium in which Shakespeare realizes his characters. One must understand both the medium and the characters—in addition to many other aspects—in order to understand Shakespeare's artistry. Such is the argument that Knobloch, Shaffer, Maus, and others are making about music. Beyond the phenomena studied in current music theory, music includes virtual social interaction.

Consider the following example of real social interaction—but not among humans. Let us follow Hans Kummer in observing a resting troop of baboons deciding where to go next. As you read this account imagine that you are a baboon situated somewhere in the middle of a troop consisting of, say, eighty members. This is what Kummer sees from his vantage point outside the troop:

> The troop performs slow on-the-spot movements, changing its shape like an undecided amoeba. Here and there, males move a few yards

away from the troop and sit down, facing in a particular direction away from the center. Pseudopods are generally formed by the younger adult males and their groups. For a time, pseudopods protrude and withdraw again, until one of the older males in the center of the troop rises and struts toward one of the pseudopods. At this, the entire troop is alerted and begins to depart in the indicated direction.

Thus a fair amount of milling about occurs in which the group ponders its options and, after due deliberation, an elder makes a decision. The troop pulls together and heads out. By comparison you might think about the opening of the final movement of Beethoven's *Ninth Symphony:* distinctly different musical ideas mill about until one of them, the Ode to Joy, takes charge.

Consider the older males at the group's center. They cannot see the entire troop in a glance or even by scanning from a fixed point of view. Each is checking out the various pseudopods and one another, glancing about, picking up indications here and there and integrating it all until one of them decides both that he's the one to signal a direction and what that direction is. Whatever the exact nature of the neural dynamics that perform these tasks, all this attending, updating, and integrating requires a pretty sophisticated control system to scan the scene and integrate tens or hundreds of indications about the state of the troop.

I suggest the neurodynamics of a single human musicker is comparable to collective decision making of this baboon troop, and that humans use their Central Social Circuitry* to track the music in the same way that baboons track their fellows. The troop's milling behavior is typical of intentional systems as they "hunt" for a stable state.[18] Unlike musicking humans, however, the baboons are not coupled in rhythmic interaction. The fact that musicking humans are coupled

---

*This term is not a standard one. Just like a theoretical biologist's use of *gene,* this term assumes the physical existence of something without making any claims about its exact nature. The brain surely has circuitry regulating social interaction, and we know quite a bit about its anatomy, physiology, and chemistry. Here we don't need to examine these details. Later on I refer to *sadness circuitry* in the same spirit.

means that the group acts in a unified way that is impossible for a baboon troop.

Imagine then that it is May 7, 1824, and you are attending the premiere of Beethoven's Ninth Symphony at the Kärthnerthor Theater in Vienna. On the stage you see not only a full symphony orchestra, with its strings, woodwinds, brass, and percussion, but also a full chorus and four solo vocalists. As the music unfolds you have to make sense of it all. At times that is relatively easy, for only a few instruments are playing. At other times the full orchestra is playing, with the strings, brass, and woodwinds all playing multiple parts—and then we have the chorus and soloists as well. The problem you have is not unlike that of the older males at the center of the baboon troop: you face a complex system of sonic activity and must make some integrated sense of it and maintain your own sense of direction amid all the hubbub. The difference between you and the baboons, however, is that everyone around you is effectively an older male scanning the scene, even the musicians.

You direct your attention here and there. Now you're listening to the violins, then the cellos attract your interest, then the flute, which gives way to the French horn, only to be supplanted by the tympany, and so forth. Even as you attend to this or that specific musical line you remain aware of other lines.

Perhaps one thing that pulls your attention here and there is a mismatch between what is currently happening in a specific part and what you were unconsciously expecting based on what you previously heard. One can imagine all sorts of things. If Beethoven has done his job as composer, then all the interacting strands of melody will be where they need to be when you check on them. The music will flow naturally and you'll hardly be aware of all the effort you're expending to track all those sounds.

The parallel between our baboon troop and our Beethoven premiere is not an exact one and has certainly been pushed to its limit. The principles of Equivalence and Ensemble State Collapse show how music allows a human group to function with the coherence of a single brain. Together they constitute the forge in which the Central Social Circuitry shapes the forms of group interaction and individual neurodynamics into a coherent culture.

At a more humble level, one where we have experimental evidence, consider the possibility that subcortical structures in your brain treat each instrumental line as the activity of a single human actor, a virtual being. This is what Albert Bregman's book *Auditory Scene Analysis* suggests.[19] The human auditory system evolved to segregate the soundscape into separate auditory streams, each of which is presumed to reflect the activities of a single causal agent somewhere in the world. Many of these causal agents are other animals, perhaps prey or predator, or fellow humans. When this system is presented with music, it operates in the same way, identifying streams and treating them as signs of actions by various agents. When you hear Beethoven's music your brain is responding to a carnival of virtual beasts, cavorting and fighting, licking their wounds, meeting and greeting old friends, gathering at the water hole for a drink, nuzzling, and snoozing the night away.

VIRTUAL ACTION

The term *virtual* has become ubiquitous. Computer folks talk of virtual memory, virtual circuits, and virtual reality, while other folks refer to the virtual office, virtual classroom, virtual corporation, virtual team, and virtual community.[20]

The sexiest virtuality is that of reality. *Virtual reality* is the term for a variety of computer technologies that allow a user to mimic the effect of operating in the real world. The basic idea is that, if we can use artificial means to provide a complete array of sensory input, then one can act as though one were, shall we say, searching for the source of the Nile with Richard Burton, when in fact one is sitting at home connected to a computer that is stimulating one's eyes, ears, skin, and perhaps nose and tongue as well. This "reality" is not real but virtual.

In listening to music, I submit we are running our Central Social Circuitry in virtual mode. It handles inputs in the standard way, but those inputs don't come from their normal external source, the social signals of other humans. Instead they are derived from music; that music may well mimic the expressive gestures of human interaction, but it is nonetheless something quite different. The feelings, forces, and virtual agents in music are not people, and in responding to them one is not engaging in social interaction.[21]

Virtual operation is native to our nervous system. A child pretends that a doll is alive or that toy truck is a real truck and interacts with it appropriately, even though the doll cannot speak and act autonomously, and the toy truck is considerably smaller and slower than a real one. The child supplies in imagination what the play objects lack in reality. When we dream, the brain creates a rich, if often confused, sensory and motor world of which we often know nothing. Recent research reveals that the sensory and motor areas of the brain are quite active during dreaming, as though we were actually out and moving about. Motor impulses are stopped, however, at the brain stem.[22] While we are relaxed and motionless the brain conjures up and moves about in its own world.

That the brain can do this is not so strange. While psychologists and neuroscientists disagree on many matters both superficial and deep, and admit to considerable ignorance concerning the operations of mind and brain, most agree that brains are active and seek input rather than being passive recorders. Our creative brains use the same neural structures for imagining and thinking that they use for perceiving and acting.[23]

When the brain is dreaming, its mechanisms are responsible only to the sensations and rhythms of the dreamer—that is, itself. The mechanisms have no need to synchronize with sensory input from the external world, though the brain must continue to regulate the inner world of the viscera. When the brain awakens, however, things are different. It must now align its activities with sensory input from the external world. When that brain is making or merely listening to music, it is aligning its activities with sound waves.

All of expressive culture occurs within some virtual space. Any action or sequence of actions that happens in reality is available for reenactment within some socially sanctioned virtual context. This is most

obvious in the case of drama, where actors imitate actions that may
well have been performed by real people. Such virtual actions are
cloaked in conventions that clearly mark them as virtual: the cos-
tumes, makeup, conventionalized motions, and speech patterns of a
particular dramatic tradition. The same is true of opera, where the addition of song heightens the virtuality of the events. Imagine that the
same is true of instrumental music, where we have no ostensible characters or actions. Rather, the performers give us the intentional and
emotional residue of actions and desires as they are embodied in musical sound.

SING A SAD SONG, WHY?

Given that music embodies virtual actions, let us consider a standard
problem in aesthetics: Why do we like music that elicits negative
emotions such as sadness? This problem entails three questions:

1. Do we in fact listen to music that evokes sadness?
2. Why do we do that?
3. Why is it pleasurable, not painful?

The first question is not much of an issue, for anecdotes abound.
For example, in his recent book *For the Love of It* on the joys of amateur musicking, Wayne Booth frequently talks of being moved to tears,
both through listening to performances by others and by performances
in which he is one of the players. Similarly, Crafts, Cavicchi, and Keil
have published interviews of a number of people who report being
moved to tears by music.[24] John Sloboda reports a study where sev-
enty-six college students were asked to check which twenty-five listed
emotions they had experienced while listening to music.[25] Sadness was
the single most frequent emotion at 96 percent, followed by 93 percent for joy, 92 percent for "liking," through 49 percent for sympathy,
43 percent for resignation, 17 percent for shame, and 13 percent for
gloating. A group of North American college students hardly constitutes a random sample of the world's peoples, but the results suggest

that almost all humans have experienced sadness while responding to music.

Why? The nature of sadness and crying is obscure. Scientific speculation agrees with common experience that the emotion (and crying) is a response to separation from a beloved, most typically the response of an infant or child separated from a parent. Paul MacLean has gone so far as to suggest that "the so-called separation cry may be the oldest and most basic mammalian vocalization." Human attachment and separation have been much studied in recent years and it is clear that the emergence of strategies for dealing with separation is critical for human psychological development.[26]

It is thus suggestive that music can quiet chicks that have been separated from their mother. Further, Panksepp has undertaken several studies of a particular physical response he describes as "a shiver up and down the spine, which often spreads down the arms and legs, and, indeed, all over the body."[27] He finds such chills particularly associated with sadness and suggests that sad music may have acoustic features especially effective in eliciting them. They seem especially strong during intense crescendos. The brain centers involved utilize endogenous opioids as well as oxytocin—neurochemicals known to mediate social bonds. A recent study by Anne Blood and Robert Zatorre has used brain imaging to demonstrate that phylogenetically old core brain structures mediating social behavior are especially active during chill-inducing music. The neurobiology of music and the neurobiology of social attachment appear to be intimately intertwined. We sing sad songs and dance with grief because they are part of our social life.

Yet unlike real grief, such songs and dance are pleasurable. Thus we must ask: How is it that, when the same brain circuitry that responds to separation is activated during music, the subjective feelings have such a different valence? Jerrold Levinson has suggested, for example, that our "responses to music typically *have no life implications,* in contrast to their real counterparts."[28] In this respect our Johnny Carson example is not as pure as we would like, for the decision to leave the show had major consequences for Carson himself and minor ones for his loyal audience.

In any case, what does it mean, concretely, to say one's response to music has no life implications? When your sadness circuitry has you crying in response to the death of a spouse, parent, child, or good friend, you are mourning a genuine loss. You will never again have conversations with that person or do things with them. Certain activities may disappear from your life altogether, at least for a time. When your sadness circuitry has you crying while listening to music, the state of the circuitry may be much the same, but the supporting neural context will be different. Your sadness is only virtual, but that virtuality is a function of the whole neural context in which the sadness circuitry is functioning, not of what is happening within the circuitry itself.

Levinson also suggests that "By imaginatively identifying our state with that of the music, we derive from a suitably constructed composition a sense of mastery and control over—or at least accommodation to—emotions that in the extramusical setting are thoroughly upsetting . . ." Surely this sense of mastery is related to the fact that one's auditory system is actively tracking the music, that one's motor system is perhaps imaginatively dancing or otherwise moving to the music—that is, if one is not actually dancing. Beyond this, when you are listening to such music you might be comfortably seated in a concert hall with a group of friends, or perhaps curled up on the sofa at home. In either case the general situation is one of comfort and intimacy with no worries for the future. That is a very different context from that of real grief.

This line of reasoning can be applied to any emotion. None of them, positive or negative, is under our direct control. If one gets a sense of mastery over grief by deliberately evoking it through music, why not extend that sense of mastery to the full range of emotions? Thus we can imagine, on the one hand, sequences of events in real life that bring one joy, anger, grief, hate, sex, love, and so forth. Now imagine that sequence of emotions independent of the particular life events that occasioned them. Imagine instead a group of people engaged in rhythmic vocalization, perhaps dancing and clapping as well, with the singing and body movements modulated by the appropriate essentic forms. We've got the same sequence of emotional states, perhaps compressed into a shorter time span, experienced as part of a deliberate group activity. In this context the emotional states do not have the same valence as they do in real life. In real life such emotions are part of the process whereby individuals negotiate their lives with their fellows, but in this ritual they are part of a shared affirmation of their group life.[29]

Even if we decided to adopt this story, I am not entirely sure it answers the needs of those philosophers, such as Levinson, who worry about the aesthetic attractions of sad songs. In real life sadness feels painful. In sad songs it does not. Why? Granted that the virtual feelings of musical experience reflect a deliberate act, how does the attendant sense of mastery alter our subjective experience of sadness? Why does the activation of the sadness circuitry feel different?

I don't know. It is a mystery—and mysteries, as someone once remarked, are to be experienced. This distinguishes them from puzzles, which are to be solved. I don't know how to turn this mystery into a puzzle, much less how to solve it, but I can tell you where I would expect to find the puzzle that corresponds to the mystery.

In the previous chapter we identified the mind with the global state of the brain. One's sadness circuitry may operate the same way in coping with a death in the family as it does in participating in a musical performance, but our subjective experience of that sadness is different because the supporting neural context is different—a matter we will touch on in the next chapter. We are dealing with two macroscopically distinguishable mental states. Both involve the activation of sadness circuitry, but they are otherwise different. Moreover, *no brain circuitry explicitly regulates these macroscopic states.* Circuitry exists for sound, motor control, sadness, and so forth, but no circuitry coordinates all the others. All we have are circumstances, customs, and practices. The various bits of brain circuitry do what they must, and some overall brain state emerges. When we understand the forms of neural weather at play in the macroscopic state of the nervous system, then we will understand why sad songs are pleasing, while the sadness of real grief threatens the end of the world.

RHYTHM
METHODS: PATTERNS
OF CONSTRUCTION

Rhythm is not a matter of the ear or of the finger only; it is a matter of
the two fundamental powers of life, namely, knowing and acting.
—Carl Seashore, *In Search of Beauty in Music*

THE TUMBUKA OF Malawi, in southeastern African, have an origin
myth that is coupled with a thigh-slapping routine. The myth concerns Mupa, who discovered the rhythms used in *vimbuza* music, the
music played for the trance dancing central to Tumbuka healing.
Mupa discovered the rhythms while slapping his thighs. He began
with a simple alternation—slap the right thigh with the right hand,
left thigh with the left hand, in even, alternating strokes—but that
quickly grew boring. So he began figuring out more interesting ways
to generate rhythms. I won't recite the whole story—you can find it in
Steven Friedson's book *Dancing Prophets*—but I will briefly describe
the thigh-slapping routine that Mupa developed.[1]

First, take a comfortable seat with your feet resting on the floor.
Gently slap one thigh (say, the right thigh with the right hand) and
then the other; do this repeatedly with an even rhythm at a comfortable tempo. Now, group your strokes into groups of three by slapping

your knee on the first of each group of three. You will probably have to count to do this. You could use numbers and say "one two three" but any three syllables will do. Just repeat the sequence over and over and slap your knee on the first syllable in the series. Not only is the physical gesture a little different from before, so is the sound. Notice that the initial stroke in your groups—set in **bold** type—will alternate between your right and left knees:

(1) **R knee** (2) L thigh (3) R thigh (1) **L knee** (2) R thigh (3) L thigh

A full cycle is thus six strokes long, divided into two groups marked by initial knee slaps. Emphasize the knee slaps so that they are just a little louder, thus strengthening the triple grouping. Practice this at a comfortable pace until you can do it with little or no thought. Then you may want to pick up the pace and see how fast you can go.

Next we are going to superimpose THREE (two-stroke groupings) on the TWO groupings that consist of three strokes each. We will do this merely by thinking. Continue the same pattern but now concentrate on only one hand at a time, perhaps your right. I find it helps simply to look at the appropriate thigh. In the following representation the right strokes are in **bold** while the initial strokes of the two groups of three are in *italics:*

(1) R knee (2) L thigh **(3) R thigh** *(1) L knee* **(2) R thigh** (3) L thigh

One could also choose to concentrate on the left-hand strokes:

(1) L knee (2) R thigh **(3) L thigh** *(1) R Knee* **(2) L thigh** (3) R thigh

Either way, you get six beats divided in two different ways. When you use knee slaps as your marker, the six beats are divided into two groups of three beats each. When you use left or right side as your marker, they are divided into three groups of two beats each. Further, you can switch your concentration back and forth from the right-hand strokes to the left-hand ones.

If you are not already practiced in this sort of thing, you should be slow and deliberate. As you become comfortable, pick up the pace. You will reach a point where you no longer explicitly think in six, with overlays about how each stroke must be executed, and think instead in three–two.

The pattern of physical gestures you establish by practicing this exercise can then be applied to playing the *ng'oma* drum, the lead or master drum of Tumbuka music. The thigh stroke and knee stroke of the exercise become two different ways of striking the drum. But the basic pattern that Mupa left his people forms the core pattern of Tumbuka drumming; all other patterns derive from it.

Mupa's story illustrates two of the three themes we will explore in this chapter. The major themes are rhythm and structure in music. Practice is the minor theme, for it takes practice to train the brain's looping circuitry to serve as a bank of oscillators regulating music's rhythms.

OSCILLATORS AND CLOCKS

How might a brain go about executing Mupa's patterns? We have already encountered one plausible device, the oscillator. When you slap a hand against your thigh at regular intervals, that is an oscillator. That you can do this at various speeds means it is a variable speed oscillator as well. It is thus reasonable to believe that, at some level of operation, the underlying neural circuitry takes the form of an oscillator—though you don't have to read very far in the neural literature to realize that various models have been proposed for how such an oscillator might be constructed, with no strong evidence one way or the other.

But one oscillator only accounts for one hand slapping. How do we get two hands slapping in alternation? One possibility is to add a *counter* to our oscillator. The counter counts beats and so allows us to execute different actions on different beats. In this case, we only need a two-place counter. We slap with one hand on the first beat, the other with the second beat. Then we reset the counter.

The counter, of course, is a different mechanism from the basic oscillator. While I don't think we can get very far without counters of some sort, we can get this simple left–right alternation without resort to a counter by employing a device we've already seen, the coupled oscillator. Instead of one oscillator driving both hands, we have two, one for each hand—a scheme supported by a variety of experimental evidence.[2] These oscillators would then be coupled out of phase—recall the discussion of Kelso's experiments in chapter 3. In this scheme each oscillator would have a period that is twice that between successive slaps. Figure 6.1 depicts this situation, with the individual slaps indicated in the center.

Of course, your ears get to hear the rhythm your hands create. You hear a regularly spaced slapping sound at twice the frequency of either of the oscillators driving your hands. To hear this rhythm—to understand it—you must entrain an internal oscillator to the rhythm of the external sound. This implies that the auditory system has a third oscillator, one that is entrained to the slapping sounds produced by alternating hand motions. Perhaps this auditory oscillator is providing the coupling function between the oscillators driving the left and right hands. That is to say, output from this oscillator goes to the two hand oscillators and keeps them exactly at opposite phase.

We are thus talking about three oscillators, one for each hand and a third driven by the sounds the sounds create. Recall, however, that the brain is bilaterally symmetrical. We might in fact have two auditory oscillators, one in each hemisphere. Still, experimental evidence indicates that it is the left hemisphere that perceives metrical rhythms while the right hemisphere is better at nonmetrical rhythms.[3]

All of this, of course, is completely speculative, though to our credit we are sticking to a fairly limited-parts list. But even this degree of speculation is not sufficient. Recall that there are two kinds of slaps, one to the knee followed by two to the thighs. We could produce this by having two three-place counters on the hand oscillators. Or we could imagine another pair of oscillators operating on a period three times as long as that of the basic oscillators. That would move the hands forward to the knees and back (see figure 6.2).

At the center we have a representation of the sounds, with the knee slaps in a darker shade. Each knee slap marks the beginning of a long-period oscillation in either the right or left hand. The idea then is that

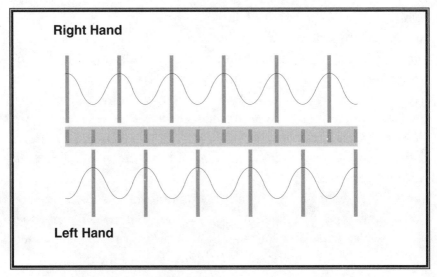

Figure 6.1　An oscillator for each hand.

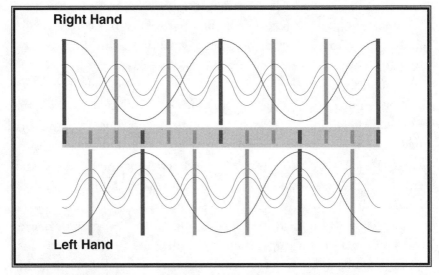

Figure 6.2　Oscillators at two different frequencies.

one generates a knee slap when the beginning of a long-period oscillation coincides with the beginning of a short-period oscillation.

I know of no experimental evidence favoring one of these models over the other. Different investigators have made computer simulations of meter and rhythm perception using banks of oscillators with different frequencies, and there has been analytic work on the use of multiple oscillators in generating actions, but I don't know of any experimental work that bears directly on the question of whether the nervous system uses multiple oscillators, counters, or both. I do have a prejudice, which is that, during practice, the *conscious* direction of motions in effect uses a counterlike mechanism mediated by language, albeit silent, inner speech rather than fully vocalized language. Such a "virtual counter" generates syllables at regular intervals and also has a mechanism to "bind" different syllables to each available execution "slot"—and we'll examine other such schemes later on. Yet the mechanism that *executes* such patterns during skilled performance consists of oscillators of various frequencies. There are no counters in the mature execution system. As I said, I know of no evidence on this; but it is the hypothesis with which I would start an experimental investigation.[4]

My prejudice in favor of oscillators is fairly easy to explain. For one thing, we know that even relatively simple physical systems can oscillate, and we know that nervous systems have special oscillatory circuits called central pattern generators.[5] Beyond this, it is easy to think of the brain as a bank of oscillating circuitry. If you ask, "Just where in the brain do we find oscillators suitable for generating and tracking rhythmic behavior?" you might answer "Everywhere." The nervous system is full of looping circuitry. Still, this does not mean that all of these circuits are oscillators. As Frank Wilson has noted in his delightful account of music making, "we probably do not possess a timing system that is anatomically distinct, in the sense that the auditory and motor systems are." But much activity is exquisitely timed as a matter of course, and the brain is rich with circuits that exhibit rhythmic behavior. I suggest that in musicking, much of this circuitry is recruited to support music's multiple rhythms.[6]

The practiced execution of periodic rhythmic patterns, then, involves multiple oscillators operating at various frequencies. You learn to execute such a pattern, however, by using some verbally mediated counter to train the brain's oscillator banks—a dynamicist might say that the counter sets an *order parameter* for the execution mechanism.

The story of Mupa is an elaborate way of motivating such a counter, or rather a set of successive counters as Mupa makes ever more elaborate experiments.

Mupa's tale is also a simple way of motivating practice. As you tell yourself Mupa's story and imitate his moves, you are practicing. You are using verbal skill to organize motor systems into a bank of oscillators that can execute complex rhythms without the need for conscious control.

THE NATURE AND
FUNCTION OF PRACTICE

Consider what you had to do to execute these various arm and hand motions in the correct patterns. You had to explicitly think about what you were doing; you may even have given yourself verbal cues of some sort (something children often do, as we will see in the next chapter). If you kept practicing, however, the need to think about what you were doing would diminish, and if you persisted long enough, it would disappear entirely. If fact, to get to the point where you could execute the patterns while explicitly attending to either the left-hand or right-hand strokes, you have to be able to execute the basic pattern without attending to physical motions.

What interests me is simply that, to begin learning this skill, you have to think about it, but with practice it becomes automatic. What is going on in the brain during these two modes? Is there a difference?

Work done by Steven Petersen and his colleagues at Washington University suggests that the thoughtful practice of a task involves a different pattern of brain activation from the skilled *execution* of the task.[7] Petersen's group used PET scans to measure brain activity while subjects were both learning a simple skill and executing it after having learned it. One task was verbal and involved reading nouns and generating appropriate verbs. The other task involved tracing a path through a simple maze using touch alone for guidance, as the maze was not visible. While these tasks elicited different patterns of brain activity, in both cases the pattern during initial performance was different from the pattern after several minutes of practice. The differences were both cortical and subcortical.

Petersen and colleagues proposed a "scaffolding-storage" model of learning. When a task is being learned—"unskilled effortful perform-ance," as Petersen calls it—the brain establishes neural scaffolding to meet the demands of the new task. Just which regions perform as scaf-folding will vary from task to task. Once learned, the task is per-formed more efficiently by other brain regions where task schemas are permanently stored. Petersen suggests that the scaffolding and storage regions may well function in parallel. During the early phases of learning, the scaffolding bears the major burden of actually executing the task while the storage region operates in the background, learning the task. As the task is learned the burden of control shifts.

If you are raised among the Tumbuka, the story about Mupa and his rhythmic investigations is your scaffolding. As you repeat the thigh-slapping routine time after time, those rhythms become easy and natu-ral for you. But Western music, which emphasizes simple two- and four-beat patterns, is quite different.

The scaffolding is of a different nature: toe tapping and counting. You learn to tap your foot to the music's beat, thus using it as an oscil-lator, and learn to use syllable sequences to count toe taps and subdi-vide beats. These routines presuppose that you've been extensively drilled in counting and can do so easily and automatically.

In effect you use components of your neuromuscular system to cre-ate a virtual clock. The overt behavior is that of an oscillator (the toe tapping) coupled to a counter (the verbal syllables). When you per-form music you know well, of course, you don't consciously think about either the toe tapping or the syllables. You simply play.

As far as I know, no one has observed just where in the brain you direct your toe to tap. But the need to deliberately learn it and con-sciously think about doing it—until it becomes automatic—suggests that it is somewhere in the neocortical motor cortex. The fact that foot tapping is used to time actions executed variously by the throat, tongue and lips, the arms and fingers, and the lungs suggests that the oscillation is in a cortical region that isn't directly linked to the leg and foot, but that can access any set of muscles. The oscillation is probably not in primary motor cortex, then, but in secondary motor cortex. There is, in fact, considerable evidence that repetitive movement is regulated by a secondary motor region called the supplementary motor area (SMA). The SMA is one of the cortical regions where Petersen and his colleagues found an increase in metabolism during skilled performance.

Now, which foot taps? The toe tapping will be controlled by the contralateral hemisphere—left hemisphere for right foot, right hemisphere for left foot. I'm right-handed and tap my right foot, but different people tap differently.[8] I know of right-handers who tap the left foot, left-handers who tap their right foot, and so on. There are people who tap both feet, one foot on the strong beats and one on the weak. Given these possibilities, I leave to you to figure out which hemisphere is active in these different tapping regimes. Note, however, that regions in one hemisphere generally have direct connections to the mirror region in the opposite hemisphere.[9]

In Western music, and many others as well, individual pulses are grouped in repeating units, generally of two, three, or four beats, or simple combinations of these (e.g., two groups of three). This grouping is called meter, and each individual grouping of beats is called a measure. Thus if there are four beats in a measure, you mentally count "one, two, three, four." We also use syllables to subdivide a single beat. Thus "one ee and ah" divides the first beat into four units while "two ee and ah" divides the second beat into four units, and so forth. For our purposes the details are not important. What is important is the simple use of the linguistic system as a source of clock "ticks" in training the music system.

Let us consider one last tradition of rhythm pedagogy, the *karnataka* tradition of South India. This rhythm discipline, called *solkattu*, is a vocal–manual discipline that is particularly important for drummers but is applicable to all musicians. I became acquainted with *solkattu* by observing a class taught by Ramnad V. Raghavan, a *mridangam* drummer who was, at the time, on the faculty at Wesleyan University in Connecticut.

Solkattu involves reciting syllable sequences while indicating the rhythmic framework with hand gestures: a clap, a wave, and finger enumeration. Each gesture marks one beat in a *tâla*, the basic unit of repetition in South Indian music. *Tâlas* can have varying numbers of beats, usually ranging from three to the midteens. The individual beats have the same length and are generally subdivided. Thus we have *chapu tâla*, consisting of five beats: 2 + 3. It is counted as follows:

Beat	Gesture
1	clap
2	clap
3	nothing
4	clap
5	nothing

In the *solkattu* exercises one superimposes syllable patterns over the manual *tâla*. Here are a few such patterns out of thousands:

ta / di / tom / nam
ta – ki ta / ta ka di mi / ta lan gu
di / tan – ki ta / na kan tan gu / ki ta ta ka / tom

The *solkattu* patterns can have varying numbers of elements and can interact with the underlying *tâla* in complex ways. For instance, one can cycle a succession of different syllable patterns, each of a different length, over a single repeating *tâla*; and one can double or even quadruple the tempo of syllable repetition with respect to that of the *tâla*.[10]

Karnataka music has a distinct flavor that is different from that of the *vimbuza* music of the Tumbuka and the various musics in the Western tradition. While these musics differ in many ways, above all they differ in fundamental rhythms, the way they structure the groove. Each culture has its own physical routines for training the musical body and recruiting neural loops to its characteristic rhythms. Thus a rhythmic pattern that is easy for a young African child may be difficult for adult Western musicians.

TWO STREAMS: GROOVE AND GESTURE

In addition to cyclic repetition, music also "tells a story," to use a phrase many jazz musicians use when talking of a particularly good solo. Music thus involves two interacting streams of activity, a common notion I got from Manfred Clynes, thus:

Two Streams Hypothesis: music involves "two simultaneous streams, one stream the repetitive and hierarchical pulse, and the other the evolving, emotionally meaningful 'story' of the music."[11]

Clynes notes that one of the ways musical idioms differ is in the way they develop these two streams. While all musical idioms employ these two streams, some, such as Western classical music, elaborate the "evolving" stream, while others, such as the polyrhythmic musics of West Africa, elaborate the "repetitive" stream.

Perhaps the most neutral terms for these streams would be *cyclic* (repetitive) stream and *phrase* (evolving) stream, for it is in the evolving stream that musical phrases are elaborated. However, I often prefer to think of the repetitive stream as the *groove* stream, after Charles Keil's analysis of musical grooves, and the phrase stream as the *gesture* stream. The notion of musical gesture is an old one, employed by both Keil and Clynes.[12]

In thinking about these streams I find it useful to think about history, by which I mean the succession of states in a dynamical system, whether it be the weather in Boise, Idaho, the roll of the dice at a Monte Carlo gaming table, or the succession of states in a nervous system. Each brain has a unique history, which means, as Freeman argues, that each engages the world in a unique way. But when a group of people commit themselves to a musical performance, they are committing themselves to share in one history. By Wallin's hypothesis (about the likeness between music and neurodynamics), that shared history is the same for each, at least at the level of the dynamics of transitions from one state to another.

It is one thing to talk about successions of states and another thing to talk about a system's memory, where memory is understood, in

Edelman's phrase, as the system's "ability to repeat a performance." More deeply, Edelman talks of structures "that permit significant correlations between current ongoing dynamic patterns and those imposed by past patterns. . . . What all memory systems have in common is evolution and selection."[13] Consider the oscillators we talked about earlier. An oscillator is a simple memory device, one that simply repeats the same succession of states over and over until it either runs out of energy or is stopped. The span of such a memory is equal to the period of the oscillator. Given that one of Clynes's two musical streams is repetitive, we can identify it with an oscillator-type memory system.

It is clear, however, that oscillators are not adequate vehicles for "evolution and selection." We need other mechanisms to handle that. I am not particularly concerned right now with what these mechanisms consist of, only that they are needed—for I want to identify Clynes's other musical stream with this other type of memory, the type involving evolution and selection.

The function of the groove stream, with its limited time depth, is to suspend history and to create the psychological space in which music happens. The cyclic repetition of a pattern creates the virtual world in which the drama enacted through a succession of musical gestures takes place. The evolving collective brain states involve both the groove and gesture streams. Clynes's sentic forms come into play as modulating forces on the gesture stream. In ordinary life, there is no groove to accompany one's sadness, anger, joy, love, grief, or hatred. These affective structures, as they are activated during music, are operating in virtual mode and it is the cyclic groove that creates that virtuality. But it is not as though these structures have some kind of a mode switch with Real and Virtual settings. Rather, *it is the absence of direct personal interaction coupled with the ongoing groove that makes the affective experience a virtual one.*

Imagine you are a performer in a musical piece that consists of nothing but the groove. Let us assume a number of distinct parts are being played—as is the case in the polyrhythms of African and African-influenced music. Once you start playing your part in the cycle, your auditory system converges on the complete sound of the cycle while your motor system converges on your particular part. Your brain moves through the same succession of states with each cycle. The same is true of the other players. All of you hear the same sounds, though each plays a different part.

In the language of dynamics theory, the cyclic pattern is a type of attractor.[14] Each person in the group, of course, is moving toward the same attractor. While the performing group is involved in this periodic rhythm, the collective system's historical "depth" is quite shallow. Individuals are no longer taking irreversible trajectories through their individual state spaces but are involved in a collective effort that converges on an attractor in the collective state space.

Consider again the bell choir I talked about at the beginning of chapter 2. Three of us played our individual parts, time after time after time, without any change, but the fourth player, the leader, did something else: he improvised short phrases against our cyclic background. None of the phrases was very long, but many of them cut across the boundaries between one period in the cycle and the next. Thus our leader imposed an irreversible temporal structure on the repeating one. His part evolved and thereby forced the ensemble state to evolve as well.

This is also typical of African musicking. The specific instruments will vary, as will the parts played by each performer, but the fundamental situation is the same. One group of musicians maintains the pulse stream while at least one other musician, generally the so-called master drummer, elaborates phrases. Where the music is played for dancers, as it often is, the dancers may well be telling a story in their dance. That is to say, the dance structure may be evolving and irreversible rather than simply cyclic. We may also have a vocalist, for example, who is improvising verses in praise of an important leader or simply telling one of the traditional tales. Whatever happens in the narrative stream, however, is ultimately entwined with the groove stream and thereby lifted from the ongoing events of one's life. The trajectory of this shared evolution is discontinuous from the separate trajectories each individual mind evolves outside of musicking.

Psychological experiments show the state dependency of memory. In one, subjects were asked to memorize a list of words while music was playing in the background. Later they were asked to recall the list. Researchers found the subjects' recall was helped if the same music was playing, even though that music was irrelevant to the memory task. Further investigation has shown that the music's tempo—the groove stream—was most effective in aiding recall. The memory traces for the words on the list seemed to have become entwined with the rhythmic dynamics of the music's groove stream, making the overall task performance dependent on the brain's overall state. Of course, the events in music's own narrative stream would be even more tightly coupled with groove stream dynamics, for they are created specifically in coordination with those dynamics.[15]

NARRATIVE GESTURES

The oral epic straddles the border between music and literature. In the classic research on this subject, reported in Albert Lord's *The Singer of Tales*, Lord and Milman Parry discovered that contemporary Yugoslav storytellers construct their improvised narratives using a large number of stock phrases. So too, they find, did the ancient Greek master known as Homer. These narratives are constructed in verse form, which means that storytellers must construct lines of a certain length and rhythm, and having words that rhyme and alliterate.

The basis of verse, of course, is meter, music's groove stream. Oral epic has a groove stream as well, and it is often sung. The Yugoslav poets Parry and Lord studied—sang their epics, creating simple horizontal melodies (which we'll examine in chapter 8). The rural blues traditions of the southern United States involve the oral improvisation of standard narratives using a variety of stock phrases, as does the rather different and more recent Nigerian tradition of Jùjú.[16]

Stock phrases are needed because oral poets must satisfy metric constraints in real time, without the writer's leisure to consider alternatives. These gestures, if you will, each have certain rhythmic, syntactic, semantic, and acoustic properties. Part of learning your craft is learning a large repertoire of such formulas so that you can call on them quickly and easily in the act of telling your tale. Of course, each story also has a standard set of characters and plot elements, which one must also know—but that's another matter. When you tell your story, you use these verbal formulas to realize the characters and events of the story at hand. Since only the characters and general plot are fixed, you can vary the details of your performance to suit your audience.[17]

Such formulas occur in all oral storytelling traditions. For example, we find them in the toasts of African-American tradition, oral tales centered around characters such as Signifying Monkey, Stackolee, and Dolomite. This tradition in turn has influenced hip hop. Most hip hop performances, according to my informants, use the same lyrics as in the recorded versions. In something known as freestyling, however, the MC (master of ceremonies, i.e., the rapper) will improvise lyrics in real time, and the DJ will then work his turntable magic in real time.[18]

There is a considerable body of musical analysis in which melodies are broken down into core gestures, called *motifs*. Early in the last century, the musicologist Heinrich Schenker theorized that the "motif, and the motif alone, creates the possibility of associating ideas, the only one of which music is capable."[19] One can create complex melodies from a simple motif or two by varying the motif in simple ways—for example, moving it up or down in pitch, turning it upside down, or reversing it end-for-end—and combining the variations. Perhaps the best-known example of such melodic development is the opening movement of Beethoven's *Fifth Symphony*, which employs a single four-note motif. These derivational processes are the meat and potatoes of the study of counterpoint in the Western classical tradition. But there is nothing specifically Western about them. One can analyze many melodic lines into component fragments derived from a small set of basic motifs. Every musical tradition has a large vocabulary of motifs—in jazz they are called riffs or licks. These motifs are thus similar in function to the verbal formulas that Parry and Lord have found underlying oral epic narrative.[20]

In oral traditions the story itself provides overall continuity in the gesture stream. What does the functional work performed by the story or theme in purely instrumental music (or music with only nonsense syllables in the vocal line)? The answer remains a mystery. To be sure, we have the well-explored themes of expectation and anticipation introduced by Leonard Meyer in his classic *Emotion and Meaning in Music.* Meyer's basic idea is simple enough: the melodic and harmonic structures of music achieve their effects by playing on our tendency to project into the future. Through a wide variety of mechanisms, musical phrases create expectations; the beginning of a phrase creates expectations about how the phrase will continue and end; one phrase creates expectations about subsequent phrases, and so forth.[21] Beyond this some recent theorists have found plots in Western classical music, but these plots depend on specific structural practices, and whatever insight they give us into those particular compositions, it's not clear what they tell us about the global structure of music in stylistically different traditions.[22]

Taken in sum, this work does not give us deep and specific insight into large-scale musical form and structure, nor is it well integrated with the theoretical and experimental work that has been done on the groove stream. A deeper understanding of musical narrative, I believe, can emerge only from a deeper understanding of the underlying neural mechanisms.

GERSHWIN'S NARRATIVE: "I GOT RHYTHM"

Short of that deeper understanding, we can at least consider a specific instance of how music structures the gesture stream. I want to consider a typical example of what many musicians know as a *standard:* these are mostly by North American composers of the first half of the twentieth century, and many of them were originally written for Broadway shows. The song I want to examine is George Gershwin's "I Got Rhythm." This tune remains a favorite of jazz musicians, who have kept Gershwin's "Rhythm" changes while creating new melodies, thereby conferring memetic status on that pattern of chords. Duke

Ellington's "Cottontail," Charlie Parker's "Anthropology," Dizzy Gillespie's "Salt Peanuts," Thelonius Monk's "Rhythm-a-Ning," Miles Davis's "Oleo," and many others are all based on "Rhythm" changes.

Such tunes are generally thirty-two bars long. "I Got Rhythm" is actually thirty-four bars long, with three eight-bar sections followed by a final ten-bar section. Jazz musicians generally shorten the final section to eight bars. The following analysis is based on the jazz version.

We can depict the structure of "I Got Rhythm" as a tree as shown in figure 6.3.

The structure of such standards is generally identified by the third level, which consists of four eight-bar phrases. This form by convention is known as an AABA form. *A* designates the first eight-bar phrase that is repeated in the second and fourth position, while *B* designates a contrasting phrase that appears in the third position.

Figure 6.4 shows the melodic contour of the A section.

The shaded background indicates the two-bar sections that frame the melody. The four melody phrases are in black, with a node for each note (the notes' relative durations are not indicated). Finally, the overall contour is shown in medium grey. Notice that the final note of the whole phrase is higher than the beginning note, giving the phrase an overall ascending shape.

Figure 6.5 shows the B section, generally known as the bridge, or channel.

The development here is similar to that in the A section. Relatively simple two-bar phrases are joined, by simple means, into four-bar phrases, and those into an eight-bar phrase. Here, however, the last note of the phrase is lower than the first, so the phrase, unlike the A section, is a descending one.

The overall melodic contour thus consists of two eight-bar rising phrases, an eight-bar falling phrase, and a concluding eight-bar rising phrase as shown in figure 6.6.

There is more to the structure of this tune than its melodic contour. We also need to consider its harmonic structure, but only briefly. Think of harmony as the sonic background to a melody. It arises from the relationship among pitches that are sounded simultaneously. Standard

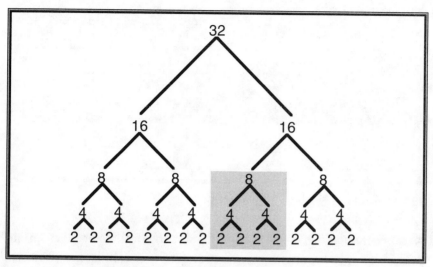

Figure 6.3 Binary structure for "I Got Rhythm."

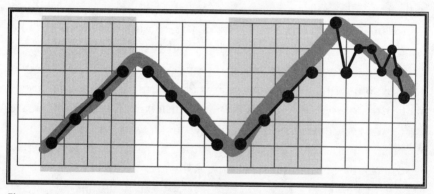

Figure 6.4 A-section contour for "I Got Rhythm."

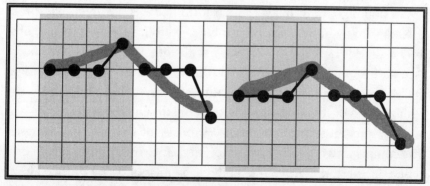

Figure 6.5 B-section contour for "I Got Rhythm."

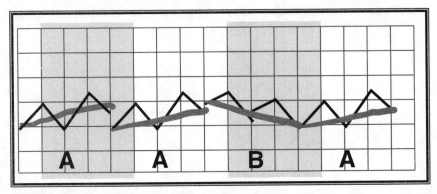

Figure 6.6 "I Got Rhythm" melodic contour.

Western harmony is based on chords consisting of three or more simultaneous pitches. In roughly three centuries of musical practice, Western musicians have worked out various sequences of chords that make sense to the musical ear.[23]

"I Got Rhythm" employs a few of these standard sequences. The important point, though, is that the A and B sections have distinctly different harmonies. Quite independently of their melodies, the two sections sound quite different and it is that harmonic contrast that has made this song so interesting to jazz musicians. When they create their own song based on "I Got Rhythm," jazz musicians keep its overall harmonic structure while providing a new melody, which may be structurally quite different from Gershwin's.

Let us think about this structure a bit. What would happen if, instead of the contrasting B section, we had another A section? The song would no longer be a thirty-two-bar form nor even a sixteen-bar form; it would simply be an eight-bar form played four times. It's the use of a bridge that creates the thirty-two-bar form. Other forms have been used to fill out thirty-two bars. "Embraceable You" and "How High the Moon" have an ABAC form; "Autumn Leaves" is AABC; and "Yesterdays" is ABCD. In each case the constituent parts are eight-bar phrases, and those in turn generally consist of two four-bar phrases that comprise two two-bar phrases. This basic structural principle underlies an extraordinarily large body of popular and jazz music. These thirty-two-bar forms are simplified expressions of the harmonic and structural principles developed in the high-art tradition of Western classical music. Just as the constant use of "Rhythm" changes confers memetic status on that particular harmonic structure, so the constant use of thirty-two-bar forms confers memetic status on those various devices.

The most obvious of these is hierarchical organization, one of the handful of principles that Herbert Simon identified in his classic series of essays *Sciences of the Artificial*. The best way to build large complex structures is to use smaller structures, each with its own integrity and order, and each of which in turn is built of still smaller structures.[24] Music is rich with such structures at every scale of organization, from hundredths and tenths of seconds up to tens of minutes and hours. One is reminded of Richard Condon's hypothesis that behavior is a wave phenomenon. Music certainly seems to be; some of the waves are very short, others are longer. But at every scale we see repetition and variation, expectation and fulfillment.

WALK THE INNER WALK

It goes without saying that the nervous system must coordinate the two streams. In the groove stream, rhythm is cyclical and repetitive, with the basic period no longer than a few seconds. In the gesture stream, rhythm has to do with the structures of phrases and so is concerned with longer stretches of time. Where are the neural structures that handle this timing?

Let's begin with the groove stream by recalling Wilson's remark that the brain doesn't have a separate timing system. For the most part we're going to have to get our rhythms from systems in which accurate timing evolved as an intrinsic aspect of other functions. We can, however, start with some circuits that are specifically rhythmic: the so-called central pattern generators (CPGs).

CPGs—circuits that generate signals at regular intervals without any sensory input—have been studied in invertebrates, fish, amphibians, reptiles, and mammals.[25] While CPGs are capable of generating simple periodic pulses necessary for motor action, it is clear that, for example, the multilimb coordination involved in walking requires extensive involvement of higher-level motor structures, including the cerebellum, the basal ganglia, and the cerebral cortex. The cerebellum seems to operate on a timescale with an upper limit of a second or two, while the basal ganglia operates in tens of seconds or even minutes, suggesting that it may be involved with the phrase stream as well.[26]

Following Clynes's remark that the pulse stream seems related to gait, and recalling music's intimate relationship with dance (and marching), it seems reasonable to speculate that the timing mechanisms for this stream are based on the mechanisms for locomotion or other motor action.[27] Thus in the Western tradition foot tapping provides the basic pulse, which is then supplemented with counting mechanisms both to group pulses into longer units and subdivide them into smaller units. The *karnataka* tradition uses hand gestures, and the Mupa storytellers use thigh slapping, in a similar way. Every tradition, it seems to me, must employ the same or similar mechanisms to handle the internal timing of musical gestures that must be executed within the rhythmic framework established by the groove stream.

But this doesn't tell us where the music's going. Given that a musical gesture—a phrase or a riff—has been selected, it doesn't tell us anything about *how* gestures are selected and, shall we say, "scheduled" for execution. What connects the groove and the gesture streams?

Let's continue with the notion that the groove stream is based on the mechanisms of locomotion. To get from one place to another you need a navigation system. I therefore suggest that it is the brain's navigation system that links the two streams, thus:

Path: neural machinery for navigation guides the gesture system on a path through a gesture "space" at a pace and rhythm set by the groove system.

Consider, for a moment, the routine descriptive language we use to talk about music. Pitches are high or low, intervals wide or narrow, an improviser has a horizontal or a vertical style, and different keys are said to be more or less distant from one another. Thus a melody will wander up and down, from one tonal territory to another, until it finally returns to the home key—just as an animal has a home base that serves as a point of departure and return. In light of recent work on metaphor this language gives one pause.

Over the past two decades George Lakoff, Mark Johnson, and others have been pursuing the idea that abstract concepts—such as those used to talk about music—are derived from concrete concepts through metaphor. Concepts used to articulate some abstract domain are given meaning by relating them to some concrete domain. The navigational domain—they talk of the journey—is one concrete domain that has played a central role in these discussions. On a journey one has goals and subgoals, requires resources, encounters obstacles, often uses various sorts of vehicles, and so forth. In a famous example, one talks of "driving in the fast lane on the highway of love"—which is, I believe, a song lyric.

The course of love is not a journey in any physical sense. But concrete imagery having to do with journeying provides an immediately intelligible way of talking about the otherwise intangible experience of love.[28]

Suggestive though this is, the fact that concepts *about* music use navigational imagery doesn't mean that mechanisms executing music itself use the brain's navigational circuitry. Nonetheless, I want to explore the notion that the machinery we use to guide our way in the physical world also links the groove and gesture streams in musicking. Unless the brain has special-purpose machinery exclusively for implementing music (for which there is no evidence), music must be implemented by neural systems that arose to serve other functions.[29]

Navigation, while it takes place in space, is not only a spatial activity. Navigating by dead reckoning, for instance, is also a temporal activity. In dead reckoning you keep track of your position by noting your direction, your speed, and your elapsed time on each heading. The advantage of dead reckoning is that you are not dependent on landmarks, hence its use by mariners.[30] The disadvantage is that you need accurate timekeeping, both to judge your speed and to judge elapsed time.

While animals do use landmarks and odor traces, dead reckoning seems to be at the heart of their navigation skills. Several decades of experimental work make it clear that mammalian navigation is regulated by a set of structures in the limbic system that are closely connected with the basal ganglia (which, as we saw, are involved in the groove stream). Among these structures, the hippocampus seems particularly interesting. The hippocampus is a part of the old mammalian brain (recall MacLean's terminology from chapter 2) that has extensive connections with the rest of the brain.

In 1978, John O'Keefe and Lynn Nadel's *The Hippocampus as a Cognitive Map* established the recent agenda in hippocampus research. More recently, A. David Redish has built on their work with *Beyond the Cognitive Map: From Place Cells to Episodic Memory*, in which he reviews more recent research and presents his own synthesis. My speculations are built upon Redish's.

Redish's subtitle indicates the range of functions that have been attributed to the hippocampus. The idea that the hippocampus encodes a cognitive map comes from hundreds of studies in which microelectrodes are implanted into the hippocampus of a rat to monitor the response characteristics of individual neurons. Investigators discovered a class of cells that responded strongly only when the rat was in a particular place in its environment, hence the notion that these are place cells. A structure that is full of such place cells might well, so scientists reason, encode some kind of map of the environment.

A rather different view of hippocampal function comes from studies of brain injuries in humans. When the hippocampus is destroyed, one loses the capacity to form new memories. You can still recall things that happened before the brain injury, but you cannot form memories of any later events. Hence the hippocampus seems to be involved in the formation, though not the long-term storage, of what is called episodic memory.

On the face of it, episodic memory and the cognitive map are very different. There is, of course, no a priori reason to believe that a particular brain structure plays the same role in both rats and humans, for organs can change their function over the long run of biological evolution. Still, these functions seem so very different that one does pause and think. And a thought one might have is that perhaps these functions are not so different after all.

That is what makes David Redish's work so very interesting. After analyzing a large number of studies and simulations, he has created a model of mammalian navigation and of hippocampal function that makes sense for episodic memory as well. Redish concludes that "the role of the hippocampus in the navigation domain is twofold: (1) to reset an internal coordinate system, and (2) to replay recently traveled routes during sleep states. . . . Both of these functions, necessary for navigation, are also keys to episodic memory."[31] I want to delay discussion of the replay mechanism until the next chapter, where I argue that music is a kind of waking dream. So let's concentrate on item 1.

The purpose of the reset mechanism is to establish the context for action, to make a link between the animal's internal cognitive map—whatever its exact form—and the external world by using external cues. This problem is familiar to subway riders. You get off the train, walk to an exit by a path that may be quite convoluted (I'm thinking of some of the more challenging stations in the New York City system), and finally emerge on the ground. The first thing you do is look around for familiar landmarks—buildings, street signs—so you know exactly where you are and what direction you are facing. Once you've established that, you can proceed on your way, guided by your cognitive map. What happens if one of your landmark buildings has been demolished since you were here last? Or you were forced to take an unfamiliar exit because of construction in the station itself? You will take a little longer to find familiar landmarks.

Redish notes that patients with hippocampal damage have problems in maintaining and establishing context. If they are interrupted in a conversation or a task, even briefly, they are unable to pick up where they left off. It is as though the conversation or the task had never existed.

Now consider the narrative musical stream. Imagine that you are listening to *I Got Rhythm*, either *just* listening or listening while you perform your part in it. You arrive at the eighth bar, the last one in the A section, and hear the so-called tonic chord. You know you are "home," for that is how the tonic chord functions in this music. Then the ninth bar arrives and you hear what you heard at the beginning (though the

lyrics are different). So you've got to recognize the connection—identify the sonic landmarks—and reset. You can now replay the melody
you heard the first time even as you are listening to its repetition.

What happens at the seventeenth bar? Something different, that's
what, and it was probably signaled in the last half of the sixteenth bar,
which is the last one in the repetition of the A section. The sounds
you hear in bar seventeen are not only different from those in bars one
and nine but from a different tonal territory. If you are familiar with
the tune, you knew that this was going to happen, and you know
what is going to happen next. So you reset your cognitive map to the
appropriate region in tonal space and listen to the bridge unfold. If
you aren't familiar with the tune, but recognize it as following the
convention of the AABA standard, then you expected a change at this
point, but don't know what's coming up next. You treat this as new
material and absorb it. If you weren't familiar with the AABA form,
you may well have been shocked that you aren't hearing another repetition of the A. But, being a flexible and adventurous sort, you get
over your surprise and listen to the new phrases.

When the bridge comes to an end, in bar twenty-four, you know
that you've reached another turning point, no matter what your prior
experience is, for this is the end of the third eight-bar phrase. Once
again you reset. If you recognize the form, you know to anticipate a
repeat of the A section. If you don't know the form, you reset and
then, immediately upon hearing bar twenty-five, you recognize the
sonic features that identify a phrase you've heard twice before. Once
again you know what to expect.

Similar considerations apply to very different musical forms. The
râgas of Indian music, for example, have a tone that represents "home
base" and other tones that play special functions in the evolving
melody line. These tones thus function as tonal landmarks in the
sonic space of a *râga*.[32]

❧

The neural story I am proposing looks like this: as Clynes and others
have argued, music is organized into two streams. One stream carries

the underlying pulse of musical performance, is mediated by structures for locomotion, and is extremely precise. It is the source of the precision that Clynes, Shaw, and others have measured in musical performances, both real and mental. These structures are both subcortical—for example, the cerebellum and the basal ganglia—and cortical.

The phrase or gesture stream is organized by limbic structures centered on the hippocampus. These structures evolved to control navigation through the environment and are closely linked to neocortical regions that subserve accurate recognition and identification of objects, events, and so on. When used for music, the navigation system is linked to the various cortical regions supporting the recognition and manipulation of musical sound—regions for recognizing intervals, melodic contours, harmonic relations, and tone quality. These regions implement the musical "space" through which the phrase stream navigates.[33]

Still, however congenial the brain's looping circuitry is to musical rhythms, that circuitry must be trained to those rhythms, and the training is culturally specific. People who learn to count four-beat measures have a different sense of musical time than those who slap their thighs in interwined patterns of two and three. The brain's circuitry must be sculpted to the forms of a specific rhythmic regime.

PROJECTION PLUS
VIRTUALITY EQUALS MUSIC

The capacity to take the entire neural apparatus involved in locomotion and navigation and direct it to the production and comprehension of music deserves a name. *Projection* seems apt:

Projection: the capacity of the nervous system to take neural structures that evolved for one purpose and "project" them into entirely different behavioral domains on a temporary basis.

Projection, in this sense, is a capacity of the whole nervous system. As far as I can tell, the brain doesn't have some subsystem that regulates projection. Rather, it is a function of the relationship between the nervous system, the perceptual system, the motor system, and the world. If you are a performer, you dedicate your body to singing and dancing or you take up a musical instrument and play it. Your motor system directs the body in creating the sounds while your auditory system listens to them and the system as a whole acts to make the sounds variously pleasing and thrilling to the ear and feet. If you are only listening—not making music and not dancing either—then you sit or stand quietly, perhaps swaying to the music, tapping a toe, or conducting the orchestra with an imaginary baton. But your auditory system is intent on the sounds, and central motor systems that evolved to drive the skeletal muscles are entrained to the music instead.

Projection is the mechanism that allows you to create and comprehend musical structure. When the emotional circuits of the core brain and the limbic system are aroused by music, they are operating in virtual mode. Since these circuits don't have a mode switch—at least there isn't any current evidence for one—virtuality too must be a function of the whole state of the brain. The two facets of projection and virtuality—one governing our use of locomotor systems to create music, the other governing our emotional response to it—together create the pleasures of musical experience.

VII

BRIGHT MOMENTS

And music came back with the fair, music which you hear as far back as you can remember, in the days when you were small, the kind which goes on all the time here and there, in odd corners of the town, in little country places, wherever poor people go at the end of the week to sit down and wonder what they have become. . . . One hardly hears the music, one knows the tunes so well, nor the motors in motion behind the booths, making things work which you have to go and pay two francs to see. Your own heart, when you're a little tipsy with fatigue, taps away in your temples. It makes a thudding noise against the sort of velvet drawn tight round your head and inside your ears. That's the way one day it will come to burst. Let it! One day when the inner rhythm rejoins the outside one and all your ideas spill out and run away at last to play with the stars.

—Louis-Ferdinand Celine, *Journey to the End of the Night*

BETWEEN MUSICAL SELECTIONS spanning all eras of jazz history, the late Rahsaan Roland Kirk used to rap about bright moments, in music as well as in life:

Bright moments is like see'n' something that you ain't ever seen in you life and you don't have to see it but you know how it looks.

Bright moments is like hearin' some music that ain't nobody else heard, and if they heard it they wouldn't even recognize that they heard it 'cause they been hearin' it all their life but they nutted on it so, when you hear it and you start poppin' your feet and jumpin' up and down they get mad because you're enjoying yourself but those are bright moments that they can't share with you 'cause they don't even know how to go about listening to what you're listening to and when you try to tell them about it they don't know a damn thing about what you're talking about![1]

The "bright moments" I will examine in this chapter often last far longer than a moment. But, however much time they span on the clock, they nonetheless, in a sense, occupy but a moment.

The term *altered states of consciousness* (ASC)[2] came into vogue in the 1960s to designate a wide variety of mental states: dreams, hypnotic trance, mystical union, meditative states, drug-induced hallucinations, and so forth. Music is especially rich in its capacity to support our aspirations to altered consciousness. During the mid-1970s Father Andrew Greeley reported a survey in which 33 percent to 43 percent of adults reported having had a mystical experience. Of these, 49 percent indicated that listening to music would trigger the experience.[3] If you have had such an experience yourself, you have company. If you haven't, you probably know someone who has.

MUSICIANS SPEAK

Before speculating about the underlying mechanisms of altered states of musical consciousness let us remind ourselves of the wide variety of these experiences. Here is a passage from a recent *New York Times Magazine* profile of the rock guitarist, composer, and singer Neil Young:

> He pauses and looks out the window. "At a certain point, trained, accomplished musicians"—which is to say, not him—"hit the *wall*. They don't go there very often, they don't have the tools to go through the wall, because it's the *end of notes*. It's the other side, where there's only tone, sound, ambience, landscape, earthquakes, pictures, fireworks, the sky opening, buildings falling, subways collapsing. . . . When you go through the wall, the music takes on that kind of atmosphere, and

it doesn't translate the way other music translates. When you get to the other side, you can't go back. I don't know too many musicians who try to go through the wall." He stops for a moment. "I love to go through the wall," as if you ever doubted it for a moment.[4]

In talking about music beyond notes, Young is talking about the force and impact that music has when you take your mind from mundane consciousness to an altered consciousness. The sounds, no longer circumscribed by the concept of music itself, are simply there, like forces of nature.

Breaking through that wall is difficult. It helps to be exhausted. Terrance Blanchard, a jazz trumpet player and film composer, told Walt Harrington:

My best performances with Art Blakey sometimes came when I was really tired and didn't have time to think about what was going on. I'm always analyzing things. And on those occasions when I was too tired to do that, I played my best. Those were the times I was relaxed and ideas would come to me and my ego wouldn't block them. Maurice André, the great classical solo trumpeter in Europe, once said that when he plays he sometimes gets the impression there's no trumpet. He feels like he's singing! I have yet to experience that. But when I listen to John Coltrane, I hear it.[5]

Blanchard echoes a common theme, that you have to cease thinking, whatever "thinking" is. He clearly knows that there is something beyond what he has experienced himself and that he can hear it in other musicians. Maurice André's comment, that on occasion it felt like there was no trumpet, suggests unimpeded ease of execution and the complete assimilation of the trumpet to his mind and body.

Jazz drummer Ronald Shannon Jackson takes some of these themes a bit farther, getting deeper into the music and further out of himself:

I was fooling around one night after some local musicians and I had played a gig—and it happened! Everything that came to mind musically came off perfectly without me having constantly to think about it. I wasn't aware of doing it. So I floated to the back of the room and was on the ceiling watching myself play, and listening and enjoying it. So I know it could happen on the bandstand. But I had no control over how to get to that point.[6]

Again, we are late at night, after the gig, and Jackson is just fooling around, perhaps cooling down. The music just flowed. He didn't have to think to make the music happen. He became detached from his body and floated to the ceiling. Presumably he doesn't mean that he physically moved to the ceiling, but only that he seemed to be observing the scene from some remove. Such experiences have also been reported during drug-induced hallucinations.[7] Regardless of the occasion, what one wants to know is: How does the mind do that?

Drummer Mickey Hart explains how a certain kind of musical ASC takes time to develop.[8] He describes how, in his early teens, he would practice:

I would sit with my drums and slowly begin warming the traps up, exciting the low end first, the bass drum, making it beat like a heart, slow and steady. The hi-hat would start clicking its metronomic click, and I'd start mixing in the middle voice, the rhythms of the snare drums and the tom-toms interweaving with the steady pulse of the bass. This interweaving of low end and middle is the main work of a traps drummer; at the high end, the shimmering harmonics of cymbals, bells, and gongs complete the drum voice.

Ten minutes. Fifteen minutes. Twenty minutes. Then something curious would happen. I'd feel myself becoming lighter; I'd lose track of time . . . I never found it exhausting to drum for hours; it left me calm, energized, and grinning.

This state came on gradually. Hart couldn't just turn it on; he had to take certain actions and let the state develop as he continued. Note also that Hart was playing alone. Elsewhere he describes collective experiences, but group interaction, however welcome, was not necessary for him.

Ringo Starr tells us how interpersonal performance dynamics are altered:

> It feels great; it's just a knowing. It's magic actually; it is pure magic. Everyone who is playing at that time knows where everybody's going. We all feel like one; wherever you go, everyone feels that's where we should go. I would know if Paul was going to do something, or if George was going to raise it up a bit, or John would double, or we'd bring it down. I usually play with my eyes closed, so you would know when things like that were happening . . . you've got to trust each other.[9]

Much of the standard literature on ASCs focuses on individuals. The individual may feel that she has transcended her selfhood, that she has lost all sense of boundary between herself and the world, but the experience is not negotiated through interaction with other people. Yet, except for Mickey Hart's practice sessions, these musicians are all reporting group experiences. They are talking about what happened to them while they were performing with other musicians. The interactive ease Ringo Starr reports was happening in the minds (and brains) of John, George, and Paul as well. And as many musicians will be glad to tell you, the magic even extends to the listeners, with "energy," such as we saw in the first chapter with Rahsaan Roland Kirk, freely flowing between performers and audience.

These anecdotes—and I could easily supply more—reveal some common characteristics:

No Thought: thinking ceases, and the music plays itself. Note that getting beyond thought is one of the objectives of most meditative disciplines. What is this "thinking" that one can go beyond it?

Altered Body Sense: one may feel light or, in the extreme, detached from one's body. This is also common in meditation.

Sharing: one senses heightened communication with other musicians and with the audience. This is not common in meditation, for meditation typically is not interactive. Meditation often, however, engenders a sense of union with some external power.

I would like particularly to emphasize the last factor, for it situates these experiences in a group context. The literature on ASCs is primarily about individual brains, and for the most part says little about the interaction between individuals. We need to think of music ASCs as arising from coupled interaction between brains.

THE PLEASURES OF
MUSIC 2: FORM AND FLOW

Every level of neural operation, from local circuitry in this or that cubic millimeter of neocortex to the entire brain, offers opportunities for music's pleasures. We can have tension and release, expectation, failure and fulfillment, consonance and dissonance. The dynamics can flow, or not. This in some measure makes it difficult to get a more detailed grip on just how musical pleasure works. We may accept the point that musical pleasure is a property of neural dynamics, and yet have no sense of how to use that idea to think about music.

The general framework I have been developing has an affinity with the Gestalt psychology of the early twentieth century. The word *gestalt* means "pattern" and asserts the importance of overall form in perception. Perception doesn't proceed by a bottom-up accretion of details but works at the level of whole objects and events. Though mainly used in the investigation of visual perception, Gestalt psychology has been applied to sound and music as well.[10] For example, the Gestaltists gave a great deal of attention to grouping effects. Auditory streaming is a grouping process by which the nervous system segregates sounds into different auditory streams, each regarded as coming from a different source. This process has come to be known as auditory scene analysis and, according to Albert Bregman, is a preconceptual process.[11] That is to say, it is a "low level" process, not accessible to conscious intervention or learning. The neural mechanisms responsible for streaming, evolved over millions of years, are tuned to the sound properties of the natural world. Thus it should not be surprising to find out that the sounds of music, which are not natural phenomena, sometimes fool these mechanisms.

Let us start with a simple example. Imagine three tones separated by moderate intervals, for example, the NBC three-note chime. When those tones are played at the original speed you hear the familiar melody. If that three-tone sequence is repeated time after time, you hear the familiar melody repeated. You hear these sounds as part of a single sound stream, indicating that the auditory system has "decided" that these sounds come from a single source.

Now suppose you increase the tempo. For a while the melody will just get faster and faster, but at some point it will disappear. You will no longer be able to detect the order of the tones, and the single sound stream will disintegrate into three streams, each consisting of repetitions of one of the tones. The tones and their relative order are the same at the high speed as they were at the low speed. But the way we hear them changes: the auditory system has now assigned them to three different sources.

This phenomenon has been investigated extensively. In general, pitches that are far apart will cohere into a continuous melodic line only if they are played relatively slowly. The further pitches are apart, the more slowly they must be played to preserve melodic continuity. Pitches that are closer together, conversely, can be played rapidly and still be heard as elements in a coherent melody. It is thus not surprising that small intervals have been found to predominate in most melodies. Large intervals are more likely to occur between phrases than within phrases—for example, between the two-bar phrases in the bridge for "I Got Rhythm."[12]

Baroque composers exploited this particular effect—the segregation of a single sequence of tones into two streams—to create the impression of multiple instrumental lines when only one instrument was playing. Bach did this, for example, in some of his music for unaccompanied violin. You can sometimes hear a similar effect in the rhythms of conga drummers, especially when they are playing rapid patterns. The drummer will be playing only one note at a time, alternating between hands, but it will sound like two interlocked streams. While conga drummers often play on two or three drums simultaneously, a good drummer has such a variety of tones at his command that he can create the effect using only a single drum.

Let us now return to the bell choir I discussed at the beginning of chapter 2. As you recall, three musicians played simple interlocking patterns while a fourth played freely improvised patterns. The melody lines people heard contained pitches played by all four musicians. Since the bells had much the same tone quality, the ear grouped the sounds according to pitch and timing relationships. If tones played by two different people are close together in pitch and time, the ear will hear them as coming from the same source and place them in the same melodic stream. The mind thus infers the existence of virtual sound sources that are quite different from the real ones.

Streaming, in turn, gives rise to the illusion of musical motion, the idea that a musical line is moving in some direction. It is so very natural for us to talk of melody moving up or down, rapidly or slowly, that we have to stop and remind ourselves that nothing is literally moving. All we hear in a single musical line is a succession of tones. Earlier tones don't push on later tones, nor do the later tones resist or react to such pushes. The tones don't interact in any way whatsoever. The sensation of musical motion must be an illusion, but it is central to music and its pleasures.

As another example, consider the familiar notions of consonance and dissonance. In music these terms refer to intervals, pitch relationship between two tones.[13] The tones may be sounded successively in a single voice (the technical term for a musical line, whether performed by an instrument or the human voice) or simultaneously by two or more voices. The neural systems that detect individual tones are well, if not definitively, understood. But no one has proposed any centers for detecting consonance beyond those involved in detecting pitch. Nor is the nature of consonance and dissonance unambiguous. Whether a given interval is perceived as consonant or dissonant depends on the immediate musical context. Further, within the Western tradition, intervals and chords that were once considered dissonant have later come to seem less dissonant.

One way to think about consonance is to view it as a phenomenon of the neurodynamics of pitch perception. Thus Mark Tramo asserts that "the timing of a neural activity may indicate the pitch of each note and the consonance of the combination of notes."[14] An interval's degree of consonance depends on the relative timing of the neural populations responding to the individual pitches that constitute the interval. One can learn to label intervals as consonant or dissonant, but this is secondary to the phenomenon itself, which is the subjective impression of the neurodynamics of pitch perception.

Interval relationships are the very stuff of harmony, and the manipulation of harmonic relationships has been central to the development of Western high art music since the early eighteenth century. Thus, with consonance, melodic continuity, and rhythm all being functions of neurodynamics, it seems reasonable to suggest, independently of subcortical emotional arousal, that our sensations of musical pleasure are neurodynamic.[15] We take an inner walk through a territory of motifs and intervals while arousing feelings of sadness, love, anger, joy, and so forth. Our overall musical feeling depends on the balance between the subcortical affect and the cortical inner motion.

When this balance becomes all-encompassing we may lose our sense of self, of separate individuality. How can that happen? We don't really know, but in thinking about this, I find it useful to think of the self as a social construct that manages the complex of roles and statuses we examined in chapter 3. It is this self that gives rise to the sensation of "thought," and when it ceases to operate, we lose the sense of thinking.

INNER SPEECH AND THE NEURAL SELF

What does it mean to say that you cease to think? It means, I believe, that inner speech ceases to play a role in directing your activities. I am thus identifying the commonsense notion of "thinking" with inner speech.[16] Your brain certainly does not shut down when you stop thinking yet remain fully awake, attentive, and performing music. All that ceases is one process.

That process was investigated by Lev Semenovich Vygotsky during the twenties and thirties in the Soviet Union and published in 1934 in his classic *Thought and Language*. The book was suppressed in 1936 and was not readily available until a decade after World War II. Vygotsky's general idea is that as others direct the child's actions and perceptions through language, so the child comes to use language in directing her own activities.[17]

Vygotsky asks us to consider a very young child, in the second year of life, interacting with an adult. This child has some capacity to understand the speech of others but has little or no speech of her own. When you speak to her the linguistic system in her brain analyzes the acoustic input and activates the appropriate cognitive and perceptual circuits. The command "come here" will activate a plan for locomotion and the child will approach you, provided, of course, that she knows and trusts you and is not otherwise preoccupied. The command "look at the bunny" will direct her gaze at the bunny.

In time the child's own language capacity grows. During the third and fourth years her grasp of language is firm enough that she can use language to direct her own actions in the way that others use language to direct her activity. She is not, of course, obligated to direct her actions in this way, but she can, for example, use speech to plan a sequence of actions or focus her attention on some task. The child will talk to herself as she thinks things through.

As such self-directed speech becomes ever more fluent, Vygotsky maintains, it becomes silent and internal. The inner tongue can now communicate directly with the inner ear, bypassing the need to speak aloud. Given that this process starts with language that others direct to the growing child and involves mental structures for coordinating language and social interaction, inner speech is thus an inner dialogue between virtual persons. It is thus not surprising that, in his investigation of the metaphor system governing folk conceptions of the self, George Lakoff found that we conceive the self to be a multiplicity of agents.[18]

The point is that we have a capacity for self-scrutiny and self-direction that is critically dependent on language. A musician who reports that the music just flowed, that he no longer had to think about it, is simply saying that the inner voice no longer played any role in the musicking. Even in more ordinary circumstances, the inner voice doesn't play much of a role in fluid performance; hands and lips and lungs just go about their business. The inner voice does speak—perhaps looking ahead and preparing, noting a mistake, or expressing annoyance at the loud bore chatting away in the front row. But when you are completely swept up in the music, the little voice disappears.

It should be obvious that this inner voice, no matter what it may say, is not some master controller. Infants are able to act without it and so are the rest of us. It is one of the brain's creatures, not its director.

And so it is with the self. Let us consider Antonio Damasio's account of the neural self, during which he considers a neurological condition called anosognosia.[19] The right hemisphere of the brain controls the left side of the body, and vice versa. Anosognosia is generally caused by damage to the right hemisphere:

> Imagine a victim of a major stroke, entirely paralyzed in the left side of the body, unable to move hand and arm, leg and foot, face half immobile, unable to stand or walk. And now imagine that same person oblivious to the entire problem, reporting that nothing is possibly the matter, answering the question, "How do you *feel*?" with a sincere, "Fine."

This is such an astounding response that, as Damasio notes, one might consider it a form of protective denial. But that is not the case: such patients simply do not know they are disabled. Similar damage to the left hemisphere will paralyze the right side of the body and may also affect language ability. But such patients are fully, and agonizingly, aware of their affliction. They may have lost the ability to talk, but their awareness of their body state has not been damaged. In Damasio's view, "signals concerning both left and right sides of the body find their most comprehensive meeting ground in the right hemisphere." Thus the right hemisphere is dominant for body sense while the left hemisphere is dominant for language.

Body sense, however, is only one source of the neural self. The other is your personal history, which is an enormous grab bag of information: people you know, when and where you met them, what you have done together, where you went to school, with references to what you kept in your locker in tenth grade, where you work, why Henderson didn't deserve that promotion, the best concerts you ever attended, especially the one where you proposed marriage to . . . and so forth. There is nothing profound or mysterious about any of this information, but it embodies much of who you are.

What happens to that history when you repeat some particular ritual? When you attend your third performance of Bach's *St. Matthew's Passion* or listen to John Coltrane's *A Love Supreme* again? For the duration of the musicking your personal history is repeating itself, if not exactly, then very closely. Whatever state your nervous system is in as you commence musicking, as it unfolds your nervous system converges on the trajectory it assumes for this particular performance and remains there until the performance is over, at which time you return to the here and now.

Just as music's groove stream is an attractor in the sense defined by dynamics theory, so a whole performance can be an attractor. While the time-depth of the groove stream is quite shallow—on the order of a few seconds at most—the time-depth of a whole performance can easily extend over minutes or even hours. Such performances segment one's life trajectory into an overall stream that is irreversible, from birth to death, punctuated by segments outside that stream. It is as though your overall life trajectory were moving to and from these stretches of musicking, which thus become "home base."

We have little recollection of events early in life, before language is firmly established. This suggests that language is an important means of organizing and accessing the neural self, of recalling earlier states in one's trajectory.[20] It does not, of course, imply that our autobiography is but a set of verbal reports. We remember sights, sounds, smells, tastes, and textures, not to mention motions and emotions, and we can reconstruct our personal world in sensory and motor modalities. But language and inner speech provide the mechanism for organizing these reconstructive activities.

Thus it is perhaps not so strange that an altered sense of one's own body parallels the cessation of inner speech. Think of the system for inner speech being coupled with the integrated body sense as a system we could call the Self System. An alteration in one component might affect the other as well. It is as though the mere existence of inner speech serves to anchor one's sense of intentionality in one's body. When that speech ceases, the anchor is gone and one floats free, outside one's body.

This, of course, does not constitute an explanation of the out-of-body experience that sometimes accompanies musical performance. It is merely a suggestion of where we might begin looking for such an explanation. Some other observations seem pertinent. For one thing, sensations of floating and flying are not unusual in dreams.[21] The brain seems quite capable of manufacturing such sensations. What is strange is that it is manufacturing them in the brain of someone fully awake and in touch with the external world.

We must, however, keep in mind how very much our sense of the world depends on the brain's highly evolved constructive activities. It takes many specific processes to turn raw sense data into the world we experience. Consider the sensation you have when hammering a nail. You feel the impact of the hammer on the nail head, but you have no sensory organs in the hammer head. The sense organs responsible for this sensation are located in the skin of the fingers and hand and in the joints of the arm, hand, and fingers. You must learn to project these sensations to the appropriate point in space—a process that may also involve relating these sensations of touch and movement to visual space.

Georg von Békésy was interested in such matters and performed some very interesting experiments with touch in the 1960s.[22] He used a pair of vibrating needles to stimulate the tips of two fingers. Each of the vibrators was actuated by the same series of timing pulses, but von Békésy introduced a lag between the delivery of the pulses to the vibrators. Where the delay was relatively long, three to four milliseconds, the subject experienced sensations in the two fingers, as one would expect. But when the delay was about one millisecond, the subject would feel only one vibratory sensation, in the finger that received the first click. If the delay was reduced still further, the subject located the vibrations at a point between the fingers, where there can't possibly be any sensation. Even more dramatically, von Békésy was able to obtain the same effect by stimulating a person's knees. Imagine sitting with your knees spread and feeling a sensation that you locate in the air midway between them. Nothing is there, but you feel the vibrations nonetheless.

This bit of trickery is certainly far different from feeling yourself float to a point near the ceiling, but it strikes me as being in the same general range of weirdness. Both phenomena have to do with one's sense of one's body and how touch and movement are integrated with visual awareness. These sensations converge in the parietal lobes of the neocortex. The right parietal lobe is one of the structures where Damasio locates the integrated body sense. Perhaps what we need to know is just how the sound of one's own voice becomes localized in space. How is it that you come to hear your voice as emanating from a point below your nose and between your ears? To be sure, that voice does not sound during inner speech, but knowing how it is localized might give us a clue to how one may feel outside one's body when inner speech ceases.

We have arrived back at Vygotsky's notion that language provides us with a vehicle for directing our own activities. This is where we find the will. Our will is simply the effect of inner speech on the motor system, a notion articulated by Miller, Galanter, and Pribram in their classic, *Plans and the Structure of Behavior:*

> Inner speech is the kind of stuff our wills are made of. When we will to do something, we may imagine doing it and we repeat our verbal command to ourselves, subvocally, as we concentrate on the task. It is a familiar fact, emphasized by nearly all behavioristic psychologists since J. B. Watson, that most of our planned activity is represented subjectively as listening to ourselves talk.[23]

Miller, Galanter, and Pribram make this statement during a discussion of hypnotism. They suggest that the hypnotized person has entered into a state where "the voice he listens to . . . is not his own, but the hypnotist's. The subject gives up his inner speech to the hypnotist." What if, instead of the hypnotist's voice, one gave up one's inner speech to music? That is, what if the role inner speech plays in regulating one's actions were, instead, to be taken by music?

In the conclusion to *Music and Trance*, Gilbert Rouget discusses spirit possession. In this case the ritual celebrant is not an active music maker, but dances to music made by others and, in time, becomes possessed by a spirit:

> The trance itself, in other words the period during which the subject settles himself, so to say, into his other persona and totally coincides with it, has, on the contrary, quite a stable relation to music . . . . Here the function of the music is obvious. It is due to the music, and because he is supported by the music, that the possessed person publicly lives out, by means of dance, his identification with the divinity he embodies. The music . . . is essentially identificatory. By playing his "motto" [a rhythm characteristic of a particular divinity], the musicians notify this identity to the entranced dancer, those around him, the priests, and the spectators. . . . Music thus appears as the principal means of socializing trance.[24]

Rouget was not thinking in neural terms here but about social function. The key word is *identity*. It is the music that signals the identity of the divinity. But the music is more than just another kind of name for the divinity. The identification is deeper than that. The music is a vehicle for a collective intentionality, one that slips beneath the barriers of individuality and the imperatives of autonomous selves. Music is a means of sharing what is otherwise an individual, private experience, that of trance. In music deeply shared, my rhythms and your rhythms are the same. And thus we are the one.

I want to pursue this theme in the next chapter, where I will argue that group synchrony achieved through music and dance was an evolutionary precursor to language. Indeed, I will argue that it was a necessary precursor, for without the trust engendered through such shared intentionality—a theme sounded by Walter Freeman—language would have been impossible. For the moment let's return to the brain.

MUSIC ON THE RIGHT

Just as the 1960s witnessed growing popular and scientific interest in ASCs, it also saw interest in split-brain research. In these remarkable experiments surgeons would cut the corpus callosum of epileptics in an effort to control convulsions not responding to medication.[25] The corpus callosum is a massive fiber bundle that connects the right and left cerebral hemispheres. When it is cut, the two hemispheres can function independently of one another. Researchers quickly discovered that the two hemispheres had very different functional capabilities. The left hemisphere seemed dominated by language and logic, leading to the suggestion that the right hemisphere was more holistic and emotional. Perhaps, some speculated, ASCs reflected a mode of brain activity in which the right hemisphere became dominant.

I wish to argue that music ASCs reflect right-hemisphere dominance. Where language underlies social interaction involving left-hemisphere functions, music sustains social interaction favoring the right hemisphere. But we have to be careful. By and large, everything is connected to everything else, though some linkages are more direct than others. Any but the simplest mental function involves a distributed network of neural centers. To say that language is a left-hemisphere function is not to say that the right hemisphere plays no role in language; that is not true.[26] Rather, the overall regulation of language seems to reside in the left hemisphere. Similarly, the suggestion that music is a right-hemisphere activity does not imply that it is subserved exclusively by the right hemisphere. Music seems to engage a more highly distributed network of neural structures than language does.[27]

We should look beyond music itself, however, and consider evidence that the right cortical hemisphere plays a more significant role in emotion than does the left. For one thing, the right hemisphere seems to mediate speech intonation patterns, which convey an emotional message. As we all know, you can say "I'm angry with you" in a perfectly flat tone of voice and you can also say "Pass the sweet potatoes" in an angry way (or a loving one, for that matter). While the meaning and grammatical structure of the utterance are mediated by the left cortical hemisphere, the emotional shading comes from the right. Furthermore, there is evidence that the left side of the face is more expressive than the right. Since the left side of the body is controlled by the right hemisphere, that suggests that the right hemisphere is more involved with emotional awareness than is the left.[28]

The evidence and arguments on this matter are not unequivocal. No doubt we need more evidence, but beyond that, the mind and brain may operate in ways too subtle to be adequately captured by our current concepts. Once again I must emphasize my argument is speculative. The suggestion I am developing can be supported by evidence; it is reasonable. But one could also argue against it. Thus I would like to reiterate the point I made in my introduction, that the purpose of speculation is not to hit upon the right explanation, as if by magic, but to guide subsequent research in a fruitful direction.

Whatever role the right hemisphere plays in various subprocesses of musical perception and production, I suggest that it is responsible for the highest level of musical regulation. That highest level of regulation concerns the coordination of emotional processes with musical form and structure. It is the right hemisphere that regulates the concord between subcortical essentic forms and cortical rhythm, harmony, and melody, and between the social mechanisms of the limbic system and perceptual and cognitive mechanisms of the cortex. It is the right hemisphere that guarantees that music's sensuous surface satisfies both the heart's desires and the mind's need for order.

In emphasizing the sensuous surface of music I mean to indicate that the sound itself is important, not just whatever that sound might seem to indicate. It is the sound itself that is Nils Wallin's "tonal flow of music" and that thus enters into Wallin's "morphodynamic isomorphism between the tonal flow of music and its neurophysiological substrates." Music stands in contrast to ordinary speech, where the sound itself is secondary. Meaning lies in the concepts and percepts conjured up by the language; the sound is a means of conveying that meaning, but except in specifically aesthetic uses such as poetry, it is not significant in itself. Musical sound drives both the subcortical emotion systems and the cortical conceptual systems. It regulates the brain in unified action beyond the self.

RHYTHMS OF DREAMS AWAKE

I believe that the musicking brain is operating in a mode similar to that of the dreaming brain. While the idea is hardly original (for example, recall Knobloch's ideas that we considered in chapter 4), my interest in it is motivated both by Alan Hobson's account of dreaming from his recent book *Consciousness*, and Leonard Bernstein's report that he has no recollection of what he did during ecstatic musicking. Could this lack of memory be similar to our ordinary difficulty in remembering dreams?

Hobson is interested in accounting for the differences between ordinary waking consciousness, deep sleep, and dream sleep as well as certain abnormal states of consciousness such as hallucinations and delirium. He argues that we need to consider three variables: activation, input-output gating, and processing mode, or modulation. By activation Hobson simply means the general level of brain activity. Activation is high during both waking consciousness and in dreaming, but it is low in deep sleep. Input-output gating has to do with whether the brain is attending to the external world or to its own activity. When we are awake the brain is attending to external input, but when we are in deep sleep or dreaming it is cut off from the world and focused on its own processes.

Modulation concerns brain biochemistry and it is the trickiest of these three variables to understand. The operations of the nervous system involve 100 or so chemicals, each playing a different role in the transmission of impulses and long-term modification of neural circuits. Hobson is interested in two neurochemical processes, aminergic and cholinergic, that have broad effects on almost every aspect of behavior. The chemicals subserving these processes are manufactured in a relatively small number of neurons located deep in the brain's core but they are distributed widely throughout the brain.

The aminergic processes involve two neurochemicals, serotonin and norepinephrine, that are critical for learning and memory. When they aren't present, memories cannot be made. Cholinergic processes, mediated by acetylcholine, generally facilitate behavior. There is evidence that motor pattern generators for walking and running can be turned on by acetylcholine, which also activates visual processes and emotion. These chemicals are neuromodulators, chemicals that affect the strength of electrochemical action across the gaps (synapses) between nerve cells.

Hobson defines modulation as the relationship between the concentrations of the chemicals driving cholinergic and aminergic processes. Both of these processes operate at high levels during normal waking and drop to low or moderate levels during deep sleep. Thus the relationship between the chemicals is pretty much the same during both states. During dreams the aminergic chemicals are in very low concentration while acetylcholine is at the same high levels it has while we are awake. The relationship between these chemicals is thus quite different, giving dream sleep a different modulation profile from waking or deep sleep.

During dream sleep the brain's motor systems are quite active. Since motor impulses are inhibited before they can travel down the spinal cord to the muscles, we don't execute the movements. Those impulses give rise only to virtual movements confined to our dreams. Visual and emotional processes are also active during dreaming. At the same time the lack of memory processing means that our memory for dreams is quite poor.

Now consider Leonard Bernstein's report that after he has been completely engrossed in music, he has no memory of the experience. There is no particular need for memory-creating processes to be active while you're performing or listening to music—unless, of course, you're a critic and have to write a review. A musician performing a composed work without using the score has already committed it to memory. She needs to be able to retrieve it from memory but doesn't need to lay down new memories of the performance itself. Similarly, an improviser needs to call on well-learned routines but has no need to learn new ones during performance. The listener is in a similar situation. To be sure, if the music is in an unfamiliar style, then the listener does need to learn the style in order to appreciate the music. But surely that is the point. You can appreciate the music only when you have learned the style. Once you have done that, you have no need for neurochemicals mediating learning and memory. You can simply lose yourself in the flow of sound.

I would speculate then that the neural mode for music making is like that for dreaming in that aminergic processes are at a very low level, much below that of ordinary waking consciousness.[29] But while the dreamer is motionless and dead to the world, the music maker is not; her input-output gating is quite different from that of the dreamer.

The musician's auditory system is attuned to the music dancing against her eardrums while her motor system is intent on manipulating an instrument, or her voice. The movements she makes are often difficult and awkward, but they have been made graceful by years of practice. The sounds, of course, have been crafted to mesh with inherent structures and processes in the brain. In particular, music demands very precise timing across an extensive hierarchy of timescales. Musical sounds are timed so that the neural reverberations in various parts of the brain converge and harmonize at just the right time. Musical sounds are thus quite different from the ordinary sounds of the world. Beyond this, when making our way through the waking world we must use all of our senses, while music requires only that we attend to sound. Thus while the musician attends to external stimuli like a waking person, her central processing requirements are different. Music is not like the buzzing and booming confusion of ordinary life.

Jaak Panksepp, a specialist in the neuroscience of emotion, observes that while dream sleep is almost universal among mammals, it is lacking in fish and reptiles and only sporadic in birds. Suggesting that dream sleep is unlikely to have evolved from nothing, Panksepp speculates that the relevant core brain mechanisms "originally controlled a primitive form of waking arousal. With the evolution of higher brain areas, a newer and more efficient waking mechanism may have been needed."[30] Among these higher-brain areas, of course, is the neocortex, the chief repository of learning. The more neocortex an animal has, the more important the neurodynamics and biochemistry of learning become. The emergence of the neocortex is thus not simply a matter of more neurons in a certain region. It also involves a significant change in brain chemical dynamics.

Panksepp goes on to speculate that dream mechanisms

> originally mediated the selective arousal of emotionality. Prior to the emergence of complex cognitive strategies, animals may have generated most of their behavior from primary-process psycho-behavioral routines that we now recognize as the primitive emotional systems . . . . These simple-minded behavioral solutions were eventually superseded by more sophisticated cognitive approaches that required not only more neocortex but also new arousal mechanisms to sustain efficient waking functions within those emerging brain areas.

Dreaming is thus a kind of neural palimpsest: the evolutionary vestige of the system that once regulated the waking state but has since been overwritten. Panksepp concludes by suggesting that dreaming now serves to integrate the emotional impulses of old brain systems with the cognitive capacities of the new brain systems.

I would like to recast Panksepp's speculation in a more colorful way: when we dream, the ancient animals within go out romping in the neocortex. The core brain systems of our reptilian heritage treat the neocortex as an environment and set out to explore it. Imagine the neocortex as some lush jungle setting or perhaps a grassy savanna, in which a small animal may bask in the sun, pursue prey, and enjoy a warm meal. To put it another way, dreaming is your inner lizard running free in the dance hall of the mind.

With memory systems deactivated in dreaming, the neocortex isn't learning new patterns. Rather, the core systems are exploring patterns already stored in the neorcortex. From an information-processing point of view this exploration is much like a real lizard acting in the world. The inputs to the "inner lizard" come not from the external world but from the neocortex, which stores patterns derived from past experience. Similarly, the outputs generated by this inner lizard don't affect the external world but rather serve to activate different neocortical patterns. The neocortex is providing the inner lizard with virtual experience.

When musicking, however, we do have external inputs and outputs. But these tend to be closely structured and strictly subordinate to the requirements of musicking—though we typically retain enough residual consciousness to give some peripheral attention to nonmusical comings and goings. In musicking the external world is assimilated to the inner rhythms of a collective dream, a dream being enacted in that public space where we share our inner environment with others.

Let us learn once more from Panksepp. Noting that both play and dreaming are cholinergically active, he suggests that "play may be the waking functional counterpart of dreaming." For me as a musician, the easy execution of physically difficult music feels like rough-and-tumble play. To be sure, I'm not rolling around, jumping and running (that's dance). But the overall feel is much like that of a child climbing a tree, chasing after others, tussling a bit, and jumping in a pile of leaves. By projection (as defined in the previous chapter), the broad physical scope of rough-and-tumble place is focused on the fine control of arms, hands, fingers, and mouth and tongue as they make music.

Music thus becomes a means of communal play, of communal dreaming. It is a group activity in which the interactions between individuals are as precisely timed and orchestrated as those within a single brain. The individuals are physically separate but temporally integrated. It is one music, one dance.

ECSTASY AND ETERNITY

Finally, we must consider a problem. Why is self-possessed inner speech the baseline state of waking consciousness? Given that ecstatic states can feel so very pleasurable, why can't we just flip into such states at will?

I don't know. But my guess is that self-possession is the baseline state because we are social creatures and we need an active self structure to manage our interactions with others. Thus when we undergo long periods of isolation, the self structure begins to dissolve, and we hallucinate and become disoriented.[31]

But that still doesn't explain why self-loss is so difficult. I suspect it is a matter of large-scale neurodynamics. For reasons that we do not understand, the transition from a state of self-possessed inner speech to one where both inner speech and the sense of a separate self are lost is not symmetrical with the transition from self-loss to self-possession. The latter is easy but the former is difficult.

Whatever the case may be, there is no doubt that music affords us deep and powerful experiences, experiences that challenge our ordinary sense of reality. Thus musicking has moved Wayne Booth, a distinguished professor of English recently retired from the University of Chicago, to write about his experiences as an amateur musician, an avocation he shares with his wife, Phyllis. In November of 1969 Booth was grieving the death of his son four months earlier. In the process of "trying, sometimes successfully, to regain his lost affirmation of life" Booth began drafting a book about life, death, and music. Concerning a performance of Beethoven's *string quartet in C-sharp minor,* he said:

> Leaving the rest of the audience aside for a moment, there were three of us there: *Beethoven . . . the quartet* members counting as one . . . Phyllis and me, also counting only as one whenever we really listened . . . . Now then: there that "one" was, but where was "there"? The C-sharp minor part of each of us was fusing in a mysterious way . . . [contrasting] so sharply with what many people think of as "reality." A part of each of the "three" . . . becomes identical.
>
> There is Beethoven, one hundred and forty-three years ago . . . writing away at the marvelous theme and variations in the fourth movement. . . . Here is the four-players doing the best it can to make the

revolutionary welding possible. And here we are, doing the best we can to turn our "self" totally into it: all of us impersonally slogging away (these tears about my son's death? ignore them, irrelevant) to turn ourselves into that deathless quartet.[32]

Each aspect of this account—the merging of selves, the separation from everyday time and space—has a physical interpretation in the theory I've been elaborating. If, contra Heraclitus, we can dip into the same stream time after time, it makes little difference whether our dips are separated by two days of mundane time, or a century and a half. If distinctions between one self and another are lost in this stream, then it makes little difference that it was Beethoven then and Phyllis and Wayne Booth now.

Learn the culture, enact the moves, and your mind converges on the performance attractor we call Beethoven's quartet in C-sharp minor. I leave it as an exercise for the reader to ponder whether or not such attractors thus qualify as a physical interpretation of the concept of eternity. From the point of view of an external observer there is nothing special about these attractors. That is not, however, the only relevant point of view. What about the system itself? What is our subjective experience of such states?

PART III

THE EVOLUTION
OF MUSICAL CULTURE

VIII

THE PROTOHUMAN
RHYTHM BAND

. . . we marvel when we hear music in which one voice sings a
simple melody, while three, four, or five other voices play and trip
lustily around the voice that sings its simple melody and adorn
this simple melody wonderfully with artistic musical effects, thus
reminding us of a heavenly dance, where all meet in a spirit of
friendliness, caress and embrace.

—Martin Luther

How is it possible for something to come from nothing? This basic
question underlies any inquiry into origins. Of course, we are not directly concerned about the origins of humankind. At least within the
confines of this book, we are interested only in the origins of music—
but that is hardly a comforting thought. We understand so very little,
and so very many things came into the world along with us: music,
language, campfires, tools, clothing, cooking, ritual, masks, graves,
footwear, makeup, fermented beverages, domesticated plants and animals. Regardless of our particular focus, we pretty much have to think
about the whole phenomenon of human culture.

Our inquiry into origins is everywhere plagued by our inability to
observe. If we could build a time machine and thus witness the first
musicking, we could record those sounds and analyze them, and note

the situations that prompted them. No doubt these observations would provoke detailed and learned arguments about just which activities qualify as Real Musicking.

But we can't make those observations, for music or anything else. We have bone, which tells us about our ancestors' bodies, including skulls and skull fragments that give us information about their brains and throats. We also have stone weapons and tools. And we have the remains of living and work sites and of graves. These remains give us a general index of cognitive capability, but they tell us next to nothing about music.

But direct observation does establish a loose temporal framework. Our task is to establish a set of events and capacities to place into that framework. It is generally agreed that fully modern humans emerged between 100,000 and 50,000 years ago. We assume that the lifeways for these people would have been comparable to those of the simplest extant human societies. I note that this is an assumption, for beyond material artifacts, we have no direct evidence of these people's activities. It is not, however, an unreasonable assumption. Merlin Donald notes that "the pygmies of the African rain forest, and the Bushmen of southern Africa when first contacted by Europeans still had the same type of tool culture associated with the very earliest modern human remains."[1] That isn't much evidence from which to infer a way of life, but it is what we have.

A TIME LINE

So let us start with what we've got. The first hominids, while capable of upright walking, had brains roughly a third the size of ours, did not make stone tools, and lived in East Africa. That last fact is quite important. As a number of observers have noted, the current great apes—the creatures who descended in the line that branched from ours eight million years ago—all live in tropical rain forests, which provide very stable environments. We are the only large-bodied primates to thrive outside the tropics. This contrasts with the carnivores (cats, dogs, and bears) and ungulates (hooved mammals, such as cattle, deer, and sheep). Large carnivores and ungulates live in a full range of habitats, from the tropics to the arctic. If those large animals can live outside the tropics, why can't large apes?

Both Valerius Geist and John M. Allman identify the steppe as the ecological barrier that kept large-bodied apes from spreading to Europe and Asia almost 2 million years ago.[2] Steppes are relatively dry, making food and water scarce, particularly for females who must provide for their young during long periods of gestation and lactation. The seasonal aridity drives plant foods underground, beneath very hard, dry soils while the lack of trees exposes the apes to predators, especially at night, since they cannot escape by climbing. Roughly 4.5 million years ago the earth's temperature plunged and entered a phase in which glaciers alternately expanded and contracted, forcing worldwide climate changes. This activity intensified about 2 million years ago. During the periods when the glaciers expanded, much of what is now forest in lowland Africa desiccated and became steppe.

Thus our ancestors had to cope with the steppe in order to survive and to move out of East Africa. By about 2 million years ago *Homo erectus* had solved these problems and spread to Europe and Asia. *Erectus* had a considerably larger brain than the earlier *australopithecus* and manufactured stone tools. Stone tools are useful for shaping sticks for use in digging up roots beneath the hard, dry ground surface and in building protective shelters. Geist and others have also argued for social adaptations, such as food sharing and monogamy, which together ensure that the male's provisions will benefit his and only his offspring.

Following Geist, I will argue that imitation of animal calls is one of the adaptations that allowed *erectus* to survive in the steppes. Imitation requires voluntary control over the vocal apparatus, a necessary precursor to music. This control in turn implies a modified vocal apparatus to facilitate the creation of a wide variety of sounds—a matter discussed by Philip Lieberman among others—and the development of the requisite neural centers.[3] Since *erectus* crossed the steppe almost 2 million years ago, it follows that this first step toward music must have taken place before then. That is to say, vocal control must have begun, though it is not clear how far it had gotten.

We do know, however, that it still had a way to go. The development of that neural control has left a trace in the fossil record. The tongue is controlled by the hypoglossal nerve, which passes through the hypoglossal canal in the skull. In a recent study Richard Kay, Matt Cartmill, and Michelle Balow report that this canal is 1.8 times larger in humans than in apes to accommodate a larger hypoglossal nerve.[4] We need more nerves controlling our tongues to give us more flexible and differentiated control over tongue movements. This control, necessary for speech, is just as necessary for music. After examining several fossil skulls (from Neanderthals and early *Homo sapiens*) Kay, Cartmill, and Balow concluded that the hypoglossal canal reached its current size about 300,000 years ago.

That fact in itself tells us nothing about what kind of vocalizations hominids produced or how they used them. But it does tell us when the evolutionary pressures for better vocalization ceased. By 300,000 B.C.E. the neural, muscular, and skeletal apparatus for vocalization conferred a sufficient survival advantage that further development was not worth the cost. That seems as good a point as any to locate a major event in our evolutionary story, but what event?

I would suggest two other milestones in the march to music. One of them is a *Gestalt* switch in which rhythmically coordinated group musicking emerges from vocal mimicry and associated activities. The other is the differentiation of language from musicking. At least one, if not both, of these events probably occurred before the hypoglossal nerve had reached its full size, and so played a role in driving the evolution of vocal control. But I see no way of hazarding a guess about when this happened.

The details of timing are not as important as the overall sequence of events. I am arguing that there are three milestones between ape mentality and culture and human mentality and culture:

1. Vocal mimicry
2. The origins of musicking
3. The differentiation of language from musicking

Let's examine them in turn.

VOCAL MIMICRY, MIMESIS, AND RHYTHM

As we noted, the glacier-induced steppe environment of the African lowlands was a difficult one for our large-bodied ancestors. How did they survive? Since we will never develop a rich body of direct evidence we may never know, but we can speculate. One factor that may have helped is social bonding. Familial bonding—parent–child, parent–parent—supports the relatively long period of growth and development large-brained infants need if they are to become competent adults. The mother needs extra food during pregnancy and while nursing her child, and even when the child is done nursing it is still incapable of provisioning itself. Enhanced cooperation among adults, the story goes, would support more sophisticated strategies for hunting and foraging.[5]

Speculations about protolanguage behavior generally play a role in these stories. Intimate interactions are facilitated by protolanguage use and provide occasions for its use. I have no objection to such stories, but I want to consider a rather different one. The neocortex must develop flexible control over the vocal apparatus before protolanguage can emerge. The same vocal control could also be used in musicking.

My favorite suggestion on this matter comes, independently of one another, from Nils Wallin and Valerius Geist. Arguing in rather different ways, both propose that early humans used vocal mimicry of animal calls to influence animals on behalf of humans. Thus:

Geist–Wallin Hypothesis: our hominid ancestors got voluntary control over their vocal apparatus through the mimicry of animal cries.

Of course, this only gets us part of the way to music. We'll need other means to complete the journey.

In making his argument about mimicry, Wallin undertook an extensive review of the literature on the acoustic properties of animal calls and of their underlying neural structure, and for that I recommend his book to you. He chose to focus, however, on the manipulation of animals under domestication. I see no reason why vocal mimicry would not apply in this case—he provides a fascinating analysis of protomusical Scandinavian herding calls that are still in use—but as far as we know, animal domestication occurs too late in human evolution to get our ancestors across the steppe and out of Africa. Geist locates his story back in the Pleistocene era.[6]

Given the connotations that surround notions of primitive man and human origins, I want to emphasize that we are talking about deliberate, voluntary actions. Our hominid precursors were not letting themselves go in paroxysms of unrestrained passion. To imitate the cries of wild animals our ancestors would have had to avoid their own natural (wild) calls and exert deliberate control over their vocal apparatus. Just how this control got started is not clear, but I note that eating required voluntary control over the mouth and we do have some voluntary control over our breathing. These are necessary components. That fact that we are here, of course, implies that this problem was solved.

As for the adaptive value of this hard-won vocal control, Geist notes that one of the challenges large primates face on the steppes is nocturnal safety. In forests or savannahs they seek safety in the trees, but steppes don't have trees. So our ancestors—*Homo erectus*—needed some other protection against nocturnal predation. One aspect of this protection, Geist argues, was to transfer nest-building skills from the trees to the ground. By building a domed "nest" from thorny branches our ancestors put a wall between themselves and predators. This would require some tool use, which *erectus* would have had. While a nest does not seem like much protection, Geist notes that predators tend to be very cautious and do not risk any attack where there is some chance that they will be harmed. A painful barrier—perhaps containing long, sharp thorns—would thus have been useful, along with sharp sticks for jabbing.

Beyond this, Geist notes that one can generate threat calls that would make approaching predators hesitate and disperse. If you can growl and roar like a lion, you can threaten animals that are threatened by lions. Lions themselves would interpret such a threat call as meaning the prey already was claimed by another lion. The same mimetic capacity, by allowing you to attract suitable prey, would help you secure a high-protein meal for your group and thus would enhance your social status. Today, a good repertoire of animal calls is standard equipment for hunters the world over. Geist is simply arguing that the capacity is almost 2 million years old.[7]

Vocal mimicry, as an adaptive skill that requires voluntary control over the vocal apparatus, thus seems to be a logical precursor to music and language. I find this proposal attractive for three reasons:

1. It is mimetic. It doesn't require protohumans to invent something from nothing. It requires only that they figure out how to imitate sounds they hear animals making. That is quite enough for a first step in a long evolutionary journey.
2. It does not require semanticity. The utterances do not have to consist of words that refer to arbitrary objects and events through some process of categorization.
3. Such mimicry is a natural starting point for more extensive mimicry. If you are going to imitate an animal's cry, why not imitate its movement and behavior as well? This could lead to ritual and dance.

As Geist points out, dance is good exercise. A large kill might provide food for a month, but a hunter cannot afford to allow weeks to pass without a vigorous workout. Ritual dance would thus serve at least the adaptive purpose of keeping the dancers in good physical condition. Loud dancing and vocalizing might also have made predators keep their distance.[8]

So let us imagine an ancestor who spends some of his time learning to mimic animals and who would also play with these sounds, as a means of learning them but also simply for the pleasure of it. These same calls could be used for signaling purposes among one's fellows, thus giving our ancestors the capacity for deliberate vocal communication, something both Geist and Derek Bickerton have emphasized as a necessary precursor to language. Vocal mimicry would certainly be used in play—as part of the routine for learning the sounds—and could be used competitively to distinguish oneself from one's fellows and thus move up in the group's status system. Vocal mimicry is thereby useful for protection and hunting, for signaling, and for status competition, and it may well be pleasurable in the sense we defined in chapter 4.[9]

This musicking then is a variety of what Merlin Donald has called *mimesis*, as opposed to mere imitation. In his influential book *Origins of the Modern Mind*, Donald talks of the culture of apes and monkeys as being episodic while that of preliterate humans is mythic. While both types of cultures have been extensively studied by others, Donald's major innovation was to offer an account of the mimetic culture of protohumans, creatures more sophisticated than living apes but not so sophisticated as we are. In Donald's view,

> Mimetic skill or mimesis rests on the ability to produce conscious self-initiated, representational acts that are intentional but not linguistic . . . reflexive, instinctual, and routine locomotor acts are excluded from this definition, as are simple imitative acts and conditioned responses.

That certainly describes vocal mimicry as we have been discussing it.[10]

Yet realistic animal calls, no matter how useful, are not music. They lack the regular and sustained oscillations that are characteristic of music and that allow for the mutual entrainment of musicians and dancers performing together. Vocal mimicry developed our ancestors' voluntary control of the vocal apparatus. We need to augment that vocal control with rhythm, and with group interaction, to have music.

Donald regarded rhythm as the paramount means of integrating mimetic skills. "Rhythmic ability is supramodal; that is, once rhythm is established, it may be played out with any motor modality, including the hands, feet, head, mouth, or the whole body," a statement akin to our equivalence principle from chapter 3. Thus we have:

Rhythm Hypothesis: the cultural precursors to humankind used voluntary control of rhythm as the mechanism that integrated their activities at the highest level.

As we have seen, human behavior and physiology are replete with rhythm. The heart and the lungs do their work to a steady beat and each individual gait has its characteristic rhythm, not to mention the rhythms of sucking and drinking, of chewing and swallowing food. The trick is to introduce rhythm into sound, to deliberately and voluntarily synchronize with one's fellows and then to *abstract* rhythmicity from the various movements that embody rhythm. Much animal rhythm is mediated by core brain mechanisms and is mostly involuntary, for example, breathing, heart beating, digestion (contractions of muscles in the stomach and intestines). Other rhythmic activities, such as locomotion and chewing, are voluntary. Making music requires isolating the fact and pace of the rhythm from the particular motor patterns that embody the rhythm.

Learning to imitate the movements of an animal requires that you focus on the animal's rhythms and differentiate them from your own. That would foreground the rhythm and make it independent of the particular muscles and joints that execute the movement. Beyond this, we should consider the rhythms involved in creating and using the stone tools that our ancestors have had for over 2 million years. To be performed accurately and efficiently, cutting and chopping must be done to a regular beat; so must the movements one executes in flaking stone blanks into tools. One must learn to use one's arms, hands, and fingers with the same rhythmic precision that is typical of walking and running. The net effect of practicing and mastering these new modes of rhythm might well be a generalized capacity for rhythmic control that is independent of any particular behavior.

GESTALT SWITCH 1. SACRED PLEASURE

So now we have bands of protohumans using their animal calls, and their animal moves as well. Group musicking would surely be common. I can imagine it starting more or less spontaneously around significant events. A lion is beaten off, a female comes back from the bush with a new infant, a death, a fresh kill, a water hole is found after a two-day search, a quarrel breaks out and is resolved. I'm imagining a group of folks going about their business and then something dramatic happens that captures the attention of more and more individuals; they begin milling around while chattering and gesturing. Then gestures, footfalls, and cries begin intersecting one another, creating ever denser patterns of sonic and gestural coincidence—the dynamics might have been a bit like those of the clapping we examined at the end of chapter 3. That, I believe, is how group musicking emerged.

For generations upon generations, this musicking may have been opportunistic and haphazard. But the particular patterns of group interaction became easier and easier to trigger, the catalytic requirements less and less, and somehow the activity began happening without any particular catalyst at all. It just happened that on this or that occasion enough individuals gathered together in a small space, one of them began a rhythmic stomp and the others joined in, for the fun of it. In this context, every once in a while—and, over time, more and more frequently—magic could happen. People would have fun and, perhaps, anxiety would be dissipated as well.

Recall that all of this mimetic activity is controlled by the neocortex. That makes it quite different from the system of innate calls, which is limbically mediated. Thus our protohumans were *intentionally* traipsing about with their nervous systems coupled together in collective dynamics. That was new, and it engendered new patterns of neurodynamics. It is these new neurodynamics that, under the influence of rhythm, underwent a self-organized change in dynamics, a *Gestalt switch* if you will, that would later give birth to the human mind and to human culture. The important point is that this new dynamic pattern did not require any changes in the neural equipment. The new dynamics is realized by the *existing* brain as it functions in a new environmental circumstance, synchrony with conspecifics.

For the first time our ancestors experienced a new kind of very intense pleasure. They would surely have worked at repeating and perfecting the techniques that gave them such wild pleasure.

We have thus arrived at a hypothesis close to that advocated by Alondra Oubré in her book *Instinct and Revelation*, where she asserts that "transcendental awareness . . . [is] both a catalyst and a by-product of continually evolving hominid consciousness." Because the word *transcendental* has unnecessary metaphysical implications, I want to re-formulate Oubré's notion using a different term.[11]

Oubré's Hypothesis: the human mind first emerged when musicking gave rise to group-synchronized neurodynamics. Such states are both a by-product and a catalyst of the continuing evolution of hominid consciousness and culture.

They are a by-product because they result from mimetic activities originally governed by more directly adaptive purposes. They are catalytic because they feed on themselves and lead to further cultural developments.

We have not yet arrived at music proper. At least, I don't think we would recognize these hominid sounds, if we heard them, as music. We have rhythmic vocal activity that takes place in groups and may well involve dance. The argument so far is a version of an argument that has been given its most thorough exploration by Steven Brown. The idea is that music proper and language were preceded by something that was neither one nor the other but partakes of both. The final emergence of music and language, then, would result from some process by which, over a period of time, this activity would differentiate into the forms we presently know.[12]

GESTALT SWITCH 2.
MUSIC AND LANGUAGE DIFFERENTIATE

In his account of language origins, Derek Bickerton distinguishes between *on-line* thinking and *off-line* thinking. On-line thinking occurs when the brain is attending to the external world and is directed to that world. In Bickerton's view, most animal thinking is like this. Off-line thinking occurs when the brain is focusing on matters that are not physically present.

Bickerton contrasts on-line and off-line thinking in the following way:

Just as calls are environmentally triggered and in turn trigger a response, so must be the identifications of other species on which calls are based: see a member of another species and you flee it, drive it away, eat it, or ignore it, depending on what species you determine it to be. You do not, if you value your evolutionary future, go into a long dialog with yourself on whether to do anything about it, and if so, what. . . . To enjoy the luxury of off-line thinking, you need a reasonable margin of safety between you and extinction.

So far as we know . . . only humans are capable of this luxury. Only humans can work on problems that do not immediately confront them (but might, at some time in the future); only humans can assemble fragments of information to form a pattern that they can later act upon without having to wait on that great but unpunctual teacher, experience . . . it is this capacity for off-line thinking . . . that endows our species with its unique and uniquely creative intelligence.[13]

I agree with this. Given the existence of musicking, how could language and off-line thinking develop?

Musicking is an on-line activity but an entirely social one. It is oriented toward other people and the sounds you are creating with their help and cooperation, rather than toward arbitrary objects and events in the nonhuman world. The ritual musicking that we have been discussing was practiced by hominids who had survived the long journey through the steppes, a march that required them to become virtuosi in the techniques and technology of group safety. Ritual musicking is on-line in its dependence on highly specific sensory input, but it takes place in the circumstance of physical safety that is necessary for off-line thinking to function. The trick now is to figure out how such primitive musicking could differentiate into more specific activities, some of which—music, dance, religious ritual—would remain on-line while language and thought became off-line.

The on-line activities surely will remain in place as language evolves, nor should we forget that the production and perception of speech *sounds* is an on-line activity. And the behavioral and dynamic differentiation that gives us language will elaborate music and dance.

So let us concentrate on language and return to music later. One can imagine any number of suggestive just-so stories.

First of all, these hominids made and used stone tools and weapons and probably made other things as well, though these objects have not survived in the archeological record. It is not hard to imagine that someone making a spear would imagine the animals to be hunted with it, perhaps in moments of pause from the hard work and concentration of flaking the stone point, stripping the wooden shaft, or binding the point to the shaft. The hunter would certainly imagine the animal as he practiced throwing the spear. Perhaps he even creates a target, perhaps from a log, or some sticks and branches bound together. This target would be a proxy for the animal itself, a physically real substitute for the animal which, because it is physically present, can support on-line mentation and yet, because it is obviously not the animal, is also symbolic. If you will, the difference between what the target actually is and the animal it represents must be constituted by proto–off-line thinking.

One can spin similar stories around the props that would have been used in the rituals, the tail suspended from a belt, the horns or antlers on a mask, the teeth strung in a necklace, the pelt draped over the shoulders. At the same time the mimetic vocalizations fill the air like the liquor that binds the ingredients in a stew. What would it take to associate the mimetic cries with the artifacts alone? Beyond that, what would it take to *replace* the artifacts with mimetic sounds, sounds perhaps more thoroughly subservient to the demands of rhythmic segmentation, yet that still retain the off-line connection to the form and actions of the animal?

Another *Gestalt* switch would do the trick. Instead of being one component of a mimetic complex that also includes artifacts and the animals associated with them, vocalization becomes a trigger that evokes the others. This switch might come about simply because vocalization is always available. Animals come and go as they please, though their actions can be manipulated. Ritual artifacts, though more tractable, are not always at hand. But the mimetic sound can be uttered at any time, in any place. It is completely under the individual's control. That alone should be enough to separate it from the rest of the mimetic complex.

At this point our foreparents are very close to having words that designate, in a rich and undifferentiated way, animals and their actions, and their uses and significance for the band. What then would it take to apply this principle to other objects and actions? Very little, it seems to me. Thus we have the origins of what David Hays and I called the indexing principle:

> Within the context of natural intelligence, indexing is embodied in language. Linguists talk of duality of patterning . . . the fact that language patterns both sounds and sense. The system which patterns sound is used to index the system which patterns sense. The names of concepts, the signifiers, to use Saussure's . . . term, index those concepts. Linguistic concepts fall into two broad classes, contentives (nouns, verbs, modifiers) and functors (determiners, conjunctions, pronouns, prepositions, etc.). Loosely speaking, syntax orders functors and contentives so that the functors are relations over the places occupied by the contentives. Of course, the functors themselves occupy places in the system, and those places are addressed by the appropriate signifiers.[14]

At this point, of course, we have not arrived at syntax or a large and diverse vocabulary, but we are on the way. On-line voluntary vocalizations are used to reference and manipulate off-line nonvocal mental structures. That is the beginning of language proper. Once the process starts, syntax and vocabulary will develop apace.

In thinking about this evolution, we need to realize that these activities would not have been confined to adults. Children and adolescents would be involved as well. And vocal games would surely enter into the play between mothers and infants. With infants and children in the mimetic circle we begin to see the catalytic effect to which Oubré alluded. Once mimesis has been initiated by adults, who did not themselves grow up in a mimetic culture, it becomes part of the external environment that shapes the nervous systems of infants and children as they mature. Of course, their actions can only be shaped to the models provided by adults, but if those actions are learned earlier in life they will be more deeply embedded in the microstructure of the children's brains, which means that the neurodynamics may be more stable. Thus the mimetic capacities of adults will show incremental improvement from one generation to the next as their brains become more intimately sculpted to the requirements of the task. Improved mimesis in turn encourages further innovation and differentiation.

Now let us consider, for a moment, the overall neural dynamics of conversation. A number of dynamic systems are operating simultaneously, not all of them consciously. A certain amount of activity is devoted to maintaining the general body state and tracking the environment. As long as things are going fine, this activity stays far in the background. One must also follow and maintain the social aspects of conversational interaction, keeping track of turn taking and status. Then we have the physical generation of speech and decoding of speech sounds. Finally, there's the activity devoted to the meaning conveyed in speech. The speaker has to assemble that meaning, while the listener has to decode it.

What is the relationship between the last two "islands" of neurodynamics, physical regulation of speech sounds and regulation of meaning?

In ordinary conversation, the neural structures subserving meaning may well be completely without external support. Even when the conversation is about things that are immediately visible, it may well refer to other matters that are not at all present. The physical production and interpretation of language sounds is, by contrast, supported by the sounds themselves. The neural effort that goes into the physical production and interpretation of the speech stream is very considerable. And it is this activity that is closely coupled in interactional synchrony. Yet in ordinary conversation this activity remains mostly in the background, unconscious.

Linguists say that language exhibits duality of patterning and arbitrariness. Duality means that a very small set of "particles" of sound can be combined in various ways to convey a very large set of meanings. Arbitrariness means that the relationship between the sound of a word and its meaning is arbitrary. These two features are obviously interdependent.[15] What this means for dynamics is that the coupling between these two dynamic streams is fairly loose. There will be some global rhythmic correspondence, but that is about it. Thus when two people are engaged in conversation, their nervous systems will be coupled at the level of producing and hearing speech sounds, but there will not be any coupling between their semantic systems.

An inevitable result of this process in which language differentiates itself from musicking, will be the emergence of the Vygotskian Self, the internalized Other. And virtuality is the other side of this Self. It is the Self that maintains the distinction between operating in the physically present external world and operating in any of various imagined worlds. That is its neurodynamic significance. To say so, of course, is not to explain how the self does this. However much I wish I could do that, I am afraid that is beyond our scope. But I would like to continue with the self in the context of other selves.

We are now in territory we explored before: in chapter 3, where we talked about the social self, the persona; the brief discussion of death at the end of chapter 4; and in our main discussion in chapter 7. Each person in the group has a considerable (highly distributed) chunk of neural tissue devoted to representing other people in the group and their mutual history.[16] The group devotes time and energy to rituals that bring their mutual representations into alignment and that may even suspend anxiety driven by knowledge of one's inevitable death. These rituals also affirm the group's symbols and customs. Musicking allows individuals to couple their nervous systems together while language gives them an access to one another's minds that is impossible for other animals.

As these activities become routinized, some individuals in the group emerge as shamans, ritual specialists who are particularly adept at regulating their neural dynamics. These individuals develop the capacity to set the Self aside in particular rituals and thereby function as healers.

SING A SIMPLE SONG:
MELODIES, TUMBLING AND HORIZONTAL

Once language has differentiated itself from the mimetic complex and virtual functioning has become firmly established, how would these developments affect music? We do not, of course, have any direct evidence on what happened, and we probably never will. The best we can do is to reconstruct what might have happened.

In his discussion of early music the ethnomusicologist Curt Sachs asserts that there are two kinds of basic melody, one tumbling, the other more or less horizontal. The tumbling melody is characterized by an initial leap to a high note followed by a stepwise descent. The horizontal melody moves to and from a prominent tone in relatively small steps, though in the extreme, such melodies may have only one tone. Sachs suggests that the tumbling melody is "derived from the violent howl" while the horizontal melody is derived from recitation. Since "there are at least two roots of mere melodical urge," he asks, "not even counting the motor impulse of rhythm—how can one possibly search for 'the' origin of music?"[17]

Given our previous discussions, it is not too difficult to speculate about the neural underpinnings of these two song types, but let us first get a better fix on these melodic types. We could depict the tumbling strain as shown in figure 8.1.

We see the high rise at the beginning and then the tumble down. That illustration, however, makes it look like the tumbling strain just slides from pitch to pitch without ever nailing any of them precisely. And indeed, that surely must have been the case originally. However, the tumbling-strain melody type persists to this day, often in a more cleanly articulated form.

To consider some examples from the musical cultures of the United States, the slow section of Louis Armstrong's "Gully Low Blues" opens with a succession of five tumbling strains. Each begins on a high note and descends approximately one to two octaves. Armstrong teases each phrase on the way down, dallying here and there, even moving back

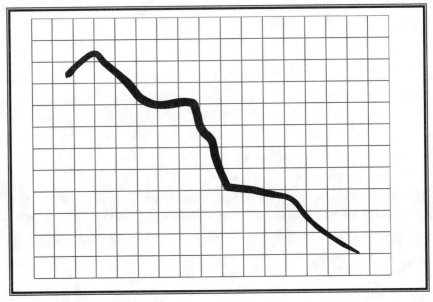

Figure 8.1   Tumbling strain.

up, but always ending below his starting point, only to leap back up to start the next phrase. As another example, consider "Over the Rainbow." The first two lines go like this: "Somewhere over the rainbow, way up high/ There's a land that I heard of once in a lullaby." The melody leaps a full octave on the two syllables "somewhere" and then wanders down until it rests on the starting tone with the final syllable of "lullaby"—though it dips below that point on "there" and "that."

The two diagrams in figure 8.2 depict horizontal melodies.

Note the limited number of pitches in each line. It is common to have horizontal melodies with only two pitches. They may also have five or more. The fundamental characteristic of these melodies is that they are organized around a single pitch with periodic deviations up or down from it.

Many chants are of this type. Operatic recitative also seems to be of this type. The rather less elevated "Old MacDonald Had a Farm" is also horizontal, especially in the refrain where one makes the animal noises, and so is Woody Guthrie's well-known "This Land Is Your Land." Turning to the Tin Pan Alley repertoire, two of Harold Arlen's

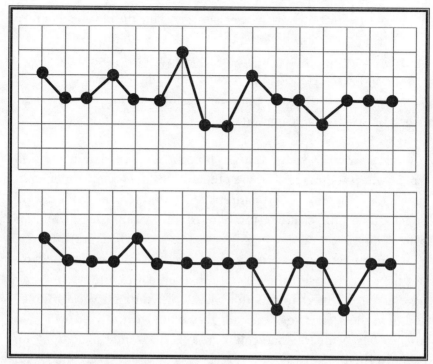

Figure 8.2   Horizontal melodies.

best known songs, "Come Rain or Come Shine" and "That Old Black Magic" are constructed of such melodies.

Sachs notes that both melodic types can exist within the same tribe and even within the same piece. He suggests that each type inevitably develops toward and commingles with the other:

Tumbling strains, I said, "recall savage shouts of joy or wails of rage." They are not passionate but highly naturalistic; they first repeat, then merely imitate, and at last only suggest the unbridled outbursts of strong emotions familiar both to the singers and to the listeners. Horizontal melodies, on the other hand, being sometimes a steady repetition of the same note, sometimes a ceaseless repetition of two notes at different pitches, remind us much of those unassuming, primitive ornaments which iterate the same little dot or dash around the rim of a bamboo quiver or zigzag across the osiers of a basket, without any intention of imitating or expressing the inner and outer experiences of man. Either type develops away from its own to the opposite type: tumbling strains move from natural genuine wails to tame and neat stylizations; horizontal types adjust themselves to the correct inflections, meter, and meaning of the words they carry and become realistic speech melodies . . . .

If we take seriously Sachs's hints to link the tumbling strain to a "violent howl," it follows that we are probably dealing with the prelinguistic vocal call system our primate ancestors used to communicate with one another. One creates a tumbling strain by imposing a rhythmic pattern on a vocal call.[18]

We are talking about primate calls here, the calls of our ancestors, not their imitations of the calls of other animals. Our ancestors may have taken the mechanisms they developed through vocal mimicry and used them to rework the calls they employed in their own social interactions. Similarly, one could create a horizontal melody by imposing a rhythmic pattern on speech, or at least on speech-like vocalization. Songs in the simplest societies tend to have rudimentary lyrics often consisting of a few repeated words or phrases, or even nonsense syllables. Still, the important point is that we are modifying a functional system, speech, by imposing rhythm on it.[19]

ADAPTIVE FUNCTION

So far in this chapter I have offered only one adaptive argument. Following Valerius Geist and Nils Wallin we have the vocal mimicry of animal calls evolving for protection and provisioning, and then being extended to interindividual signaling. This idea does not address music but one of its necessary precursors, voluntary control over the vocal cords. Given that the human vocal apparatus is costly—it makes us more vulnerable to choking on our own food—vocal mimicry has to be very useful in order to justify this cost. Geist's argument is that it is one of a number of adaptations that made it possible for *Homo erectus* to cross the steppes of northern Africa.

Our discussions of ritual and anxiety in chapter 4 suggest another adaptive argument. Given the importance that social life has for primates, Walter Freeman's hypothesis that strenuous ritual is a means of reorganizing neural tissue for the purpose of adjusting social relations implies that such ritual is biologically adaptive. Further, if anxiety is a symptom of poor neural "traffic flow," an activity that can alleviate this symptom may also be adaptive in that it may "relax" the conflicted systems enough that people can solve problems more effectively. To the considerable extent that human anxiety is caused by social tensions, these may be one and the same effect.[20]

These possibilities invite a number of observations. In the first place, if the ritual activity does not impose any costs on individuals or the group—comparable, say, to that imposed by the human vocal tract—then adaptive value is unnecessary. The group would engage in the activity simply for the pleasure it affords. In the second place, even if we grant the behavior's adaptive value, that is not the *proximal* cause for that behavior. The proximal cause is surely pleasure or anxiety relief. That may also explain people's willingness to undertake the tedious practice needed to learn the calls and moves required by the ritual.

My third observation is that the neurochemical mechanism Freeman proposes appears to involve the *cultural* appropriation of a *biological* process for a *social* purpose. The social purpose lies in better interpersonal relations, while the cultural mechanism, of course, is the ritual activity. The biological process is the use of oxytocin to dissolve or weaken interpersonal bonds so that they can be "reset" along lines carried in the ritual and in subsequent activity. As we saw in chapter 5, oxytocin seems to facilitate bonding between parents and infants and between pairs of mated adults. The release of oxytocin in groupwide ritual activity is not within its biological design specifications. Animals do not engage in groupwide ritual activity at all. Thus we have a case where the culturally mediated pursuit of pleasure is recruiting a biological mechanism to serve a new function. To be sure, this function is closely related to its basic biological function; but it is not the same function.

At this point we have crossed the line from animal mind and culture to human mind and culture. The plastic brain is structured through its interaction with the external world. Whatever is there will affect the brain's maturation. The brain has no way of knowing or caring whether an external circumstance is biological or cultural. It can mold itself to either one.

This means, of course, that in certain critical ways, the *functional structure* of the brain is influenced by culture. What, for example, are we to make of the fact that the brains of literate people seem to make special provisions for the interpretation of written symbols? Writing did not exist on the African steppe 2 million years ago; it was not a component of our environment of evolutionary adaptedness. Writing is entirely a product of culture. But it molds brains—think of what your infant is learning as she plays with alphabet blocks.[21]

Part of what makes brains so useful is their capacity to be molded by the environment. That is, after all, how learning happens. But ordinary learning seems to involve only modification of synapses. The massive pruning of synapses that is typical of human cortical development is a different and deeper process. That is what allows the human brain to adapt to culture on a timescale measured in years rather than in hundreds of generations.

In any event, it does seem that biological adaptation played a role in the evolution of musicking's precursors and perhaps of musicking proper. But that evolution also had a cultural component in which the pleasures of musicking spurred further development and practice. I am thus proposing that musicking and the brain have coevolved, just as Terrence Deacon has proposed that language and the brain have coevolved.[22]

But the biological component in the evolution of musicking doesn't quite do the job. Adaptive explanations in biology are understood to explain variations among species. If you want to know why the Galápagos finches have differently shaped bills, look to their food supply. One species must crush seeds, another catches insects on the wing, and yet another sips nectar from flowers, and their bills reflect these differences.[23] But if we think the purpose of music is to facilitate social interaction, a purely evolutionary explanation tells us very little about the variations among music and the music of different groups.

The problem we face here is one of timescale. Biological evolution takes place over generations, through the mechanisms of genetic inheritance and physical reproduction. For human beings those mechanisms produce change on a timescale of tens of thousands of years. In the contemporary world—which is admittedly an extreme case, but one that cannot be dismissed—musical styles emerge and die on a scale of tens of years. The mechanism for that change cannot be biological. The mechanisms of music are implemented in biological material, the human body and its regulating brain, but they are not fully of that biology. Musical variation belongs to culture and to history. From a biological point of view that variation is just random noise. From a cultural point of view, that variation is us.[24]

MIND AND CULTURE

Life is about physical survival. To survive an organism must maintain its structural integrity in the face of all those physical forces that work to degrade that integrity. When the organism dies, that integrity is lost and the organism's structure starts deteriorating. Successful organisms, however, leave progeny. And those progeny can continue organizing matter and energy into living form. Darwinian evolution is a theory about this ongoing biological process.

Human beings are organisms and, as such, came into being through a Darwinian process and continue to evolve according to the laws of that process. However, human brains, acting in concert, gave rise to a new domain, that of the human mind and culture. That new domain has processes of its own.

One of those processes is an evolutionary one, cultural evolution. The question then arises: does cultural evolution have the same causal structure as biological evolution, is it a Darwinian process? That is an idea that various people, Richard Dawkins and Susan Blackmore among them, have been pursuing over the past three decades. When I introduced Dawkins's concept of the meme at the end of chapter 2

I tossed this theory into that ring. It is now time to continue with that line of reasoning.

The meme is the cultural analog to the biological gene; it is the unit of inheritance. In my version of cultural evolution memes are in the external physical world, and I have given examples of musical memes, whether simple phrases, chord structures ("I Got Rhythm"), or even musical forms (AABA, AABC, etc.). What is the cultural analog of the biological organism, the phenotype?

That issue is as difficult, obscure, and contentious as the nature of memes. Some theorists, Susan Blackmore among them, deny the need for a phenotypic entity at all.[25] In contrast, David Hull has cast scientists themselves into the phenotype role in his treatment of science as an evolutionary process. Influenced by Hull, William Croft assigns the speaker and her grammar to the phenotypic slot in language evolution.[26] Given both the difficulty and the preliminary nature of this theorizing, these are reasonable choices.

In the case of musicking I take a more abstract view:

Performance-as-Phenotype: the phenotypic role in music's evolution is played by performance-level attractors.

Note that in identifying musicking's phenotypes in this way I have not introduced a new entity into the theory; I have simply assigned an existing theoretical entity to a role in a different theory, that of cultural evolution. For we have already discussed performance-level attractors in the previous chapter. A performance-level attractor is simply a trajectory in a group's collective neural state space that specifies a whole performance. As such, it is a different object from the groove-stream attractors we discussed in chapter 6, though a performance's groove-stream attractor would be a component of the overall performance attractor. Performance attractors are thus properties of brains-in-process, whether a single musicking brain or a group of brains coupled through musicking. They cannot be thought of as being inside brains in the way viruses are inside their hosts. They are self-organizing emergent phenomena arising when people make music.

While music's performance attractors are not compact physical objects like biological organisms (phenotypes), they are bounded in space and time, as are organisms. They come into being at a certain time and in a certain place and continue on for a finite period of time. Their constituent memes, however, can persist (be reconstructed) from one performance to another just as genes survive from one generation to the next. Further, individual memes can be used in distinctly different performance attractors just as individual genes can be in the genotypes for different organisms. Thus the analogy seems to hold in certain basic ways.

Most importantly, a performance attractor can be successful or not, just as organisms can. Success is the subjective experience of pleasure in the musickers while the lack of pleasure is failure. People will be motivated to repeat pleasurable performances, but not lackluster ones, much less performances engendering anxiety—excluding, of course, the case of performances considered to be practice or rehearsal for "real" performances. Any memes contributing to a pleasurable performance are likely to be repeated in other performances, while memes contributing only to unpleasant performances will drop out of the repertoire.

Performances live in the ebb and flow of human couplings, two by two, ten or twenty people at once, a hundred or three hundred, for a minute, ten minutes, or an hour, three hours, a day, and so forth. Varying numbers of people, varying periods of time, couplings of all kinds, some happening on a regular basis while others happen opportunistically, these are the stuff of human culture. The repeatable couplings of culture must be repeatedly assembled—to use a term coined by Linnda Caporael.[27] In these couplings our nervous systems link together, our minds interact and are brought into convergence through music.

The emergence of culture created a long-term dynamics that is new in the history of life on earth. When I introduced dynamic concepts back in chapters 2 and 3, I focused on relatively short-term interactions, seconds, minutes, and hours. That is the timescale on which musicking happens.

We now need to think in terms of weeks and months and years and centuries. Those are the timescales on which human groups, and groups of groups, come together in ritual and also in conflict, and go their various ways. From week to week and year to year the rituals are pretty much the same, but over the course of centuries they change. That long-term evolution of collective dynamics is a new phenomenon.

It is cultural evolution. Cultural survival depends on the neurodynamics and couplings that carry the culture. These mechanisms work much faster than do biological evolution. Yet they are no more subject to our direct and intentional control than those of biological evolution.

IX

MUSICKING
THE WORLD

The sacred performance is more than an actualization in appearance only, a sham reality; it is also more than a symbolical actualization—it is a mystical one. In it, something invisible and inactual takes beautiful, actual, holy form. The participants in the rite are convinced that the action actualizes and effects a definite beatification, brings about an order of things higher than that in which they customarily live.

–Johan Huizinga, *Homo Ludens*

ACCORDING TO FANNIE Berry, an ex-slave, Virginia slaves in the late 1850s would sing the following song as they felled pine trees:

> *A col' frosty mo'nin'*
> *De niggers feelin' good*
> *Take you ax upon yo' shoulder*
> *Nigger, talk to de wood.*

She went on to report that:

Dey be paired up to a tree, an' dey mark de blows by de song. Fus' one chop, den his partner, an' when dey sing TALK dey all chop togedder; an' purty soon dey git de tree ready for to fall an' dey yell "Hi" an' de slaves all scramble out de way quick.[1]

The song thus helped the men to pace and coordinate their efforts. Beyond that, Bruce Jackson notes, "the songs change the nature of the work by putting the work into the worker's framework . . . . By incorporating the work with their song, by in effect, co-opting something they are forced to do anyway, they make it *theirs* in a way it otherwise is not." In the act of singing the workers linked their minds and brains into a single dynamical system, a community of sympathy. By bringing their work into that same dynamic field, they incorporate it into that form of *society* created through synchronization of interacting brains.[2]

What is the tree's role in this social process? It cannot be active: it cannot synchronize its activities with those of the wood choppers. But, I suggest, "putting the work into the worker's framework" means assimilating the trees, and the axes as well, into social neurodynamics. The workers are not only coupled to one another; by default, that coupling extends to the rest of the world. What does it mean to treat a tree or an ax as a social being? It means, I suggest, that you treat them as animate and hence must pay proper respect to their spirits.

Thus we have arrived at a conception of *animism*, perhaps mankind's simplest and most basic form of religious belief.[3] In this view animistic belief is a natural consequence of coupled sociality. In effect, the nonhuman world enters human society as spirits and, consequently, humans perform rituals to honor the spirits of the animals they eat, or the trees they carve into drums, and so forth. With that in mind let's consider a passage from Bruce Chatwin's *The Songlines*, an intellectual and spiritual journey into Australia's Aboriginal outback. In this passage Chatwin is talking with Arkady Volchok, an Australian of Russian descent who was mapping Aboriginal sacred sites for the railroad. Much of the outback is relatively featureless desert, and navigation is a problem if you don't have maps and instruments, which, of course, didn't exist until relatively recently. The Aborigines used song to measure and map the land:

[Arkady] went on to explain how each totemic ancestor, while travelling through the country, was thought to have scattered a trail of words and musical notes along the line of his footprints . . . as "ways" of communication between the most far-flung tribes.

"A song," he said, "was both map and direction-finder. Providing you knew the song, you could always find your way across country."

"And would a man on 'Walkabout' always be travelling down one of the Songlines?"

"In the old days, yes," he agreed. "Nowadays, they go by train or car."

"Suppose the man strayed from his Songline?"

"He was trespassing. He might get speared for it."

"But as long as he stuck to the track, he'd always find people who . . . were, in fact, his brothers?"

"Yes."

. . . .

In theory, at least, the whole of Australia could be read as a musical score. There was hardly a rock or creek in the country that could not or had not been sung. One should perhaps visualise the Songlines as a spaghetti of Iliads and Odysseys, writhing this way and that, in which every "episode" was readable in terms of geology.

. . .

"Put it this way," he said. "Anywhere in the bush you can point to some feature of the landscape and ask the Aboriginal with you, 'What's the story there?' or 'Who's that?' The chances are he'll answer 'Kangaroo' or 'Budgerigar' or 'Jew Lizard,' depending on which Ancestor walked that way."

"And the distance between two such sites can be measured as a stretch of song?"[4]

We are now prepared to answer that question in the affirmative, as Arkady Volchok did. Given the nature of navigation by dead reckoning—that it requires accurate estimates of elapsed time—and the temporal precision of musical performance, it makes sense that one would use song to measure one's path in a desert with few discernible features. Given our further speculation that music's narrative stream is regulated by the brain's navigation equipment, this Aboriginal Song-as-Map seems like a natural development.

Yet we should be wary of getting wrapped up in the practicality of it all. For that hardly explains the mythology, the fact that this or that feature of the landscape is a sacred place, that the Songlines were traced by culture heroes of animal nature. None of that is necessary for the merely practical end of accurate timekeeping, though it might be useful to have a story to give some content to the narrative stream. To measure a long stretch of time, and thus a long distance, one could simply count to some sufficiently high number while walking and singing at a steady pace. Counting to an arbitrarily high value, however, is a relatively recent human accomplishment, one not present in preliterate cultures.[5] One could also use very long strings of nonsense syllables, but they are very difficult to memorize accurately, as thousands of undergraduates in decades of psychological experiments know all too well; such things simply don't have much purchase in the human brain.[6] So one sings the song of a culture hero's journey, while tracing that journey oneself, and in the process, one becomes that hero. We are in the world Val Geist hypothesized, in which our ancestors imitated the calls of animals in order to manipulate animal behavior. In the process of imagining the wilderness through the persona of an animal one assimilates that wilderness to the categories and needs of human culture.

In a good story, the episodes are interesting in themselves and give the narrative the intrinsic structure necessary to facilitate ready recall and reconstruction. Yet this statement is a far cry from asserting that the narrative content of the Songlines is subordinate to their practical value as navigation aids. Some compelling narrative content may well be necessary for Songlines to function in this way, but that requirement says nothing about what the compelling content must be. Its nature is relatively unconstrained by the practical purpose it serves. It is thus open to pleasurable creation and embellishment.

Cultural Freedom: while all human societies must ensure the biological survival of their members, there is considerable leeway in how that is accomplished. This creates a zone of cultural discretion that is constrained only by the group's collective capacity for coupled neural interaction and desire for pleasure.

To state this in the language of dynamics we introduced in chapter 3, what's at issue is a society's trajectory through its collective state space. Biological needs certainly place strong constraints on that trajectory. But that state space is so very large that it still leaves many degrees of freedom to be patterned by the pleasures and anxieties of the collective neural tissue. By choosing what designs to inscribe in those degrees of freedom, the members of a society impose their will on the world.

Beyond story and song we have ritual.[7] These activities are the means by which our ancestors reconstructed life's activities *within* the sphere of social synchrony. Through myth and symbol, song and dance, through ritual, activities become socially *real* as the actions taken by culture heroes. Somewhere in one of the stories a culture hero will eat the traditional food, prepared in the traditional way, for the first time. That story provides the cultural authority that justifies eating that food, but only if it is prepared in the way prescribed in the story. And so it is with all the artifacts and events and processes of human life. Each must be provided for in the society's complement of myth and ritual. The biological body cares nothing for these stories, but the cultural body, with its mindful brain in synchrony with other mindful brains—it cares deeply about these things.

PRELITERATE SOCIETIES: FROM BANDS TO THE CHURCH-STATE

Given our conception that music is grounded in coupled sociality, we need briefly to consider anthropological work on the nature of human society in preliterate cultures. As Alan Merriam notes in his classic text, *The Anthropology of Music*, such peoples use music in many contexts—working up courage for battle, celebrating a marriage, grinding grain, divining the future, praising a wealthy leader, toilet training, narrating tales, grieving for the dead, paddling a canoe, easing an infant to sleep, beseeching divine beings, accompanying children's games, celebrating one's clan, drinking, healing disease, and so forth—so many that it seems as though our ancestors would have musicked for every occasion. One of the standard refrains among ethnomusicologists is that music pervades life in preliterate societies. That is why we need to take a brief look at how such societies are organized and how they function.

An extensive literature exists on the forms of preliterate social organization. Despite the usual disagreement on details, there is general agreement on a scheme that ranges from small bands, with membership of a few dozen living in a relatively small territory, to church-states, such as the Aztec, covering thousands of square miles with a population in the six figures and ruled by semidivinities. In these societies kinship ties, both real and mythic, provide the main mechanism for organizing social life. Your position in society is largely determined by your genealogy.[8]

At the lower end of this spectrum, society is egalitarian. There are no full-time leaders and little or no task specialization among adults, beyond the division between men's work and women's work. Each adult possesses more or less all of the culture's general knowledge: how the natural world works, how one comports oneself in society, and how to behave toward the spirits. The simplest societies are loosely organized and subsist on foraging activities and so are known as hunter-gatherers. People live in bands of twenty or thirty people that range over a relatively large territory. These are the people with whom you would interact daily, and thus your personal history is intimately intertwined with theirs. Beyond this, a number of these bands may live in a region—all speaking the same language, having the same myths and rituals, and related to one another by blood or marriage. These bands will meet seasonally for major ceremonies.

In a recent synthesis and review of work on human groups Linnda Caporael argues that the band, which she calls a *deme*, and the group of bands, which she calls a *macrodeme*, are basic units of organization that appear in all human societies.[9] We see demes and macrodemes in their most basic configuration in hunter-gatherer societies, but they persist even in the most sophisticated. Thus, drawing on David Hull's work on the social organization of science, Caporael suggests that scientific "in-groups" devoted to certain ideas are demes, while somewhat larger "invisible colleges" are macrodemes that meet with one another at yearly meetings of scientific societies.

Caporael's analysis extends to smaller groups as well. Many tasks typically fall to groups that are smaller than bands. Courtship, mating, and child rearing involve intense interaction between pairs—technically referred to as dyads. One obvious characteristic of dyads is that they permit a very high level of coordination between people; consider an infant interacting with her mother, or a courting couple. Other activities require "handfuls," work groups of a half dozen or so individuals. Here, coupling is generally looser than in dyads. Thus when a handful of men go out hunting they may agree on the type of game and the general direction of the hunt but otherwise function fairly autonomously, at least until game has been spotted.

Caporael treats these core configurations—dyads, "handfuls," demes, and macrodemes—as basic units of social organization. I will assume her framework for the rest of this book. For the past ten or fifteen millennia, however, humans have been living in societies larger than thousands of individuals. How do we construct societies larger than the largest core configuration, a macrodeme of some hundreds of individuals? We need a new mechanism—permanent leadership—and as we will see later on, that mechanism requires musicking for its social construction and maintenance.

In hunter-gatherer societies leadership is only temporary, often for waging war.[10] We see the emergence of permanent leadership with the emergence of village society. The leader is not just one of the boys or girls, but has authority over all villagers, though not very much. As groups of villages become organized into chiefdoms and chiefdoms into kingdoms, leadership is consolidated and becomes differentiated into distinct levels. At the upper end of this spectrum we may have three or four levels of social organization above the local. In parallel to this political structure we see a division of labor, including full-time craft specialists of various sorts, ritual and political specialists, and even full-time musical specialists. This specialization, of course, requires more complex means of distributing the physical goods of society. It also requires a more complex ritual life.

Societies with well-developed patterns of leadership have different patterns of musicking from societies that lack formalized leadership.

Before describing these differences, however, I should point out that this leadership cannot be reduced to the biologically based dominance we see in many animal societies. If leadership were simply a matter of dominance, we would see it in hunter-gatherer societies, but we do not. Those societies are relentlessly egalitarian.[11] That does not mean that all men, women, and children are "equal" in these societies, only that no one has permanent and unquestioned authority over others. Such authority is socially constructed by methods unique to human society.

Without this authority, large complex societies would be impossible. Authority is important, not only for leading war parties but also for settling disputes within the group and for redistributing food and other goods. When cultural knowledge exceeds the boundaries of one person's direct experience, specialization is necessary and specialists must be granted authority in their own domains. This is as true for musicking as for any other specialty. Certain people must be trusted to know the songs and the dance steps. But full-time musical specialists are rare in preliterate societies.

In such societies some may be better at musicking than others. Some may be part-time specialists and, as such, have considerable expertise. But the gulf between highly skilled virtuosi and unskilled laity typical of our society is unknown in preliterate societies. If music is a mystery, it is a mystery familiar to all.

MUSICKING IN SOCIETY

Let us then take a brief look at some kinds of musicking in preliterate cultures. There is so very much musicking, of such various kinds, that we cannot hope for a complete survey. But we can consider a few examples.

Let us begin with the child's first exposure to song. Some research indicates that caregivers in all cultures sing to young children. In particular, they sing young children to sleep.[12] Why? The relation between a child and her mother—who, in most cultures, is the primary caregiver—is among the most important in human society. While a mother typically has more than one child and a child has more than one caregiver, mothers and children spend a great deal of time in one-to-one interaction, the form of interaction most conducive to micro-synchronized behavior. In a sense, this interaction begins even before the child is born. The fetus is certainly aware of mother's heartbeat and her motions, and mother is aware of and responsive to fetal movements. Once the child is born mother and child interact much more extensively and intensely.

Much of that interaction centers on physical care—feeding, clothing, dealing with the infant's urine and feces, bathing—much of it is play, and some of it centers on sleep. Neonates spend two thirds of their day in sleep, but that sleep is not concentrated in a single long period. It is intermittent, forcing parents to interrupt their own sleep to attend to the infant several times a night. One of the major tasks for parents and infants during the first three months is to help the infant consolidate much of its sleep into a single period that spans the night.[13] Given our technical conception of the mind as global neurodynamics, this process comes down to helping the infant to control her mind. Strange as it may seem, that is what sleep consolidation is, perhaps the most basic form of mind control we have.

It is in that context that we must understand lullabies. How do they help the infant regulate her mind? I would like to believe lullabies are neurodynamically helpful above and beyond mother's comforting presence, but we do not know. We do know that rocking at just the right frequency—about one cycle per second—will calm crying infants; and rocking too is often part of the sleep ritual.[14] Perhaps gentle song helps an infant to sleep by giving her something to attend to that is not, however, arousing and so does not demand or elicit any response. It thus helps the nervous system become decoupled from the external world.

Beyond this, consider our earlier discussion of the emergence of the self through a process in which the young child internalizes the activities of caregivers. In this context, the lullaby is a way of maintaining the presence of this self structure as the mind settles into sleep. What capacity does the infant have to keep the repetitive song streaming in her mind's ear after mother has stopped singing it? Could this be the foundation on which the later internalization of a verbal self is constructed?

As I said, we don't know. But the question is an important one as it has to do with mind control, and mind control is basic to human culture. But it also suggests something about the significance of music dealing with love and grief. Musicking provides an opportunity to reenact one's first social relationship, to slip beneath the bonds of verbal category and commitment and restructure the world. Just as musicking preceded language in the phylogenetic emergence of humankind, so it precedes language in ontogenetic development.[15]

Beyond this, we know that lullabies are a distinctive kind of song with features shared across cultures—simple repetitive structures, falling pitch contours, repeated syllables. Their performance style is also distinct, not only for lullabies but for all songs directed to children. These distinctive features—higher pitch, slower tempo, a distinctive timbre, and others—seem to increase the song's emotional expressiveness.[16] We should also consider the various hand games and dandling that are often a part of adult musicking for children.

Just as adults have a special repertoire of songs they sing to children, so children have their own repertoire, which is often connected with physical games and dancing.[17] The children's repertoire is generally simpler than the adult repertoire, often using short phrases repeated time after time with little or no variation, and using three or four pitches within a narrow range. That is to say, such music frequently makes use of the horizontal melodies analyzed by Curt Sachs.

In a classic ethnographic account, John Blacking collected, transcribed, and analyzed the children's repertoire of the Venda, an agricultural people living in and around the Zoutpansberg Mountains of South Africa.[18] Counting songs, in which children count with their fingers, are among the first ones they learn, and they often use them to select just who is to perform some disagreeable task. Most such songs have ten lines, one for each finger, though Blacking recorded one six-line song generally used to count the extended legs of seated children. The words in these songs have little to do with the Venda numbers and may include words borrowed from other languages, including Afrikaans and English.

Other songs accompany children's work activities, various games—headstands, hopping—and there are songs of mockery, songs for danced "amusements," and songs that accompany a story, which is often told by an older child or an adult. The latter songs often have obscure lyrics, though no one is much concerned about them. Blacking thinks they may be "stories set to music which have become corrupted with the passage of time." Remarking that this is true of children's music in many cultures, Bruno Nettl suggests that children's music often seems left over from old rituals that are no longer performed. Finally, both Blacking and Nettl suggest that children's music marks children as a separate social group.

The anthropologist Dennis Werner has observed adult musicking among the Mekranoti Indians of the Amazon rain forest.[19] While they do engage in hunting and gathering, the Mekranoti live in settled villages and do some gardening as well. Thus they are not hunter-gatherers in the strictest sense—there are few hunter-gatherer peoples left in the world. Theirs is a more complex culture, though not much more so.

Werner describes how the women would sometimes spend

> hours painting each other's bodies with genipap dye in dramatic, but delicate, striped designs . . . Just before daybreak, and again just before nightfall, the women also joined together in the central plaza to sit on palm leaves and sing one tune after another, their arms rocking to and fro to the steady rhythms. This was part of the women's *bijok* ceremony, I was told. The singing would continue without change for several months, before preparations began for the ceremonial finale.[20]

The *bijok* ceremony is sponsored by parents wishing to give special ceremonial names to their daughters. The women of the village would spend six months singing together in the morning and the evening, singing in unison, swaying back and forth in steady rhythm, infants strapped to their bodies. These preparations culminated in a four-day festival in which everyone participated, men, women, and children. Bodies painted, decked out in ceremonial finery, people would stroll the village in pairs and groups, singing and dancing, well-fed on tortoise pies supplied by the ceremony's sponsors.

The men had their own singing responsibilities. Every morning before dawn, they would gather in the men's hut—the center of political life—and sing for two hours.

> At first the men sang perfunctorily . . . as the men's house filled they began to sing with more gusto, aggressively swinging their arms to and fro in a cradling motion that rhythmically accompanied all Kayapo melodies. Most of the tunes were in a regular 4/4 time . . . . The men sang in the lowest bass they could manage, heavily accenting the first beats and punctuating them with glottal stops that made their stomachs convulse to the music. . . . Hounding the men still in their lean-tos was one of the favorite diversions of the singers . . . . Sometimes the harassment grew personal as the singers yelled out insults at specific men who rarely showed up.[21]

Sometimes the singers would harass the laggards by yelling that they've already been attacked "and you're still sleeping." Small groups are vulnerable to attack, and early morning is a standard time for such raids. The men had similar, though generally shorter, song sessions in the evening.

What is so striking about this singing is the amount of time both sexes devoted to it, two hours in the day of a society of limited means. Yet while it is possible, as their taunts indicate, that the men's morning singing serves to protect the group from attack, what are the women doing? Is there any reason to think they are doing anything more than simply controlling their neural weather while maintaining the fabric of coupled sociality?

In the case of *bijok* singing, we have two distinctly different phases. We have the daily routine that goes on for half a year, and then we have the four-day concluding period when everyone in the village gets dressed to the nines and has a grand party. This distinction, in a standard terminology, is between ritual, or sacred music and actions, and secular actions. Each ritual has its characteristic songs, rhythms, and dance steps. People behave differently during ritual periods than otherwise, often "protected" by masks or elaborate makeup. Life thus moves back and forth between ordinary time and ritual time.

We can talk about this in the dynamical language we used in our early discussions of the nervous system and coupled interaction. The state space is that of the collective neural tissue of the entire group, and the trajectory, the history, is that of the group. There are times when group members will be loosely coupled or even completely independent. But during groupwide ritual, they will be closely coupled—recall the principle of ensemble state collapse from chapter 3. Each different ritual describes a distinct path through that state space; but, roughly speaking, each performance of a given ritual is like other performances of that ritual. Each ritual has its own performance attractor.

However, where we were thinking about individual brains in chapter 7, when we introduced the concept, now we are thinking about the coupled brains of the group. The concept of the performance attractor, however, is the same in each case—the trajectory toward which musicking performances converge. Just as a performance attractor acts as a psychological "home base" for an individual, so it is for the group.

Whenever the group performs a ritual it enters a distinct region of the state space, with different regions for different rituals. We can thus think of a group's history as a path that moves to and from the ritual attractors of the state space. When we also consider that major rituals often occur at regular intervals—often seasonally—it becomes clear that a group's trajectory through its state space is not at all random. On the contrary, it is highly structured. We can think of the annual journey through state space as the pattern of the group's culture.

RITUAL DESIGNS

We are interested in the distinction between the sacred and profane as it is understood by anthropologists, not theologians. The sacred is a realm of being into which you enter through a ritual process, while the profane or the secular is simply life as you live it outside ritual performance. These are collective states, different modulations in the synchronous social consciousness of a society. The sacred and the secular are two different kinds of collective neural weather.

In a piece entitled "Two Essays Concerning the Symbolic Representation of Time," Sir Edmund Leach characterized the social motion between the sacred and the secular in terms originally stated by Émile Durkheim.[22] Durkheim referred to four "states of the moral person":

1. Secular Life, that is to say, the various states of one's ordinary daily existence. You leave this through a
2. Rite of Separation, in which you undergo a ritual that detaches you from your daily existence and introduces you to the sacred realm, which you experience in:
3. the Marginal or Liminal state, where you are now in a sacred world discontinuous from the secular world, to which you return through
4. a Rite of Aggregation, or desacrilization, often symbolized by rebirth.

Arnold van Gennup described a similar sequence of states in his classic study *The Rites of Passage*. More recently Victor Turner has elaborated on these ideas and related the marginal or liminal state to Csikszentmihalyi's notion of flow, familiar territory by now.[23] Individuals in the marginal or liminal phase of the ritual are linked to one another through a synchrony that is deeper or more pervasive in the nervous system than that required for ordinary conversation and interaction. At its most profound, that interaction is mediated through music and dance.

These rituals have been termed rites of passage because so many of them mark passage from one social status to another: child to adult, unmarried to married, living to dead, unborn to born, entry into the priesthood, entrance into a secret society, ascendancy to a leadership position, and so on. When a person's status changes is this way, so does the set of roles she can enact. Thus much of the special instruction associated with these passages is about the roles required by the new status. But because social roles come in reciprocal pairs, when a person changes status, everyone in society must change the set of roles they enact with that person. These changes are implemented in neural tissue that is distributed throughout the society. Ritual, as Freeman has suggested, is the mechanism by which groups make systematic changes in the collective neural tissue.

But Freeman was interested in more than changes in status. He was, if anything, even more concerned about realigning social bonds simply for the health of the community. With that in mind, let's think about a tribe of hunter-gatherers, humankind's simplest society, having approximately 500 individuals. Because resources are widely scattered, hunting and gathering societies cannot support single bands of that size.[24] Assume they live in ten nomadic bands of roughly fifty people each.

It is relatively easy to get fifty people all singing and dancing to the same beat. The youngest children can participate from their mother's backs while the older children can dance, clap, and sing, if not directly with the adults, certainly in their own way and to the same beat. That takes care of social coherence in the individual bands. But if the tribe consists of 500 individuals in ten bands, rituals confined to individual bands won't do the job. We know that such tribes have periodic gatherings where all the bands meet in one place and have a big ritual bash.[25] This is one mechanism for achieving coherence across the entire tribe.

But we need not gather all the individuals together at once. We can have smaller interband meetings. One obvious occasion for this would be a wedding. Typically marriages happen between members of different bands. The bands are of kinfolk and incest taboos prevent you from marrying your kin. The practice of exogamous marriage (as it is called) thus guarantees that individuals in any given band have close relatives in other bands—and anthropologists typically discuss exogamous marriage in terms of these social alliances.[26] Given that marriage is typically the occasion for a major ritual, however, exogamy also guarantees that members of different groups participate in rituals together. Exogamy thus ensures that one important kind of ritual maintains a circulation of individuals through the individual occasions of that ritual.

I do not mean to offer this argument as an alternative to the idea that exogamy is about securing alliances between bands. I see no reason why exogamy cannot do both, as well as maintain the integrity of the gene pool by reducing inbreeding. Surely social practices that serve multiple functions are a good thing. Or, switching our point of view, surely memes—the artifacts and behaviors of interband rituals—that serve several purposes are more likely to survive in a culture than memes that serve only a single purpose, or none at all.

Marriages are, of course, a recurring event in the cultural life of the tribe, but they are not the only occasions for interband rituals. Births, deaths, and adolescent initiations also involve such rituals, as does warfare. Whatever else such rituals accomplish, they attune the members of the society to one another and to the memetic fabric of their common culture.

Important though they are, rites of passage are not the only rituals. Another kind deals with healing, diagnosis, and treatment of illness. These rituals are particularly interesting because they often involve trance and possession, states of consciousness involving a radical manipulation of the sense of self.

HEALING: TRANCE AND POSSESSION

Shortly after the end of World War II a young Russian emigrant journeyed from her new land, the United States, to the Caribbean country of Haiti. There she would become a participant-observer in the religious rituals of Voudoun (also spelled Vodun), practiced mainly among the poor. Along with Candomblé (in Brazil), Santaria (in Cuba), Voodoo (the United States), and others, Voudoun is one of several New World religions in which a West African worldview and deities take on some of the forms of Roman Catholicism.[27] Thus George Eaton Simpson reported:

> In the Plaisance region [of Northern Haiti], there are three schools of thought concerning the relationship between the loa and the Catholic saints. One view is that there is a spirit "under the water" to correspond to each saint of Heaven. Since God is too busy to listen to the pleas of

men, the loa and the saints meet at the half way point on the road between Heaven and earth, and the loa tell "their brothers" what their human followers want. The saints then return to God and report on the appeals of men, and God grants or refuses the various requests. . . . A second group believes that the saints are loa, although they hold that not all loa are saints. A third point of view is that the saints and the loa are bitter enemies. According to these vodunists, the loa are fallen angels who are worshipped by those who have been chosen by them.[28]

However one explicates the relationship between the African divinities, the loas, and the Christian saints, the ritual practice of Voudoun is more African than European.

Maya Deren documented Voudoun rituals on film, sound recording, and in a book, *Divine Horsemen: The Living Gods of Haiti*. She became a participant in the culture she observed and was allowed to extend her participation to the point of becoming a celebrant in a possession ritual. Thus she was ridden by Erzuli, goddess of love who is identified with various saints, including Mary, as the horse by a rider—the metaphor used by the practitioners themselves.

Before reading Deren's description of her possession, let us remind ourselves of some obvious things. We are dealing with ritual practice, a set of actions undertaken by a group of people in accordance with procedures they have learned from their elders and culturally designed to achieve one end: possession. While possession itself happens to one or several focal celebrants (usually a priest or priestess), it requires the coupled interaction of a group, some playing drums or other percussion while others sing, clap, or dance. To paraphrase Hillary Clinton, it takes a village to make a divinity. The rhythm must be just so, and there are different rhythms for different divinities. The priestess does not play an instrument, nor does she sing. She dances. When she has been dancing long enough, when her brain has become properly attuned, the Self disappears and the divinity takes over:

The white darkness starts to shoot up; I wrench my foot free but the effort catapults me across what seems a vast, vast distance, and I come to rest upon a firmness of arms and bodies which would hold me up.

But these have voices—great, insistent, singing voices—whose sound would smother me. With every muscle I pull loose and again plunge across a vast space and once more am no sooner poised in balance than my leg roots. So it goes: the leg fixed, then wrenched loose, the long fall across space, the rooting of the leg again—for how long, how many times I cannot know. My skull is a drum; each great beat drives that leg, like the point of a stake, into the ground. The singing is at my very ear, inside my head. This sound will drown me! . . . The white darkness moves up the veins of my leg like a swift tide rising, rising; is a great force which I cannot sustain or contain, which, surely, will burst my skin. It is too much, too bright, too white for me; this is its darkness. "Mercy!" I scream within me. I hear it echoed by the voices, shrill and unearthly: "Erzulie!" The bright darkness floods up through my body, reaches my head, engulfs me. I am sucked down and exploded upward at once. That is all.[29]

This is one of seven or eight occasions on which Deren became possessed. She remembers nothing about what she did while under possession (as you may recall, Bernstein required several minutes to return to himself if he had become possessed while conducting). Erzuli rode her, but she does not remember the ride.

Deren is hardly a typical celebrant of such rituals. She was not a Voudoun priestess. The Voudoun priest or priestess is born into the culture and undergoes training for possession rituals. It is not something she does in order to satisfy intellectual and existential curiosity about a facet of human experience. Further, as a relatively recent cultural hybrid, Voudoun cannot be casually taken as representative of the type of religious practice that might have occurred, say, ten thousand years ago in a village. It is, however, closely related to the cultures we will be examining in the final chapter, the African-American cultures of the United States.

All of this notwithstanding, Deren's account is consistent with other accounts of possession in a number of respects.[30] In the first place, as we have seen, the priest or priestess who becomes possessed does not perform any music. Conversely, as Gilbert Rouget points out, it is rare for the musicians to become possessed; that is not their role in this situation. Their role is to provide the rhythmic context that establishes a link, a coupling, to the divinity within the priest. Second, Deren did not remember what the divinity said when it rode the rhythmic coupling to become manifest and thus to speak through her. Third, the rhythm of the dance is keyed to the divinity's identity. The person takes on the "aspect" of the divinity in her physical style and voice; she speaks with the divinity's voice, not her own.

The occasion for possession rituals is generally medical: someone is ill, or perhaps the community is in some way ill. The source of the affliction must be found and steps taken to cure it. Once the celebrant becomes possessed, the divinity will give information bearing on the matter. Just how the divinity obtains this information or, if you will, just how the celebrant obtains the information through the community, is not our concern. What is important is that possession is undertaken only for serious reasons; it is not an occasion for psychedelic tourism.

Possession is not the only mental state for medical divination. The literature also speaks of trance, typically identified with shamans. The shaman is a religious practitioner and a musician as well. The shaman will provide his or her own music, often with a drum or a rattle, while dancing and chanting until the onset of trance. At that point she may continue to make music, or that burden may fall on an assistant. In either case, the shaman undertakes a spiritual journey in her own persona, often called "shamanic flight," in which she sees and hears things bearing on the medical situation that prompted the ceremony. Unlike the possessee, the shaman remembers all that happened in her trance.

Michael J. Winkelman has done a cross-cultural study demonstrating systematic differences between trance cultures and possession cultures.[31] Shamanistic flight is characteristic of relatively simple societies, such as hunting and gathering societies, while spirit possession is common to complex societies with permanent village settlements and agricultural subsistence. Winkelman offers no explanation. There is, however, one obvious direction for speculation.[32]

That the possessee does not play an instrument, and that the players generally do not become possessed themselves, means that possession rituals involve a more highly differentiated set of roles than shamanistic rituals. We have at least four roles—patient, possessee, musician, other (who may help with the musicking)—as opposed to three roles: patient, shaman, other (who may help with the musicking). This parallels the general level of social differentiation in these two types of society. The simpler societies lack full-time leaders and religious practitioners and have relatively little craft specialization. The settled societies do have full-time leaders, often have full-time religious practitioners, and have some craft specialization. Given that the brains performing the societies' mundane activities are the same brains that, when closely synchronized through musicking, enact divination rituals, this parallel makes sense.

Making sense is not so bad, but it is only a starting point. The question of specialization is but a specific version of a more general question, that of the relationship between style of musicking and general cultural style.

Before we get to that, however, I want to make one more point about shamans and priests. How do you become one? Typically a person will undergo a spontaneous trance or possession early in life, in the form of a dream or some sort of "sickness."[33] That is taken as a sign of spiritual potential. The person can then choose whether to undertake a spiritual apprenticeship. One object of the training is to bring trance or possession under control—but not merely individual control, for the rituals are not solo events. The apprentice must learn to put his or her mind, neurodynamics, in service to the community.

Thus we have:

1. the phylogenetic origins of human society in spontaneous musicking;
2. the ontogenetic assimilation into human society through maternal song;
3. the capacity to diagnose and cure ills, both individual and collective, by using music to step outside the bounds of mundane consciousness anchored in the (linguistic) self.

In each of these cases, musicking is a fundamental source of mind control, of taking action to manipulate neural weather, individually and collectively.

CULTURES AND STYLES: CANTOMETRICS

Human cultures are not miscellaneous collections of artifacts and practices. In a way that is often difficult to explicate, a culture's modes of food preparation are consistent with its modes of dress, of interpersonal address and stance, dwelling style, weaponry, mode of subsistence, pantheon of supernatural beings, and so forth. The *locus classicus* for this idea is Ruth Benedict's *Patterns of Culture*. She argued her thesis by showing that the Pueblos of the American Southwest were Apollonian in their formality and emotional reserve, the Dobu of Melanesia were Paranoid in their bending of patterns of hostility into functioning social structures, and the peoples of America's Northwest Coast were Dionysian in their search for religious ecstasy.

Our biological heritage includes a nervous system that takes over two decades to develop and is, especially during its early phases, open to environmental influence. Nurture has plenty of opportunity to influence human nature. Because of that we must think of cultural differences as intrinsic, not extrinsic. Culture is not a thin veneer glued atop layers of biology. Rather, it is the spicy liquor that binds disparate meats, grains, and vegetables into a flavorful stew.

I suggest that cultures encode their master patterns much as holograms encode images. If you rip a hologram of a coin, for example, in half, you can still use it to view the entire coin. If you rip one of those halves in half, you can use either of the resulting quarters to view the entire coin. This is quite different from an ordinary photograph where, if you rip it in half, you get one half of the coin on one piece of photograph and the other half on the other piece. A piece of a photograph contains a piece of the image; a piece of a hologram, however, still contains the entire image. The resolution of the image, that is, its sharpness, will be somewhat reduced—the smaller the piece, the lower the resolution—but the entire image is there. A hologram is thus a way of distributing the entire image throughout the representing medium.

Similarly, the pattern of a culture is distributed throughout all the artifacts and practices of the people who live that culture. Each piece and aspect reflects the pattern of the whole.

While it has disappeared from view these days, there is a considerable body of research and theory that indicates that the brain stores information holographically. This body of work is akin to the dynamic views we examined earlier in this book.[34] If those brains store information so that each physical part reflects the pattern of the whole, then that is how they will organize culture. And the ritual process has the effect of tuning the brains of all participants to the same rhythms and symbols. It is thus at the core of the process of distributing a culture's pattern in the brains of people in a society.

Alan Lomax's *Folk Song Style and Culture* is one of the most rigorous investigations of cultural style, though it is not particularly under Ruth Benedict's influence. In the 1960s Lomax and a team of investigators conducted a substantial survey and analysis of the world's musics. Working in the tradition of cross-cultural research initiated by G. P. Murdock, they prepared a sample of over 3,000 songs, representing 233 cultures from 5 continents plus the Pacific islands, and had judges code all songs on 37 aspects of song style—nature of the performing group, relationship between vocal part and instrumental parts, melodic style, rhythmic style, wordiness, tone quality, tempo, and so on. They analyzed this information and sought correlations with measures of social structure and economic practice.

In general, they found consistent correlations. In particular, "The principal discovery in cantometrics is that a culture's favored song style reflects and reinforces the kind of behavior essential to its main subsistence efforts and to its central and controlling social institutions."[35] Of course, as the methodological mantra goes, correlation is not causation. The fact that these three aspects of culture—song style, subsistence activities, social institutions—seem to share the same pattern need not be interpreted as implying that one of those aspects determines the other two.

In particular, we have no reason to believe, in the manner of Marxists both vulgar and sophisticated, that subsistence patterns determine institutional and musical patterns. Human beings have great freedom in the way we execute the tasks of living. This freedom allows culture to serve both aesthetic and practical constraints, to be both pleasurable (in our technical sense) and utilitarian. The different cultural arenas share the same pattern because they are executed by the same brain. Or rather, they are executed by the same society of brains variously coupled from day to day, band to band, season to season.

Nor should we exaggerate the degree of fit Lomax found between musicking and society. The songs of two hunter-gatherer societies may be much the same in terms of Lomax's scoring criteria and yet be very different music. Within our own culture there are lots of rock and roll, rhythm and blues, and country and western tunes that will look very much alike on Lomax's scorecards and yet appeal to utterly different populations, populations that wouldn't be caught dead listening or dancing to one another's music. Lomax's results are far from worthless, but they reflect a rather coarse-grained view of both music and culture. To use a visual analogy, if you blur your vision a bit (perhaps simply by removing glasses) you may no longer be able to distinguish between one dog and another, but you'll have no trouble distinguishing between dogs and trees. Lomax set his methodological sights on distinguishing dogs from trees and, by and large, succeeded.

With that in mind, let us consider just two of his findings, about social solidarity and about cultural complexity.[36]

In looking at social solidarity, Lomax considered the structure of work teams. Individuals in hunting parties are relatively autonomous. They may set off together, and they may join together when game has been spotted or killed, but they spend a great deal of time looking independently for signs and following them. Gardeners and agriculturalists, however, often work in closely coordinated teams, tilling the soil, planting seeds, tending plants, harvesting, and preparing the harvested food for eating.

Lomax found that societies with closely coupled work teams favored musicking where performers blended their voices very closely and danced to the same rhythms. They sang the same pitches and intervals, enunciated the words in the same way, and matched their timbre. Societies with more autonomous working methods did not sing so cohesively. They didn't always sing the same pitches and intervals, and their rhythms were not quite together. The overall sound was more ragged. Coordinated vocalizing is correlated with coordinated work teams.

In passing, however, Lomax noted that while coherent vocalizing seems to happen spontaneously in preliterate societies, it "is achieved among Anglo-Americans only by intensive rehearsal of carefully chosen personnel under the restrictive guidance of a director."[37] Lomax offers no explanation for this difference, but one line of speculation seems obvious. The members of an Anglo-American choral group are likely to work different jobs, having different team styles, and they may not see one another daily. They do not share the solidarity one finds among performing groups who also live and work together. Coherence must be externally imposed through the authority of someone who is not only a musical specialist but a specialist in organizing and directing musical groups.

That brings us to the issue of cultural complexity, which we have already encountered in Winkelman's study of trance and possession.[38] One of Lomax's findings was that the simpler the society, the simpler its song lyrics, with the simplest societies using a great deal of repetition and nonsense syllables. Similarly, the precision of enunciation varies with social complexity; the more complex the society, the more precise the enunciation. The prevalence of solo singers, Lomax writes, mirrors social structure:

> As society grew more complex and leadership more exclusive, the solo bard began to hold the center of the stage. He preempted the communication space as the priests and kings seized and held the wealth and power of the human community. The bard, exercising exclusive dominance and enforcing passive attention through long songs, represented the dominant leaders and helped to train the audience to listen for long periods without replying. More than that, the bard, whether sacred or secular, addressed himself to the powerful leaders who more and more directed the life of ever larger social units.[39]

We are now in a position to address the question we raised earlier: How is authority socially constructed?

The relationship between the solo singer and the passive audience is fundamentally a dyadic one, like that between husband and wife or parent and child. The audience may consist of five people or five hundred. It makes no difference: they all play the same role, which is to listen. This also applies to the relationship between a soloist and the accompanying group. The soloist takes one role while the accompanying group, collectively, takes another. There may or may not be some differentiation between performers in the general accompanying group, but that group, as a whole, occupies one side of a dyadic relationship while the soloist occupies the other side.

Long-term leadership is socially constructed, I suggest, by having a group take one side of a dyadic relationship. Thus we need a principle:

Group Substitution: a cohesive social group can collectively play a single role in a role structure.

Leaders typically assume their authority through an appropriate rite of passage—think of a coronation or a presidential inauguration—and their authority is reinforced through continuing rituals of state. Thus, not only does musicking allow human society to form in the first place, but by allowing group substitution in role structures, it is also critical to extending human society beyond the boundaries of face-to-face acquaintance.

MEMES, ATTRACTORS, AND CULTURAL COHESION

In culture, as in life, we see an evolutionary process. By defining shards of sound to be memes, as I did at the end of chapter 2, I committed myself to an evolutionary model. Now I must begin to deliver on that commitment.

One problem, of course, is that it's not clear just what a meme is. That doesn't bother me very much. The cultural arena is very different from the biological arena, so there is no point in being too fastidious in constructing our analogy. Biological genes are found on strands of DNA and thus, to a first approximation, one gene is much like another. Culture's genes, the memes, are not such a homogeneous lot. Musical instruments are memes, as are performance techniques, and so are motifs, specific sequences of intervals, particular rhythms, and so forth. If something exists in the external world and can be imitated, it is at least potentially a meme. To be sure, memes are impotent unless they find their way to groups of human beings with functioning neural and motor systems. But genes are similarly useless without cellular transcription and replication machinery.[40]

Correlatively, in chapter 8 I suggested that the performance attractors function as the musical analog to the biological phenotype. As you recall, a performance attractor is simply a trajectory through the state space of a group's collective neural tissue. Performing groups are constituted as the occasion requires—Linnda Caporael talks of repeated assembly[41]—but typically consist of individuals having long-term relationships with one another. While musical instruments exist independently of their use, the memes of musical sound exist only in the act of performance (or the act of mechanical or electronic reproduction). Though more elusive than the physical artifacts, they are no less external, physical, and memetic. The performance attractor is a function of the joint interaction of group members, their instruments, and the sounds of music.

What, then, determines whether or not a performance attractor—the cultural phenotype—survives in a given group? It must meet the expressive needs of the group. But just what does that mean?

Let us consider, once again, Alan Lomax's central finding: "The principal discovery in cantometrics is that a culture's favored song style reflects and reinforces the kind of behavior essential to its main subsistence efforts and to its central and controlling social institutions." Yet this is but an observation, arrived at through a fairly complex procedure. Why should song style "reflect and reinforce" subsistence activities and social institutions? Why doesn't song style reflect something else, or nothing at all?[42]

One answer, implicit in chapter 3's discussion of social status and role, is that the same nervous system must enact both sets of activities. Given that, it is most "economical" to make these activities as similar as possible. What's at stake, then, is consistency or coherence. And just what kind of entity "cares" about coherence? Minds do, for it is minds that seek pleasure and avoid anxiety. As I argued in chapter 4, pleasure is simply the subjective experience of enacting coherent neural patterns. This coherence is an aspect of collective intentionality. It is not "in the genes" or rigidly imposed by the environment. It is chosen, and it is chosen because it feels good.[43]

In most of the societies Lomax surveyed, people's lives are dominated by subsistence activities and politics. Song style reflects social institutions because that's all there is for it *to* reflect. These populations live in relatively circumscribed areas, and most of the population derives its subsistence from a relatively small number of activities: hunting and gathering, fishing, tending animals, and gardening. Thus since most people live similar lives, they can share similar music. It makes sense for them to build their musicking using the same pool of memes organized into performances converging on the same limited set of attractors.

What happens when we consider societies, such as our own, with densely populated urban areas and a wide variety of full-time vocations requiring many different work styles? Such cultures typically support a variety of musical styles and, judging from some recent ethnographic work in the United States and the United Kingdom, individuals may adopt several distinctly different kinds of music.[44] In this more complicated world, people have more options. Many will choose the music of their fathers and mothers; or they may choose the music of their fellow workers. But some make other choices.

X

MUSIC AND
CIVILIZATION

Poets are the unacknowledged legislators of the world.
—Percy Bysshe Shelley

IN 1967, A book with an ungainly title, *The Origin of Consciousness in the Breakdown of the Bicameral Mind*, created a minor sensation with an astonishingly quixotic and original thesis: human consciousness originated in ancient Greece sometime between Homer and the Athenian Golden Age. That is to say, Homer was a Hellenic zombie telling heroic tales about older zombies. *Night of the Living Dead* had opened in Troy and was playing to a packed house.

The author, Julian Jaynes, stages this argument by noting that *Iliad* and *Odyssey* contain many episodes in which humans receive direction from gods and goddesses, and do not contain many words referring to mental states and actions. He takes the first observation at face value and concludes that the Homeric Greeks heard inner voices and acted on what they heard. From the fact that mental words had become common by the time of the Athenian Golden Age, he concludes that human consciousness had finally emerged. The inner voices were no longer necessary as their function was subsumed by consciousness; Jaynes would thus have us believe that the creation of concepts about mental states and acts gave rise to consciousness.

However skeptical I am about aspects of Jaynes's theory—for example, the idea that Sophocles was conscious while Homer was not is deeply odd—something very important clearly happened in the period he surveys. Jaynes seems to have assumed that the absence of words about mental states means there was no consciousness. I see no reason to accept such an assumption. If one thinks of consciousness the way Walter Freeman does, then rabbits and dogs are conscious.[1] But they have no words for mental states either.

If we reject Jaynes's claim about consciousness, however, we can still accept some of the reasoning that accompanies it. The important observation is that mental terms were scarce in Homeric times, but not in Sophoclean and later times. If one has few or no mental terms, one can hardly attribute much to the mind. Similarly, Sophocles' *Oedipus the King* would not have been possible in Homer's time precisely because it takes place in a mental realm. It is about mental events, acts of knowing or denial.

I submit that this change is about the emergence, not of consciousness itself, but of a whole range of new modes of consciousness, new ways to use the mind, new patterns of neural weather. Another way of talking about this change is to use Jean Piaget's concept of reflective abstraction.[2] In his studies of child development, Piaget proposed that conceptual development proceeds through a series of stages in which the mental mechanisms of later stages objectify those that were used in earlier stages. The conceptual development that Jaynes has identified is like this.

Jaynes's analysis centers on a handful of terms. As used in the *Iliad* these words refer to bodily symptoms, but they later come to have mental referents, such as mind or spirit. One of these terms is *thumos*:

> It refers to a mass of internal sensations in response to environmental crises. . . . This includes the dilation of the blood vessels in striate muscles and in the heart, an increase in tremor of striate muscles, a burst of blood pressure, the constriction of blood vessels in the abdominal viscera and in the skin, the relaxing of smooth muscles, and the sudden increased energy from the sugar released into the blood from the liver,

and possible perceptual changes with the dilation of the pupil of the eye. This complex was, then, the internal pattern of sensation that preceded particularly violent activity in a critical situation. And by doing so repeatedly, the pattern of sensation begins to take on the term for the activity itself. Thereafter, it is the *thumos* which gives strength to a warrior in battle.[3]

The next step is to conceptualize *thumos* as a container of various psychological substances such as vigor, and as an agent responsible for some class of psychological acts.[4] Once Jaynes has made similar arguments for the other terms, it seems obvious that the conceptualization of mind we find in classical Greek thinkers is constructed over sets of bodily symptoms we now recognize as being regulated by the brain centers most directly responsible for motivation and emotion.

Once the Greeks have words for these mental and physical states they can use those words in examining their experience and formulating new ideas. They can begin to think *about* their neural weather in a new way. They have, in a sense, objectified the mind.

Consider a different scenario. Imagine, first of all, a ritual of the type we examined in the previous chapter. Everyone in the community participates, but some have central roles that perhaps require more elaborate costuming and makeup, more intricate dance steps, and more singing. These people occupy the center of the ritual space. The others surround them, actively participating through song and dance, but their steps are not so elaborate, their singing more circumscribed.

You are seated in an amphitheater carved out of a hillside and are observing this scene on the stage before you, down at the bottom of the hill—perhaps the theater of Dionysus below the Acropolis in Athens.[5] You are now watching a play. The social interaction between central and peripheral ritual celebrants, the complete dynamics of a society at a given ritual moment, is now arrayed before you. The whole social system has become objectified and available for your contemplation.

This play is, in fact, an ancient Greek tragedy, perhaps Sophocles' *Oedipus the King*. The little story I told about it is, I suggest, what Friedrich Nietzsche had in mind in *The Birth of Tragedy*. Like many scholars of his time, Nietzsche was interested in the origins of things. Linguists were in search of humankind's first language, the biologists hunted for the origins of species, and classicists wanted to know where Greek tragedy came from. It came from prior ritual, they supposed, but how?

Nietzsche begins, in effect, by proposing a theory of mind, of neural weather. He sets forth his well-known opposition between "the Apollonian art of sculpture, and the nonimagistic, Dionysian art of music," asking us to "first conceive of them as the separate art worlds of *dreams* and *intoxication*."[6] The particular intoxication he has in mind is that of the Dionysian festivals, in which the celebrants get drunk on wine, song, and dance. Nietzsche thus plants himself firmly in the territory we have been exploring. Whatever his interest in historical details about when and where those festivals took place, he was most interested in understanding tragedy as a form of neural weather. That is, like Jaynes a century later, he saw a new mode of consciousness emerging.

Nietzsche's solution is, in effect, to have the Dionysian chorus frame and present the Apollonian action of the principal celebrants. He asks us to imagine "the reveling throng" as it must have existed before the development of tragedy, where "the votaries of Dionysus jubilate under the spell of such moods and insight whose power transforms them before their own eyes till they imagine that they are beholding themselves as restored geniuses of nature, as satyrs." Nietzsche then goes on to say that "The later constitution of the chorus in tragedy is the artistic imitation of this natural phenomenon" and that "there was at bottom no opposition between public and chorus."[7] That is, the chorus of Greek tragedy is a latter-day reconstruction of the Dionysian band.

Continuing on, we are asked to believe that "the scene, complete with the action, was basically and originally thought of merely as a vision," that is, as being Apollonian in character. Through his Dionysian identification with the choristers, the spectator adopts their vision—that is, the central action of the tragedy—for himself and thus enters fully into the dramatic action. Nietzsche concludes by saying that "we recognize in tragedy a sweeping opposition of styles . . . the Dionysian lyrics of the chorus . . . the Apollonian dream world."

Judged as history, Nietzsche's theory is not very good. More recent scholarship suggests that Greek tragedy is not a lineal descendant of the Dionysian cults that so fascinated him.[8] But it is by no means clear that getting the history right would have helped Nietzsche much. Nietzsche was grappling with the same subject Jaynes grappled with, a subject much more difficult to conceptualize than the provenance of the various texts and artifacts that are the evidentiary foundation of archeological and historical thinking. Nietzsche took the differences between texts and artifacts separated by relatively long intervals as evidence of a major change in the Greeks' collective neural weather.

That is not unlike our task in this chapter: to discern shifts in neural weather betokened by the evolution of music beyond what we find in preliterate societies.

AGES OF MUSIC AND CULTURAL RANKS

In his book *The Four Ages of Music* Walter Wiora looks at music as a comparative anatomist looks at the fossil record. He is a comparative anatomist of musical style. After a career's worth of study he has concluded that, in the large, musical styles have emerged in four ages in which the newly emerging styles have broadly similar characteristics. Older styles, meanwhile, continue to be performed. The process is thus a cumulative one, yielding newer kinds of music without completely eliminating the older.

It is easy enough for an anatomist of musical types to listen to live and recorded performances of existing music—that's how Lomax did his work—but only Western music has left fossils in the form of scores. We have some ancient musical instruments, but the instruments cannot tell us how they were played. We also have various written accounts of music performed in ancient literate cultures. Those accounts can tell us about the occasions for music, the number and kinds of instruments in an ensemble, the effect of the music on listeners, the general esteem in which music and musicians were held and they can give us general impressions of how it sounded; but those accounts cannot give us the music itself. We have even less evidence about the music of preliterate peoples living 5,000 or more years ago.

And yet Wiora's first age is that of "prehistoric and early times" in which he includes "survivals among primitive peoples and in the archaic folk music of high cultures." Similarly, his second age is that of "the music of the high cultures of Antiquity, from the Sumerian and Egyptian to the late Roman, as well as its manifold continuations and further developments in the high cultures of the Orient."[9] Wiora has no direct evidence of how those old musics sound, but he is willing to assume that their general characteristics are like those of musics existing among living peoples, as biologists are willing to assume that the soft tissue parts of extinct species resemble those of living species having similar bony parts. One may or may not be willing to grant Wiora this assumption, but we must recognize that it is an assumption—one that is common among students of cultural history and evolution.[10] Given this assumption Wiora compares the musics of his first and second ages with those of his third, the "musical art of the West," and his fourth age, "the technical and industrial Age, spanning all countries of the world, uniting the heritage of all previous cultures in a kind of universal museum and carrying on its international concert life."[11]

Just as a paleontologist can conduct her investigations without having to think about the nature of the process that produced reptiles about 300 million years ago and mammals about 250 million years ago, so Wiora is not concerned about the process that led from the earlier to the later types of music. He simply wants to provide a proper description of the types.

My primary purpose in discussing Wiora is, then, to present and reinterpret his general account in this and the next section. Once I have done that, however, I will go on to sketch an account of how the later types evolved from the earlier. The validity of Wiora's work, of course, is independent of my theory about the process through which music has evolved. I can be wrong without my error propagating to Wiora's typology.

〜

If you read Wiora carefully, you realize that his first three so-called ages have an intrinsically musical emphasis, rhythm, melody, and

harmony, in that order. But his fourth age does not. He talks of folk
and art music, of reproduction, of types of music being available. All
of that is true, but it confuses the issue. For that reason I want to forget about Wiora's characterization of that age, though our final chapter is devoted to some music from it.

While it is clear that music in all of these ranks (a term I prefer to
age for reasons I will explain shortly) exhibits the basic phenomena of
rhythm, melody, and harmony, there are significant differences between one rank and the next. Rank 1 is oriented toward rhythmic
elaboration. Rank 2 strongly *differentiates* the control of melody from
control of rhythm and creates techniques for elaborating melody. In
rank 3, harmony is in turn differentiated from both melody and
rhythm. Note that this ordering seems intrinsic. Music unfolds in
time. How could one gain control of melody without first having
control of the temporal unfolding, of rhythm? And how could one
have control of the simultaneous ordering of musical pitches—harmony—without first having control over the pitch patterns of individual lines?

I explicitly do not want to imply, however, that rank 1 music lacks
melody or harmony, only that rhythm is its focus. Similarly I do not
mean to imply that rank 2 music lacks harmony, only that melodic
practice is more sophisticated than harmonic. In particular, rank 3
musical form gets much of its structural variety from the practice of
modulating from one well-established key to another, but rank 2 music tends to be modal, without any modulation from one key to another in a given composition.

Since this is an important issue I want to reframe our accepted
ideas of rhythm, melody, and harmony, notions we pretty much took
at face value in the earlier chapters of this book. I submit that our basic experience of music, like all our basic experience, is holistic or
Gestalt in nature.[12] This was brought home to me a number of years
ago when a friend asked me to teach her about jazz. We would listen
to records and talk about what we were hearing. I would call her attention to what the alto sax, or the bass, or the trombone was doing
and, in the process, I discovered that she couldn't even discriminate

one line from another, much less follow whatever point I was making about what was going on in that line. She could get a sense of the whole but had a hard time perceptually segmenting the whole into the discrete contributions of various instruments.

My friend also could not, at first, hear the chord structure (harmony) of a piece independently of the melodic line. If one cannot distinguish melody from harmony it is impossible to understand that, for example, Thelonius Monk's "Bright Mississippi" is based on the harmonic structure of "Sweet Georgia Brown," or that Charlie Parker's "Thriving on a Riff" is based on "I've Got Rhythm." To hear the derivation you have to ignore both the jazz melody and the melody of the source tune; once you do that and attend only to the chord changes, the derivation is obvious. As an experienced musician I had no trouble doing this. But this was difficult for my friend—a difficulty we dealt with, in part, by singing the melody of the source tune while listening to the jazz tune derived from it. The melody, though quite different from the jazz melody, seemed to fit. And why not?—they both had the same harmonic structure.

Such listening and analysis takes practice because we don't hear rhythm, melody, and harmony and then combine them into a musical whole. Rather, we apprehend the whole first and only gradually learn to differentiate that whole into rhythm, melody, and harmony. Developmental linguists talk about the holophrastic utterances of the child (roughly from eight to eighteen months old) in which the child uses one brief utterance to designate a whole situation without being able specifically to designate aspects of the situation (such as the actors and their actions).[13] Our basic sense of music is undifferentiated in the same way.

While the neocortex has regions that seem specialized for metric and nonmetric rhythms, timbre, intervals, melodic shape, and harmony, one needs special cultural "tuning" to be able explicitly to attend to and control one or more of these aspects of musical sound independently of the others. Only through the long process of cultural evolution has control of rhythm, melody, and harmony become clearly differentiated.

I would like to introduce the idea of a functional channel to talk about this long-term differentiation. By *channel* I mean a physical link between input and output such as a phone line, a communications bus on a computer, or a radio link. In the brain, such a channel is not necessarily an anatomically distinct structure or set of structures, for example, a fiber bundle. I am not talking neuroanatomy. Rather, I am concerned about the total neurodynamics between auditory input and motor output. Differentiation of music into rhythm, melody, and harmony means starting with a single functional channel in preliterate cultures, which then separates into two and then three functional channels.[14]

Finally, where Wiora talks of an age of music, I want to talk of cultural *rank*, where rank is an attribute of the neural processes underlining musical performance. Cultural rank is the number of functional channels required to realize the music and is said to be *cultural* because it reflects the way culture molds brains, not biology.

Cultural rank has nothing to do with the number of performers required, the number of different instruments, or the number of independent musical "parts" or voices. Beethoven piano sonatas are surely of rank 3, but they require only one performer. Traditional West African polyphony may easily involve tens of performers playing a dozen different parts on as many different instruments; but in this analysis, they are realized by rank 1 neurodynamics. Their use of rhythm is quite elaborate, but melody and harmony are relatively simple.[15] Cultural rank, then, can be defined with respect to the global dynamics of a single brain.[16]

It is my contention that all music in preliterate societies is realized through rank 1 patterns of neural activity. During Wiora's second Age, the music of ancient civilizations, we see the emergence of rank 2 dynamics, dynamics requiring two functional channels. There is no reason, however, to believe that all music in these ancient civilizations involved rank 2 processing. Much rank 1 music will remain.

That is why I prefer to talk of cultural *rank* rather than *Ages*. To talk of the music of a particular age implies that all of the music in that age possesses the same defining characteristics. I don't believe this is true. Ancient civilizations were complex and highly differentiated societies, with social classes and a well-developed division of labor. They also had a differentiated musical repertoire in which a "high" musical culture emerged to serve the expressive needs of the elite. In these societies we see the increasing emergence of musical performances that are not tied to specific ritual or work contexts. Court musicians, for example, would play for the entertainment of the lord and his court without any specific ritual requirement.[17] While I would expect, for example, that the musical paradigms of the high culture are more likely to be of rank 2 than of rank 1, that has to be determined in specific cases. It is not required by the concept of cultural rank.

Similarly, a rank 3 performance is one requiring three functional channels, for rhythm, melody, and harmony. Rank 3 performances emerged in Europe during and after the Renaissance. As a highly differentiated class society, Europe had music for the court, the aristocratic salon, the middle-class parlor, the church, the village square, the city gate, the battlefield, and other settings. The rift between professional musicking and a passive public widened as people became used to attending musical performances in the company of complete strangers.[18] The music of Europe's high-art tradition became the special province of composers, who would write notes that somehow represented the music itself, which then came to be regarded as eternal, outside time and space. Thus performers became servants to composers and their music.

THE EMERGENCE OF MELODY AND HARMONY

In chapter 5, I argued that the neural mechanisms for music include a groove stream, a gesture stream, and a mechanism to walk a path from one gesture to another. Given those mechanisms, what does it mean to assert that control of melody becomes differentiated from the control of rhythm? It means the musical motifs, elementary musical gestures, are no longer manipulated and elaborated simply as a rhythmic *gestalt*. Differentiation requires that the gesture stream now have two substreams, one for the rhythmic aspect of music while another regulates the melodic aspect. Each of these streams has a path.

The classical music of India exemplifies this differentiation. The melodic stream is regulated according to the demands of a specific *râga*, which is a structure of pitch relationships used in creating melodies. The basic *tâlas* (recall our discussion in chapter 6) structure the pulse stream while variations on the rhythm are used to elaborate the rhythm substream of the gesture stream. A *râga* is defined in terms of a starting tone, a final tone, a tone that serves as a melodic center (one note can serve two or even three of these functions), scale tones, embellishments, and melodic formulas. The elements of a *râga* are thus defined entirely in terms of pitches and their relationships to one another.[19] *Tâlas* are defined separately and independently. A performer must select both a *râga* and a *tâla* for a performance.

In a typical performance the ensemble will consist of a drummer, playing a *tabla*, a *mridangam*, or some other drum; another musician playing a tambour or harmonium to provide a background drone; and the soloist, playing a sitar or vina, both stringed instruments that are plucked, or perhaps a flute or his voice. A performance often begins with a prelude in free time by the soloist. This establishes the basic melodic material of the *râga*. When the prelude is over, the drums join in and the actual composition begins. The composition will consist of a theme, a second subject, development, and a coda. The themes and subjects are improvised, as are, of course, the developmental variations. Much of the artistry in performing this music lies in the interplay between the percussionist and the melodist as they try to outfox one another and thereby lead the listener's expectations on a merry chase.[20] Thus these two aspects of musical material, rhythm and melody, are independently manipulated and developed.

This music is a chamber music. As such it makes a fairly sharp distinction between performers and audience. The musicians are full-time professionals and the best of them are highly skilled virtuosi.[21] This is not true of preliterate societies, where we seldom encounter full-time musical specialists. With an interesting exception, the audience for a performance of classical Indian music doesn't actively participate in the performance.

That exception occurs in the South Indian, or *karnataka*, tradition. Any musicians in the audience will be allowed to sit in the front row.

This honors their expertise, and it also allows them to participate in the performance by beating the *tâla* using hand gestures, thus helping the performer keep track of the pulse stream.[22]

From melodic elaboration in rank 2, we move to harmonic elaboration in rank 3, which happened in post-Renaissance Europe. In the simplest sense, harmony is the simultaneous sounding of two or more different tones. In that sense, harmony exists in music of all ranks. Societies with rank 1 or rank 2 performance paradigms have choral singing where different singers will sing different melodic lines, with harmonies arising in the relationships between those lines. Harmony can similarly arise in the interaction of instrumental lines. However, the manipulation of these simultaneous occurrences as a constitutive principle happened only in the post-Renaissance West.

Thus to the substreams for rhythm and melody we must add a third substream for harmony. The gesture stream is now subject to three independent sources of structure.

The high-culture music of the European Renaissance was essentially polyphonic; that is, it was built on the interplay of two or more simultaneous melodic lines. In their interaction, the polyphonic lines would give rise to triadic (three-tone) chords. The first discussion of such chords appears in Zarlino's *Istituzioni armoniche*, published in 1558.[23] Zarlino, however, emphasized horizontally conceived lines, not vertical chords. With Rameau's publication of *Traite de l'harmonie* in 1722, the vertical triads move into the foreground and melodies become the temporal unfolding of vertical chords. From this point through the end of the nineteenth century, Western music is organized around vertically conceived progressions of chords.

Modulation from one key (or harmonic area) to another became important and created opportunities for manipulating expectations on a different level from the purely melodic manipulations of rank 2.[24] Much of the evolution of rank 3 music involved developing techniques for modulating from key to key.[25] While these techniques deepened our understanding of harmonic relationships between successive chords, they also permitted us to develop elaborate multipart compositional forms, the suites, sonatas, and symphonies of European classical music.

The growth of this music from the Baroque period through the end of the nineteenth century involved ever more elaborate ways of using harmonic structure to create longer and more complex musical forms. Twentieth-century composers, while experimenting with those techniques and structures, would attempt to go beyond them to fundamentally new music. The twentieth century would also produce various New World hybrids of African and European musics, such as blues, jazz, rock, tango, samba, and hip hop. We will consider this process in the final chapter.

Before that, however, I want to speculate about the mechanisms underlying the evolution of musical forms.

EVOLUTION OF MUSIC:
A DARWINIAN MECHANISM

Wiora's long-term historical account of music is only descriptive. It tells what has happened over the long course of history; but it doesn't say why it happened. My interpretation of Wiora in terms of functional channels and neurodynamics doesn't change that. That interpretation implies nothing about how that process works, only about its results. Now is the time to face that issue.

While biologists have settled on Darwinian evolution as their mechanism for explaining the long-term course of life on earth—though there is considerable controversy about the details—students of human culture and history have not reached a similar consensus. This does not mean, of course, that no ideas have been proposed—they have been, and over a considerable period of time. But nothing has taken hold.[26]

Recently, as we have already seen in the cases of Richard Dawkins and Susan Blackmore, some thinkers have been exploring the possibility of applying Darwin's evolutionary model to culture. By adopting Dawkins's notion of the meme I have tossed my hat in this particular intellectual ring though, as I have noted, my views are a bit unorthodox.

In Donald Campbell's standard formulation, Darwinian models call for a source of variation and a mechanism for selective retention.[27] In the biological case, variation is genetic, selection involves the interaction of phenotypes with the external world—often reduced to "the survival of the fittest"—and retention is a function of reproduction. Phenotypes that survive long enough can reproduce and pass their genes into the next generation; others will not and their genes will be lost. In the cultural case we have memes instead of genes; and, for music, I have proposed that performance-level attractors play the phenotype role. The fate of memes depends on whether they contribute to repeated performances.

I have already argued that performances will be repeated if they give pleasure to the musickers, where we understand that musical pleasure is a function of the collective neurodynamics of the musicking group. That gives us a mechanism for selective retention. While I have yet to provide a mechanism for memetic variation, I want to sidestep that question so I can think about the structure of the group, for that is the environment to which performances must adapt. What role does musicking play in the process by which a society evolves from a hunting and gathering band (HG band) to a chiefdom with well-established permanent leadership?

Before we get to that question we are faced immediately with another question: What drives groups to evolve in this way? That is a deep and complex question, occasioning considerable discussion and debate that, alas, has not yet converged on an answer.[28] A moment's consideration, however, makes it clear that I don't need that answer in order to think about the role musicking plays in the process. That such evolution happens is sufficient.

How does the evolution from HG bands to chiefdoms affect patterns of interpersonal encounters? Let's characterize these encounters with respect to *similarity* of cultural knowledge and personal *familiarity* between individuals. In HG bands all individuals have pretty much the same cultural knowledge. The major distinctions are between men and women, and between adults and children. Likewise, as everyone knows everyone else, encounters between strangers are few and far between. To be sure, you know your bandmates better than individuals in neighboring bands, but you still know individuals in neighboring bands on a face-to-face basis.

Our chiefdom has tens of villages and some division of labor. Such a society will be illiterate, but it is considerably more complex than a basic HG society, with a larger population numbering in the thousands or even tens of thousands. Most members of a chiefdom will have some interaction with craft specialists, and so will have some consequential interactions with people whose cultural knowledge is different from their own. Further, the larger population means they need to be comfortable interacting with both complete strangers and individuals whom they do not know at all well and with whom they share no kinship. The chief and his staff will have interactions with everyone but wield power that ordinary members of the society do not have.

The need to interact routinely with strangers requires a major change in the neural mechanisms for social interaction. In the world of HG bands meetings between strangers frequently end in violence.[29] This would be disastrous in a society where meetings between strangers occur routinely. Society needs a legal system that guarantees justice. Chiefs and their staff constitute that legal system, settling disputes where individuals and their kin cannot. Conversely, individuals need a sense of identity that allows them to feel comfortable holding a limited range of interactions with strangers. If you live in an HG band, your identity is your place in the kinship system. But that identity is not sufficient to negotiate your way in a civilized world. There you need some notion of citizenship or subjecthood. The chief guarantees interactions between his subjects. If you share subjecthood with a stranger, you can safely interact in certain ways. In particular, commercial transactions are possible.

Similarly the fact that you must interact with individuals having different cultural knowledge means that your different bodies of knowledge must be mutually consistent. You must recognize that not everyone shares your specialized knowledge and make appropriate adjustments in conversation. You must thus differentiate your specialized knowledge from a body of common knowledge that you assume for all subjects living in the same society—what George Herbert Mead called the generalized other (GO).[30]

In an HG band each individual will have a persona (recall figure 3.1) in the collective neural tissue. Each individual will also have some neural tissue devoted to the system of roles associated with the statuses in the kinship system (recall figure 3.2). Individuals in our chiefdom, however, will have two statuses unlike any in HG bands, one for the GO and one for chiefhood. These statuses will be outside the system of kinship statuses. Thus you can interact with anyone using the knowledge and scripts associated with the GO status; you need not have any kin relationship at all. Similarly, everyone must interact with the chief in the same way, regardless of how they interact with one another. The chief's status seems to be that of the GO *plus* the power and authority that allow the chief to enter into dyadic interactions with the entire community considered as a collectivity. That is forbidden to the ordinary GO, and that is what allows the chief to speak for and represent, to lead, the community.

I imagine these two statuses developing over a period of generations as the population grows and social structure changes to accommodate the larger and more diverse population. Given the periodic cycling between states of closely coupled ritual activity and more loosely coupled mundane activity we can think of this as a process happening in the collective neural tissue. The GO forms through a process of differentiation. As the population grows and diversifies the collective neural tissue adapts by adding more and more personas organized by kin-based statuses. That works for a while, but as the number of personas grows larger and larger, the neural structures begin to fail. The collective neural weather becomes more and more disorderly, anxiety grows, and disputes became a problem. This "pressure" forces a massive reorganization in which each status, including the role scripts associated with it, is factored into two components: one component is unique to each role while the other component is common to all roles, for all statuses. These common components are then organized into the GO status. With this simplification neural weather calms down, anxiety decreases, and peace returns to the community.

Of course, it is not quite the same community. It is organized in a different way. Individuals now make a sharp differentiation between those they know and those they do not and between ordinary subjects and a chief.

Musicking organizes the rituals in which, over time, coupled brains create the GO and chiefhood statuses. When people take part in a ritual, they engage in playacting. There are rituals, often associated with specific calendar times, in which men act like women, women act like men, adults act like children, ordinary subjects act like chiefs, and chiefs act like ordinary subjects.[31] This is the kind of activity that is likely to produce the differentiation we need, for it gives each person's nervous system an opportunity to enact different social statuses and roles, thereby providing an opportunity to factor each into shared and unique components.[32] That is one clue about how the collective neuropil does its work.

Another clue comes from E. E. Evans-Pritchard's classic work on the Nuer, a cattle-herding people living in southern Sudan.[33] At the time Evans-Pritchard surveyed them, the 1930s, the Nuer numbered about 200,000, but had no permanent leaders—an exceptionally large population for an egalitarian society. There were a number of individuals with specialized roles and some authority—especially the leopard-skin priests, whose major function was to restore peace after homicides— but no one with permanent, institutionalized authority. However, there had been, in recent memory, a small number of prophets who came very close to having such authority across all of Nuer society. These leaders were religious figures who, in moments of possession, "spoke the directions of the spirits of the air for raids on the Dinka [a neighboring people] and for resistance to the slavers and the administration and made sacrifices to them."[34] Given that the Nuer also had priests who played the therapeutic role, I speculate that the Nuer body politic simply reconfigured that role to serve a different function.[35]

These two clues suggest that ritual creates a cultural space where social innovation takes place. During periods when a society is under no particular stress, ritual serves to confirm and maintain the existing order. But when the society comes under duress, ritual allows new social mechanisms to emerge. As societies grow and their structure differentiates, musicking continues to play the role it had in humankind's beginning: the forge in which new forms of social being emerge.

Now, at last, I am ready to think about where memetic variation comes from. In the first place, memes can come from other groups. This has certainly been important in music, and we will examine a particular case in the next, and final, chapter. New memes may also arise spontaneously in the course of musicking. While a group may enter into a ritual intending to do what they did before, new things may happen—a new rhythmic interaction emerges, or a snappy dance move, whatever. In performances that aren't strictly scripted by a notated score, novelty is always possible. Effective and pleasurable novelty is likely to be remembered and incorporated into the next repetition.

Beyond this, I suggest that individual invention—whether spontaneous or deliberate—is another source of new memes. At first it might seem that we have now left the world of Darwinian evolution, where the variation is blind. However, the will of individual musickers is beside the point. Individuals may only offer memes for performance; it is the group that determines which performances will be repeated and by so doing creates culture. What provides pleasure for one creative individual may not provide pleasure for the group. Whatever the source, as long as a group has a plentiful supply of memes it has the raw material for cultural evolution.

MUSIC AND LITERACY

That then is my general suggestion about the role musicking plays in the growth of societies. It provides a mechanism by which the collective neural tissue can restructure its mechanisms for social interaction.

Notice, however, that the particular story I told doesn't get us all the way to rank 2 musicking. How do we arrive at the differentiation between rhythm and melody?

Let us recall two observations from the previous chapter. From Rouget we have the fact that the focal celebrants of possession rituals are not themselves making music, though they may dance. Our vatic chiefs may be on intimate terms with the spirits, but they are not the solo singers Alan Lomax found associated with a complex society having permanent leadership. When you look at Lomax's work carefully, how-ever, you realize that, for the most part, his elaborate solo singers are members of literate societies singing rank 2 music.

It would thus seem that elaborate solo song—Egypt's late Umm Kulthūm is a superb example[36]—tends to be rank 2 music. This makes sense, for the elaborate ornamentation and embellishment characteristic of solo styles calls for melodic independence from rhythm. How might this come about?

I speculate that the dynamics of the process are the same as I've postulated for producing solo music, but those dynamics are working on a different base. I say this, not because I have any evidence—I don't—but on general principle. I can't see any point in postulating another process without a very good reason to do so.

Since rank 2 music occurs in civilizations with a small elite capable of writing, let's assume the process takes place among people who can write.[37] Writing introduces virtual encounters into the web of social transactions. Whenever you read something you encounter not only the author of the text, but every other reader of the text. But these others aren't directly present to you, hence the encounter is a virtual one. This virtual encounter requires you to imagine the writer and ad-dress yourself to her without any external support other than the text itself. As strange as that may seem, writing a text is even stranger, for it requires you to generate language without any of the customary cues about how your words are being received. Given a nervous system that is organized for interaction with an external world, that's quite a feat.

I believe, then, that the process needed to maintain an imaginary other while reading and writing is similar to that needed to maintain a gesture stream with two components, one for rhythm and the other for melody. That imaginary other strikes me as being the same kind of phe-nomenon as the GO status or chiefhood; all are foci of social interac-tion. Given a population of readers and writers, I suggest that the process that created the GO early in culture's evolution will produce a differentiated gesture stream at this later time. Perhaps the neural tissue for the GO is used to track one of the subordinate gesture streams while ego regulates the other. Similarly, I suggest that the same general set of processes underlies the emergence of rank 3 music in post-Renaissance Europe, but operating on a different neurocultural base. Beyond this, I have no specific account to offer, though I conclude this chapter with some general remarks about the beginning of that evolution in the Middle Ages and its culmination in the late nineteenth century.

Instead, I want to focus on another issue, that of music and identity in complex societies. Literate societies are quite different in scale and structure from preliterate societies. They have an elaborate class structure, large urban centers, and far-flung trading relationships with many other societies. In a world where one is almost never exposed to any group other than one's own, style is invisible. In that world music may well *reflect* social and economic matters in a fairly direct way, as Lomax has argued. But as soon as one must routinely interact with other groups—different social classes, different occupational guilds, or tribesman from different provinces, and so forth—style becomes palpable; *they* walk and talk differently, *they* dress differently, *they* sing different songs, dance different steps, and may even worship different divinities.[38]

In such a world of interacting groups, I suggest, the expressive style of a group's performances becomes part of the equipment through which the group negotiates its place in the social and cultural order. In a time of rapid change this can happen from one generation to the next, as it has happened in the West over the last five hundred years. Musical styles begin to resemble *cultural species*, with adherents of a style extolling the virtue of their chosen style while denigrating other styles. Thus Baroque and Rococo, classical and romantic, swing and bebop, jazz and rock, can battle one another for cultural territory like jackrabbits and Aussies.

THE SUBLIME AND THE MUNDANE

Now let us consider two samples of recent musical practice. We've already encountered Leonard Bernstein's ecstasy, but marching bands are new. Both are examples of musicking in a highly differentiated culture with an elaborate class structure and complex government.

Let's consider Leonard Bernstein first. He has described two types of ecstasy, one while conducting and the other while contemplating the score in his study. Yet these do not fit either of the two models we examined in the previous chapter, shamanic trance or spirit possession. Perhaps there is a culture-specific component to ecstasy.

That it took him time to return to himself after an ecstatic performance suggests something like possession. But the spirit that possessed him made no pronouncements, nor was the occasion a medical ritual in which all participants played an active role. In a concert, the active musickers, the musicians, are radically distinguished from the passive musickers, the audience.[39] Nor was Bernstein's experience a shamanic trance. He reported no mystical flight, nor did he produce a running commentary of what he saw during the flight. As for his experience of being absorbed into the score–composer while contemplating it in his study, the mere fact that this is a private, individual experience differentiates it from either trance or possession.

This is not at all surprising. After all, Bernstein was raised and functioned in a very different world from either trance societies or possession societies. Why shouldn't his ecstasies be different?

If they are different, however, we need a more specific explanation than mere assertion of cultural difference. What is it about the life of a highly educated twentieth-century New York Jewish musician that supports that kind of experience? The question seems to me akin to the one Nietzsche posed when he undertook to explain the mentality of Greek tragedians and their audience. It is a question about the neurocultural construction of mental activity. And I am even less prepared to answer it than Nietzsche was prepared to answer his.

I note, for example, that Bernstein was raised in a literate culture, and that the brains of literate people have regions specialized for reading, specializations that must reflect the effects of early childhood experience—for example, with alphabet blocks or picture books—on the maturing brain.[40] But it is not at all clear how this culture's heavy reliance on written scores would affect his capacity for, and the nature of, his musical ecstasies or their nature. In that it affects the topography underlying his neural weather we can imagine that, in some way, literary culture influences his global neurodynamics—I've implied as much earlier when I suggested a relationship between literacy and rank 2 musicking. We need a much more specific understanding of the relationship between culturally induced cortical specialization and neurodynamics, an understanding that tells us how Bernstein's brain constructed his ecstasies and also tells us why they seem to be relatively rare—recall that none of his Tanglewood conducting students recognized the experience.[41] By contrast, shamans and members of possession cults seem to achieve their ecstasies more reliably. Why?

As I have said, I cannot answer these questions. I raise them only to assert that they *are* questions.

If we are intellectually defeated by the sublime, perhaps we will have a little more success with the mundane. Consider the marching band. Though we now associate them with football games and half-time shows, marching bands arose in the military, from kettledrum and trumpet units and fife and drum units that transmitted signals to the troops.[42] The basic performance paradigm and musical repertoire of the modern military band emerged in the nineteenth century, following the invention of valved brass instruments. As quasi-military organizations, marching bands partake of both military drill and music, the two cultural activities William McNeill discussed in *Keeping Together in Time*.

Unlike the symphony orchestra or even its more recent cousin, the drum-and-bugle corps, the marching band is not generally organized as an autonomous social unit. Marching bands are fielded by schools and the military and exist to help maintain *esprit de corps*. They also represent their parent organizations in community parades.

As a functioning parade and drill unit, a marching band is organized into ranks and files. This social structure is responsible for how the band moves on parade, on the drill field, or on the football field; it is, at best, loosely related to the band's musical organization. The drum major initiates activities—marching, stopping, turning, performing—while individuals at the left and right ends of individual ranks are responsible for keeping order. The drum major is simply a proxy for the band leader, who generally does not march but who has ultimate authority over the band and, as such, bears ultimate responsiblity for its performance. In the United States military the band leader is a commissioned officer while none of the bandsmen, including the drum major, hold commissions.

These responsibilities obtain both during parades and during practice.[43] A band of, say, seventy-two individuals may be organized into nine ranks of eight and be directed in its maneuvers by a drum major. The band is thus a dyad, and the relationship between the drum major and the band as a whole is an example of the basic authority configuration we examined in the previous chapter. Yet at the same time the band consists of nine groups of eight individuals each, with each group having its own leadership structure. Thus we can think of the drum major as having a dyadic relationship with a group of nine social individuals, each of which, in turn, consists of eight individual actors.

The musical organization is similar, but the units do not necessarily match. For musical purposes the band is divided into sections, each consisting of players of the same or similar instruments. To the extent possible, the instrumental sections will march together. Military bands typically have the following sections: clarinet, saxophone, flute, trumpet, trombone, baritone horns and euphoniums, tubas, percussion. Each section will have several members. The music for such bands is written so that each section will have its own part, which may differ from the parts played by the other sections. Thus we can think of each section as one social individual, where each social individual can be realized by several individual performers. The band as a whole stands, again, in a dyadic relationship to the director.

The director may conduct the band when it is more or less standing in formation. Otherwise the band performs without a conductor—the drum major is not a conductor, though he or she will initiate music.

The marching band is thus a very sophisticated social organism. But this sophistication involves only two basic groups, the dyad and the small work group of six to ten individuals. These two social forms are extended to cover groups of sixty or a hundred or more individuals through the Principle of Substitution. But getting this general principle to work in practice is not an easy matter. Marching bands do not arise spontaneously. They require much practice and discipline, and they require obedience to authority. Beyond this, they reflect an extensive body of social and musical lore accumulated over centuries. The performers do not have to discover these techniques and processes *ab ovo*; they learn them from the previous generation, who learned them from their predecessors, and so on. Each generation may add new techniques to the body of knowledge, but no generation makes it all up from nothing.

Needless to say, the marching band reflects a very complex form of society, one whose affairs are regulated by large hierarchical organizations. That is the same type of society that supported Bernstein's ecstasy, not to mention his TV programs explaining music to children. Bernstein was the archetypal romantic genius, an outsider who was highly valued as long as he knew his place. Yet his orchestra was organized in much the same way as that mundane guardian of civic pride, the marching band. In complex societies both the sublime and the mundane must dance to a tune beaten out by authority. If you want to dance to a different drummer, you're out.

THE GREGORIAN
CONTRACT AND THE PRIMITIVE

By way of transition to our final chapter, I now want to consider a specific aspect of European culture: the reexamination and assimilation of the primitive within modern cultural forms. This phenomenon is not confined to music, but is a general aspect of European culture through the nineteenth and twentieth centuries. In the cognitive sphere it gives us the discipline of anthropology. In the expressive sphere it yields primitivism, which parallels the emergence of museums of primitive art. This assimilation employs a metaphor of conquest: just as "inferior" cultures were conquered (and thus needed to be preserved from eradication) by the "superior" European civilization, so emotion was conquered by its superior, reason.

The musical version of this story starts with plainsong, the liturgical music of the medieval Christian church. During the medieval period most plainsong was used within religious communities as a daily aspect of their religious life, rather than being performed with a congregation on Sundays. While this body of music has its roots in pre-Christian music of the Jewish service, it is generally known as Gregorian chant, after Pope Gregory I, who played a major role in organizing and codifying the chants late in the sixth century C.E. These chants are generally regarded as the fountainhead of Western classical music, all of whose forms have some link to their Gregorian lineage, though many other musics are eventually put to classical use.[44] For this reason we can think of the classical music as developing under a Gregorian contract.

Plainsong is pure melody, sung in unison, utterly without pulse and meter. Closer to horizontal melodies than tumbling strains, it is, in effect, spirit without body. That is the core conception that over the course of centuries becomes stretched and modified, both by extending its own devices (e.g., the development of parallel vocal lines and then polyphony) and by assimilating other types of music, including various dance styles, whether the courtly minuet of the Baroque and Classical periods or the mazurkas beloved by Chopin.

Plainsong is also the source of Western musical notation.[45] The earliest notation appears in manuscripts from the ninth century and makes no use of the staff that became typical of later notation. The symbols representing the notes are called *neumes* and appear to be derived from hand gestures used to indicate the direction of melodic flow. Neumes indicate only relative pitch, rather than the absolute pitch of contemporary notation, and note durations are not clearly represented. We must regard this notation as a mnemonic aid, signs to help one remember melodies one has heard and sung. Without that prior experience, the neumes are deeply ambiguous. It would take several centuries for neumes to evolve into modern notation.

⟨❧⟩

Medieval Europe was a congerie of tribes, cities, and states of various cultures. But they were all, in some measure, under the sway of the Roman Catholic Church, and thus of its ritual, including plainsong. Europe was dotted with communities of chanting religious, and congregations would hear chanting at church services. Plainsong thus has geopolitical implications. While Europe's various cultures each had their own local musics, they all had plainsong as a common musical practice.

European tribes first began to distinguish themselves from the rest of the world as Christians. As such they deemed themselves superior to all infidels—such as the Arabs, who showed their inferiority by studying mathematics and drinking coffee rather than alcohol. It wasn't until the seventeenth century, after the Western Church had been split by the Reformation, that the secular concept of Europe replaced the sacred concept of Christendom as a touchstone of identity.[46]

Thus, just as humankind originated in musicking somewhere in Africa, so Europe begins to unify through the sacred musicking of the chanting religious. As that body of music begins to differentiate and develop, it moves into secular contexts and mingles with vernacular musics. From this process, over a course of centuries, emerges the high art known as classical music—at least within the Western nations. Some of that music was written to sacred ends—for instance, the cantatas and masses of Johann Sebastian Bach. Some was written for the opera in its various forms. And some was written for aristocratic patrons, a state of affairs that continued well into the nineteenth century.

During the nineteenth century this formal, learned artistic tradition embraced the idea of the "noble savage," a descendant of the earlier notion of the Wild Man living in a state of natural purity untainted by civilization.[47] We can see this idea at work in the famous remarks that the conductor Ernst Ansermet made when he first heard Will Marion Cook's Southern Syncopated Orchestra on tour in Europe in 1919:

> The blues occurs when the Negro is sad, when he is far from home, his mammy, or his sweetheart. Then, he thinks of a motif or a preferred rhythm, and takes his trombone, or his violin, or his banjo, or his clarinet, or his drum, or else he sings, or simply dances. And on the chosen motif, he plumbs the depths of his imagination. This makes his sadness pass away,—it is the Blues.

Ansermet goes on to single out one musician for special praise:

> There is in the Southern Syncopated Orchestra an extraordinary clar-
> inet virtuoso who is, so it seems, the first of his race to have composed
> perfectly formed blues on the clarinet. I've heard two of them which
> he had elaborated at great length . . . they gave the idea of a style, and
> their form was gripping, harsh, with a brusque and pitiless ending like
> that of Bach's second *Brandenburg Concerto*. I wish to set down the
> name of this artist of genius; as for myself, I shall never forget it—it is
> Sidney Bechet. When one has tried so often to rediscover in the past
> one of those figures to whom we owe the advance of our art . . . what a
> moving thing it is to meet this very black, fat boy with white teeth and
> narrow forehead . . . but who can say nothing of his art, save that he
> follows his "own way," and when one thinks that his "own way" is per-
> haps the highway the whole world will swing along tomorrow.[48]

Taken together, these passages reveal an astounding blend of admira-
tion and condescension. Ansermet recognizes the power of the music
he heard and the extraordinary skill of one musician, whom he compared to one of the canonical figures of his own tradition. Yet it is
quite clear that Ansermet considers himself superior to both the music
and the musician.

Such was the attitude of the cultivated European at the end of the
nineteenth century. Europe's colonies and ex-colonies spanned the
globe; its museums displayed artifacts from an extraordinary range of
cultures.[49] Its scholars were writing ethnographic studies of primitives
the world over while Freud was theorizing about the primitive impulses in the minds of proper Viennese gentlefolk. The triumph of
reason over emotion was seen as the hallmark of the civilized.

Throughout most of the nineteenth century romanticism thrived
in music, and with it the notion of the romantic genius—an idea
clearly conflated with that of the noble savage in Ansermet's account
of Bechet. Romanticism, in turn, produced nationalistic music, in
which composers sought out and incorporated folk tunes and dances
into their works. With composers such as Borodin, Mussorgsky, and

Rimsky-Korsakov, the Russian school was one of the most prominent among the nationalists. Igor Stravinsky was Rimsky-Korsakov's most famous student, and his early ballets, *Firebird*, *Petruska*, and *Le sacre du printemps*, were in the nationalist tradition, making extensive use of folk songs and dances. Of these, *Le sacre*, with a scene in which an adolescent girl dances herself to death in a pagan celebration of spring, represents the strongest break from previous tradition. The insistent rhythms shattered the Gregorian aesthetic contract in which music was inscribed in a world where the mind and heart were divorced from the body.

That contract had been eroding for some time. For example, the rolling rhythms of Beethoven's last *piano sonata, Op. 111,* seem to presage boogie-woogie piano figures, Chopin's dance-inflected polyrhythms threaten the conventions of Western meter, and the waltz was raising temperatures in ballrooms across Europe. Yet these and other works only challenged the Gregorian contract. Stravinsky shattered it.

The 1913 premiere of *Le sacre* was a scandal, one of the most notorious in the history of Western music.[50] The scandal was relatively short-lived, and Stravinsky's place in twentieth-century Western classical music was readily secured. But the place of that body of music in Western concert halls has never been secure. Classical concerts would continue to be dominated by works that adhered to the Gregorian contract. Those who sought music outside the bounds of that contract looked to a different musical tradition, the one Ansermet observed in the playing of Sidney Bechet.

As Ansermet foresaw, that is indeed the highway—though railway would be a better metaphor—along which the world was to swing. Across the Atlantic, in North America, new music was brewing, not romantic, even in the sense of Nietzsche's Dionysian tragedians. Rather, Africa and Europe had been coupling, and that coupling bore fruit in various musics: spirituals, the blues, ragtime, and jazz.

XI

THROUGH
JAZZ AND BEYOND

> After emancipation . . . all those people who had been slaves, they
> needed the music more than ever now; it was like they were trying to
> find out in this music what they were supposed to do with this freedom:
> playing the music and listening to it—waiting for it to express what they
> needed to learn, once they had learned it wasn't just white people the
> music had to reach to, nor even to their own people, but straight out to
> life and to what a man does with his life when it finally *is* his.
>
> —Sidney Bechet, *Treat It Gentle*

IN 1922 LOUIS Armstrong left his native New Orleans to join his
mentor, Joe "King" Oliver, in Chicago. In 1924 he left Chicago to
play with Fletcher Henderson, who led the hottest band in New York.
There he met Don Redman, a college-educated musician who
arranged music for Henderson and was important in developing the
basic vocabulary of big-band arranging. Upon his return to Chicago a
year later, Armstrong went into the recording studio with a pickup
band to make the first in a series of five dozen recordings over the next
three years. These recordings, known as the Hot Fives and Sevens, are
among the most important and remarkable in jazz history. Armstrong's solos on several of them were transcribed and made available
in sheet music form shortly after the records appeared.[1]

The last recording in this series was made on December 12, 1928, with Earl Hines on piano, Don Redman on clarinet and alto sax, Zutty Singleton on drums, Fred Robinson on trombone, Jimmy Strong on clarinet and alto sax, and Mancy Carr on banjo. They recorded "Tight Like This," which was a musical reply to "It's Tight Like That" cut by McKinney's Cotton Pickers a few weeks earlier. Don Redman, who was now music director for McKinney, arranged the tune for this recording.[2]

The piece is slow, in a minor key, and very dramatic. Armstrong doubles up on the time in his solo—a practice that would become routine with the emergence of bebop in the 1940s. As he lays out in the fifteenth and sixteenth bars of his solo, some wise guy in the band—probably Redman or Hines—says in a falsetto voice, "oh it's tight like that Louie." At this point Armstrong inserts a two-bar lick that he then repeats two bars later in a slightly more elaborate and rapid form. This particular lick is one of Armstrong's signatures and it shows up in other solos as well, such as his standard routine on "Dinah."

When I first heard that lick I recognized it as the beginning of a children's song about French girls lacking underpants. The melody also turns up in cartoons, where it typically accompanies a snake charmer. Where did Armstrong learn it? Was it current among children when he was growing up as well?

I've made some inquiries by phone and through the Internet and found out a few things. In the first place, other people remember this tune from their childhoods and it is still in circulation. Eric Johnson told me that his daughters remember these lyrics:

> *All the girls in France do the hokey pokey dance,*
> *And the way they shake is enough to kill a snake.*

Karen Stober tells me the tune was sung by two children facing one another and clapping hands to the lyrics, which she reported as:

> *On the planet Mars all the women smoke cigars.*
> *Every puff they take is enough to kill a snake.*

When the snake is dead they put flowers on its head.
When the flowers die they say 1969! [whatever year it is].

The tune's locale has changed, but we still have a snake being killed. I found a somewhat fuller version on the web where the dance was characterized as a "hookie-kookie dance" and that triggered my own memory. The version I knew as a child included a hoochie-coochie dance.[3]

This doesn't tell us where Armstrong got his lick. That this tune is still in circulation among children suggests that it is long-lived. Perhaps it was known in turn-of-the-century New Orleans children's culture.

Following a lead suggested by my friend, David Bloom, I went out on the web looking for information about the Chicago World's Columbian Exposition of 1893. I struck paydirt.[4] The exposition's press agent, Sol Bloom, had played our melody at a press showing for "Little Egypt," a dancer who was one of the exposition's premier attractions, along with John Philip Sousa and Wild Bill Cody. Subsequently the tune was copyrighted under various names, including *Dance of the Midway*, *Coochi-Coochi Polka*, *Danse de Ventre*, and *The Streets of Cairo*. One W. J. Voges included it as the *Koochie-Koochie Dance* in the second edition of *Pasquila Medley* published in New Orleans in 1895. That puts our tune in New Orleans prior to Armstrong's birth, though it tells us nothing about how he came upon it. Perhaps more important, the fact that so many people published versions of the tune indicates that it was very popular in America at the end of the nineteenth century.

Another informant, trumpeter Jeanne Pocius, told me that this melody appears in *Arban's Complete Conservatory Method for Trumpet* as one of "Sixty-eight Duets for Two Cornets," which follows "150 Classic and Popular Melodies."[5] Our tune is number 13 and is called "Arabian Song." Arban, or Arban's, as it is known among trumpeters, is the prototypical method book for "legit" trumpet and cornet training. Jean-Baptiste Arban was a cornet virtuoso, composer, conductor, and teacher on the faculty of the Paris Conservatory. He first published his *Grande méthode complète pour cornet à pistons et de saxhorn* in 1864.[6] I have no idea whether Armstrong studied from Arban's—he doesn't appear to have been able to read music in his youth, though he later acquired that skill—but the presence of this particular melody in such a book places it firmly in a widespread print-mediated cornet–trumpet culture that predates Armstrong by half a century.[7]

But where did Arban get it? He did not compose it. Half of his method book consists of technical exercises, the other half is complete tunes and compositions, from the very simplest to complex virtuoso display pieces. That's where we find our tune. These melodies comprise what is, for all practical purposes, a European Songbook of the 1860s. While some of them were by recognized masters of the European high-art tradition—Mozart, Beethoven, Mendelssohn, Bellini, von Weber, Haydn—many were just tunes, attributed to no one. "Arabian Song" is one of those.

When we consider the lyrics this tune has attracted, its use in cartoons to accompany snake charming, and its title, it seems to be a musical icon of the Mysterious Licentious Orient, which had fascinated European peoples at least since the Crusades. It is the only song identified with the Orient in Arban's collection, but other tunes have national or ethnic identification. Thus we find a "German Song," a "Neapolitan Song," and a "Swiss Song," a "French Air" and an "Italian Air," a "Russian Hymn" and an "Austrian Hymn," as well as "Blue Bells of Scotland" and "Yankee Doodle." In compiling his collection of melodies Arban clearly wanted to present music from all the civilized nations he could think of. It is thus in the service of a truncated ethnic inclusiveness that he included an "Arabian Song"—or, more likely, the one-and-only "Arabian Song" he knew.

Beyond this, the opening five notes of this song are identical to the first five notes of *Colin Prend Sa Hotte*, published in Paris in 1719. Writing in 1857, J. B. Wekerlin noted that the first phrase of that song is almost identical to *Kradoutja*, a now-forgotten Arabic or Algerian melody that had been popular in France since 1600.[8] This song may thus have been in the European meme pool 250 years before Arban found it. It may even be a Middle Eastern song, or a mutation of one, that came to Europe via North Africa through Moorish Spain or was brought back from one of the Crusades. For all practical purposes we can consider it to be nearly as old and widely dispersed as dirt. And, on the evidence, equally fertile.[9]

We still don't know how Armstrong and this melody found one another, but that hardly matters at this point. The tune was well-known and Armstong's audience would surely have recognized his use of it.

This modest little melody still persists in the children's repertoire, which tends to be, as Bruno Nettl has observed, rather conservative. The popular songs of Armstrong's childhood have all but disappeared. We would not recognize most of them today. The same is true of many popular songs of my childhood despite their persistence on "classic rock" radio stations. The children's repertoire is more enduring, a slow-moving substrate beneath the quick flux of popular entertainment for teens and adults.

It is not surprising that music Armstrong learned as child should turn up in the music he made as an adult. Yet each time Armstrong uses it, he transforms it to meet the specific requirements of the current performance. If we think of that melodic fragment as a meme, the cultural equivalent of a gene, then Armstrong's uses would be mutations and his use of only part of the melody would seem to be a kind of memetic recombination. But what is that fragment being recombined with?

To some extent, it was being combined with other licks, or riffs, as musicians call them. These too we may think of as memes. Some of these fragments may have come from the same pool that floated the "Arabian Song" across the Atlantic from Europe. Others may have been indigenous to the United States or even local to New Orleans or Chicago. Jazz culture is full of these licks, which can come from any place.

Still, Armstrong's use of that one meme is special. He expects his audience to recognize it as a quotation. This is a common practice among jazz musicians, a form of musical play, of cultural signifyin', to use Henry Louis Gates's term.[10] That Armstrong quotes this particular meme twice in one solo—which is not a standard practice—suggests he's being emphatic about it. He seems to be saying: "That's right, you heard it, *that* kid's song. And to show you I meant it, I'm gonna' give it to ya again."

Dizzy Gillespie often inserted a fragment of the "Habanera" from *Carmen* into his "A Night in Tunisia." Dexter Gorden liked the opening phrase of "Mona Lisa."[11] Lee Morgan recorded an improvisation in which he quoted Ziggy Elman's licks from Elman's famous solo on "And the Angels Sing."[12] Morgan was too young to have seen Elman perform live and so must have learned those licks from a recording.

Jazz biographies are filled with accounts of their subjects' hearing jazz on record or on the radio, becoming intrigued, inspired, and learning from these secondary sources. These secondary sources may have been as important in jazz's evolution as direct person-to-person transmission.[13] Eldridge learned from Armstrong's recordings, Gillespie from Eldridge's recordings, and so forth. Jazz culture is thus, in part, a huge pool of memes that musicians call on in their performances. Musicians may also have licks that are unique to them, licks they use here and there, but which are not immediately adopted by other musicians. These licks may make it into a recording and so remain available to other musicians. Finally, some bits of sound simply "lay well" on a particular instrument, passages well suited to lips, fingers, and lungs. As such, they show up constantly.[14]

When jazz musicians play, they call on various intersecting pools of material that they then assemble into a performance. While jazz contains some solo performances, mostly on piano, it is primarily a collaborative art. Musicians interact to shape the current performance. What happens is spontaneous, but that spontaneity draws on a large body of well-practiced licks and routines.

The greatness of an individual musician such as Armstrong is a function, both of his power to forge compelling performances from the "raw" memes and of the existence of that meme pool. While Armstong may have been ahead of his fellows, he couldn't have been very far ahead of them, otherwise they could not have performed together. Beyond this, without a large population of music lovers familiar with the same meme pool, Armstrong's recordings would have had little effect. By the time he went to Chicago, a large population had been listening and dancing to rags and blues, show tunes, fox trots and Charlestons and marches, all with a hot pulse and raggy rhythms. Armstrong's improvisations gave them a new wild pleasure, and their collective joy made him great.

"JES' GREW" IN THE TWENTIETH CENTURY

One could tell hundreds of thousands of such stories about musicking. But however important it is that we understand the nature of individual atomic interactions, we cannot grasp the large-scale processes at the atomic level. We must also talk about aggregate phenomena.

With music we tend to focus on musical styles, canonical composers and performers, the places where they worked, and their audiences. Thus we talked of Louis Armstrong, Don Redman and others, New Orleans, Chicago, and New York, as well as Jean-Baptiste Arban and Paris, France. Arban worked in the European high-art and military band traditions while Armstrong worked within New Orleans–style traditional jazz and swing. Armstrong's audience was diverse from the beginning, and it eventually grew to include a significant fraction of the world's population, though many of those heard him only sporadically and probably didn't recognize what they were hearing. The most important thing about Armstrong's audience for my purposes is that it included both black and white folks, but we'll deal with that later.

For now, I want to suggest that the process by which jazz emerged is the same as that which originally brought music into being. That is, it involved chaotic group dynamics out of which something new emerged. Way back then that something new was protomusic and the first specifically human culture and consciousness. The situation with jazz, of course, was quite different. Music had been around for millennia and many styles had been born and died, rich meme pools floated from place to place waiting for a catalyst to trigger a new dynamic, a new style. The catalysts were, of course, the great and near-great men and women who inhabit our various musical pantheons. But like Armstrong, they all depended on their fellow musicians and their audiences to amplify their innovations into full-blown musical styles. Without that amplifying context, their genius would have been culturally impotent.

As the nineteenth century turned into the twentieth, America was saturated with hybrid music having a raggy pulse. All it took was a little magic, what the novelist Ishmael Reed called "jes' grew," and jazz began to precipitate out here and there. It jes' grew and grew and became unstoppable. Through New Orleans, Chicago, Los Angeles, Kansas City, New York, Detroit, and Philadelphia, jazz spread, spawned new styles, and mixed with polka, classical, country, mambo—and became many.

This process was one aspect of the large historical process through which European states and nations extended their will over the globe through trade, conquest, and colonization. As part of this process they enslaved African peoples, mostly from West Africa, and brought them to the New World to labor in the sugar plantations of the Caribbean, the sugar and coffee plantantions of Brazil, and the tobacco, rice, and cotton plantations of North America.

These peoples brought with them cultures that included possession cults and polyrhythmic percussion. As we noted in chapter 9, much of that religion survived, as Candomblé of Brazil, Santeria in Cuba, Voudoun in Haiti, and Voodoo in the American South, especially in Armstrong's home town of New Orleans. While the African forms of that religion were more thoroughly suppressed in the rest of the United States, the spirit survived in dramatic and emotionally demonstrative versions of Christianity that featured rocking song, speaking in tongues (possession), and dramatic conversions. During the eighteenth and nineteenth centuries this Africanized Christianity moved out of the black community and into the white community. It remains current among both blacks and whites today.[15]

African polyrhythms survived in the Caribbean and in Brazil, forming the foundation of what we think of as Latin music. But for reasons that are obscure, West African polyrhythms did not survive in the United States. The reason commonly given is that drums were banned.[16] Drums *were* widely banned (though not in New Orleans' famous Congo Square), and that would certainly make it difficult to retain the rhythms. Still, while the polyrhythms were lost, the rhythmic drive of African music was not. It spread throughout the United States in the nineteenth century, and the twentieth century has seen waves of Latin music move through the country, touching jazz in the process.

Minstrelsy, the primary form of mass entertainment during the nineteenth century, was one of the main vehicles for cultural cross-breeding. Minstrelsy was a combination of song, comedy, and theatrical sketches. Even as white performers in blackface made fun of black manners and mores, they also satirized the white upper classes. Black song and dance became a vehicle by which white performers could elude the strictures of their own society and culture. After the Civil War, black performers donned blackface and entered the minstrel circuit as well. White and black minstrelsy persisted into the first quarter of the twentieth century in vaudeville and in New York City's Broadway theaters.[17]

During the same time, starting in the second quarter of the nineteenth century, America and Europe were swept by a brass band movement. These musicians were working-class amateurs and their bands, as Trevor Herbert has written, were "the first medium in modern times through which vernacular traditions fused with the deep history and values of western music so as to change those values."[18] Every community had a brass band, as did many businesses. They gave concerts in the bandshells that adorned town parks, and they marched in parades. Of course, just as blacks played bid whist rather than contract bridge, they had their own brass bands too.[19] That is the musical culture to which Armstrong was introduced at the Colored Waif's Home.

It was not the only musical culture Armstrong knew. He spent a lot of time on the streets, picking up music from parades and from saloons, brothels, and churches as well:

Across the street from where we lived was Elder Cozy's church. . . . I can still remember the night mama took me to his church. Elder Cozy started to get warmed up and then he hit his stride. It was not long before he had the whole church rocking. Mama got so happy and so excited that she knocked me off the bench as she shouted and swayed back and forth. . . . After that mama really got religion. I saw her baptized in the Mississippi where she was ducked in the water so many times I thought she was going to be drowned.[20]

The down-home church with its rocking music appears in many jazz biographies. In fairness, not all African-American churches were like this. Some were and are more restrained in their worship. But the ecstatic style, which after all originated in Africa, was there from the beginning and remains in place to this day. As the center of black community life,[21] the church is also the institutional fountain of the exuberant energy of African-American musics, not only jazz but gospel, soul, and rock and roll.

Minstrelsy, brass bands, and the church were three arenas in which African and European musics mingled in nineteenth-century America. The fourth was work: the field hollers and work songs African-American slaves and freedmen used in the fields, the waterfronts, the roads and railroads, and in the forests—recall "Talk to the Wood"— were important as well. They began to decline in the twentieth century as people moved from the farms to the cities and work became more mechanized.[22] In each arena we find Africanisms and Europeanisms merging into Americanisms. Armstong was touched by all of this.

THE WORLD, THE ATLANTIC, AND NORTH AMERICA

In figure 11.1 the ovals represent styles or families of styles, and the arrows indicate memetic flow from one style (or family) to another— keeping in mind that a given meme can exist in many pools. It is, of course, possible for contemporary styles to exchange memes with one another. Roughly, the diagram moves from the past toward the present as we move from the top to the bottom.

At the very top we have the first music, originating somewhere in Africa long before recorded history. Through an evolutionary succession we will never know, one lineage yields the Hebrew chant, one of the sources of the Gregorian chant, which, as we saw at the end of the previous chapter, is at the core of European musical culture. Another lineage, also lost to history, yielded the polyrhythmic musics of West Africa. We do not know what interaction, if any, existed between these two lineages before the beginning of the Atlantic slave trade, though we should note that by the eleventh century C.E., Islam had penetrated deeply into West Africa.[23] The evolution of these two lineages is one aspect of a worldwide process whose most recent aspect is the broad dispersion of jazz and its descendants in the twentieth century.

By the sixteenth century C.E., we have Europe and West Africa, which I have represented as large ovals containing a number of unlabeled smaller ovals to indicate the various musical cultures in each area. Because the slave population of North America came from many different (mostly West African) tribes, the African musical contribution cannot be considered stylistically homogeneous.[24] The European sources were varied as well, though we know considerably more about them. To the right we have the musics of the Caribbean and Latin America, many of which resulted from European and African crossbreeding and which have themselves migrated around the world and to North America as well. Europe, Africa, and the Americas from the sixteenth century to the present form the Atlantic arena.

The rest of the diagram indicates part of the American arena. The stylistic designations are all standard, the distinctions between them are real but fuzzy, and the picture is hardly complete.[25] The most important thing about this diagram is its general form: once we get beyond the initial dispersion, lineages converge and cross. Whereas biological evolution is largely a process of treelike branching (see figure 11.2[26]), cultural evolution is quite different.[27] Musical styles interbreed all the time. Thus while biological species only have a single parent species, musical styles (cultural species) can have multiple parents.[28]

Beyond this, we should note that while jazz historians have a tendency to treat blues as a precursor to jazz, the emergence and evolution of blues parallels that of jazz, rather than precedes it. It is only in hindsight that we see jazz and blues as two distinct musical lineages. To those living in the early twentieth century it was all just hot music,

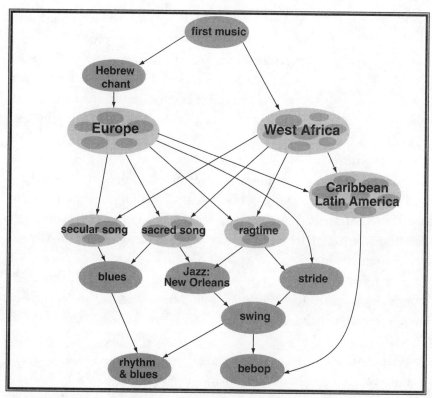

Figure 11.1   Some stylistic arenas in early twentieth-century America.

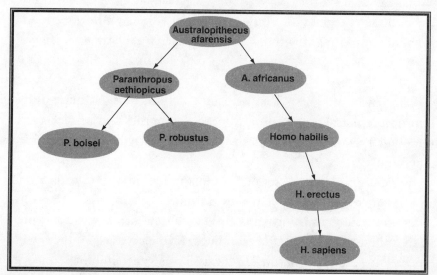

Figure 11.2   Hominid phylogeny.

with "jazz" and "blues" being flexible designations for various tunes in the mix. The two musics were and remain closely related, sharing a variety of musical devices and memes but maintaining their separate identities. During the late 1930s, forms of blues and jazz met in a small-group style known as jump blues. Two decades later jump blues would meet country music and spawn the miscegenating rhythms of rock and roll.

The rise of rock and roll, of course, is a different story, as is the rise of hip hop. But these stories involve the same social, cultural, and musical forces, white people and black people working out their lives in the United States of America. Jazz, rock, and hip hop all involve cultural cross-breeding, the catalytic emergence of styles from heterogeneous meme pools.

This relentless stylistic cross-breeding is generally acknowledged, but its implications have not been fully assimilated. Consider the following, by Marsha Bayles:

> I realize that a great many musicians and writers will reject the proposition that Afro-American music is an idiom of Western music, on the grounds that it is, root and branch, totally "black," meaning African. This attitude is usually called "cultural nationalism," but I prefer to call it "cultural separatism," because, instead of affirming Afro-American music by sharing it with the world, it takes a jealously proprietary stance.[29]

While Bayles recognizes that African-American music is quite different from classical music and European folk musics—in its devices, its emotional tenor, and its African roots—she nonetheless claims it for the West.

If we are to be at all serious about the hybrid nature of jazz and other American musics, it makes no more sense to claim them for Western culture than for African. The cultural process that has produced these musics defies the nationalistic labels we keep inflicting on them. However, this particular discussion is generally not framed in terms of Western music versus African music, but rather black versus white.[30] As far as I am aware, no current party to these debates questions the cross-breeding or the fact that African Americans have been the major innovators while the audience has been largely white—white Americans, after all, outnumber black Americans by a considerable margin. What is disputed is the abstract designation we should apply to the music.[31]

I have no suggestion for resolving this dispute, for I think it follows from mistaken ideas about culture. But I am very interested in the process that gives rise to both the music and the debate. The music itself is very attractive, and that attractiveness is ultimately rooted in our common biological heritage. However, outside of performance arenas—nightclubs, ballrooms, concert halls, or even one's own home—whites and blacks travel in different circles and have different identities imposed by enduring attitudes and institutional arrangements. Thus even as the music serves as a bridge between the cultures of black and white Americans, it also obscures and frustrates broadly sanctioned roles and identities.

DUKE'S PLACE

Not long after Armstrong began recording his Hot Fives and Sevens, Edward Kennedy Ellington, also known as Duke, took his band into New York City's famed Cotton Club, where he played and broadcast for five years. Located at 142nd and Lenox in Harlem, the Cotton Club was owned and run by gangsters—Owney Madden, Frenchy DeMange, and Harry Block. It seated five hundred people amid fake palms and real booze, and featured shows elaborately staged, often with an exotic jungle motif. The club's clientele was exclusively white, the performers exclusively black—a common arrangement in those days. This is how Ellington described the ambience:

The Cotton Club was a classy spot. Impeccable behavior was demanded in the room while the show was on. If someone was talking loud while Leitha Hill, for example, was singing, the waiter would come and touch him on the shoulder. If that didn't do, the captain would come over and admonish him politely. Then the headwaiter would remind him that he had been cautioned. After that, if the loud talker still continued, somebody would come and throw him out.[32]

While the clientele behaved impeccably, they watched light-brown showgirls dance erotically, impeccably costumed in very little. The jazz historian Marshall Stearns describes a Cotton Club skit where

> a light-skinned and magnificently muscled negro burst through a papier maché jungle onto the dance floor, clad in an aviator's helmet, goggles, and shorts. He had obviously been "forced down in darkest Africa," and in the center of the floor he came upon a "white" goddess clad in long golden tresses and being worshipped by a circle of cringing "blacks." Producing a bull whip from heaven knows where, the aviator rescued the blonde and they did an erotic dance. In the background, Bubber Miley, Tricky Sam Nanton, and other members of the Ellington band growled, wheezed, and snorted obscenely.[33]

The show was phony, the eroticism was not, and the music was hot. This glamorously absurd setting is where Duke Ellington worked out the basic elements of his musical style. He was able simultaneously to satisfy his own expressive needs and those of the white clientele. Their need for exotic jungle nonsense did not get in the way of his music.

What is so very remarkable about Harlem's Cotton Club is that black musicians of the highest caliber were able to excel in a setting where the racial divisions and accompanying stereotypes could hardly have been more extreme or explicit. Yet if Ellington ever felt that his integrity was compromised or his human dignity insulted, he never gave voice to such an opinion within earshot of anyone prepared to write about it. As far as we know, Ellington thrived at the Cotton Club. He was doing what he wanted to do, in the way he wanted to do it, and white folks were footing the bill.

However extraordinary this situation may appear, it is but a variation of a common social arrangement. As Alan Merriam observed, in societies that are complex enough for part- or full-time musical specialists to emerge, those specialists tend to be socially marginal. Their status is low, but their services are highly valued and often well rewarded.[34] That is certainly true of musicians in the United States.

Thus while Africans were brought to North America to work at hard labor, through a long, difficult, and often violent social process we had created, by the beginning of the twentieth century, a social structure in which a talented fraction of their descendants could begin prospering as musicians, comedians, dancers, and athletes. Nor were African Americans the only ethnic minorities entering this niche. Jews and Italians have been very important in both jazz and classical music, and Jews have also been prominent in theater, comedy, and motion pictures. The highly rhythmic musics of various Spanish-speaking ethnics have been consistently popular. Thus one of the many gradients ordering individuals into social and vocational classes in America is one where wealth, power, and prestige accrue to old-money people of English descent while darker-hued ethnics become entertainers and athletes.

The Cotton Club's pattern of segregation is one facet of its social function. When its well-off white patrons entered Harlem, they were leaving the mundane, disciplined world in which they worked for a living and entering ritual ground where the ordinary rules of polite society were suspended.

We are now deep in the cultural territory we entered at the end of the previous chapter, where the romantic notion of artistic genius meets the noble savage, where high art meets primitive and folk art.[35] The same cultural system that allowed the aesthetic descendants of Bach, Beethoven, and Brahms to stage a primitive ritual under the guise of *Le sacre du printemps* allowed a collateral line of descendants to construe Harlem as a primitive jungle where people lived free of the artifice and constraint of civilization. That, however, is not how Harlem was experienced by those who lived, worked, and worshiped there. For them, Harlem was a city within a city, a world within a world, and part of a nation within the larger state.

MOTOR AND EMOTIONAL STYLIZATION

Let's ease our way into jazz's expressiveness by looking at another children's song, for such games mold the brain's rhythms long before jazz sophistication is possible. Consider two versions of a child's song recorded by Leah Yoffie in St. Louis in 1944.[36] This is the version white children sang and danced:

> *Little Sally Water,*
> *Sitting in a Saucer,*
> *Weeping and crying for some one to love her.*
> *Rise, Sally, rise,*
> *Wipe off your eyes;*
> *Turn to the east,*
> *Turn to the west,*
> *Turn to the one that you love the best.*

Here is the version performed by black children:

> *Little Sally Walker,*
> *Sitting in a Saucer,*
> *Weeping and crying for a nice young man.*
> *Rise, Sally, rise,*
> *Wipe your weeping eyes;*
> *Put your hand on your hip,*
> *Let your backbone slip*
> *Shake it to the east, O baby;*
> *Shake it to the west,*
> *Shake it to the one that you love the best.*

The lines "Wipe your weeping eyes;/ Put your hand on your hip" and the phrase "O baby" jazz the rhythmic flow. But it is the physical gestures, "Let your backbone slip" and "Shake it to the . . . ." that convey the deepest difference from European-derived culture. The mobile pelvis is a feature of African dance, but until the twentieth century it has been rare in Western dance.[37]

In those two versions of that children's song lies the expressive difference between the European-dominated cultures of the United States and those African-American cultures still feeling the sway of their African ancestors. In a few paragraphs I will talk about sexuality, for jazz is certainly a more overtly sexy music than most European musics. But that easy sensuality is only a consequence, a symptom, of this critical difference.

Likewise, I could talk about mind and body, saying that Europe separates mind from body while Africa refuses to make the separation. This mode of talk and thought is authorized by intellectual tradition, but does not seem adequate to me in view of the account I have already given of mind and brain. Whatever is going on, it involves mind and body for both Europe and Africa.

The explanation I seek needs to be found in the neural material of the first half of this book. On the European side, we need to understand the neuromuscular foundations of an expressive culture inscribed within the bounds of plainsong, religious music almost bereft of rhythm. On the African side, we need to understand the neuromuscular foundations of an expressive culture growing from dance styles that require a mobile pelvis and polyrhythmic facility. Lacking these physiological accounts, we must struggle on with sex and with mind–body.

That struggle puts us in intellectual territory pioneered by Sigmund Freud, whose theories have been sources of insight and controversy for most of the past century and into the current one. Western culture is built on principles of reason, justice, and hard work. But Western culture also depends on repressing feelings and desires, a matter that Freud argued most broadly in *Civilization and Its Discontents*.[38]

The repressed desires, of course, do not disappear. They simply manifest themselves indirectly and often destructively. In his study of nineteenth-century European aggression, *The Cultivation of Hatred*, Peter Gay suggests that ethnic scapegoating was the obverse side of the coin of nationalism. The identity a people creates for itself is often a means of denying any similarity to the primitive and inferior others. Writing about World War I he suggests that for a frustrated and repressed Europe, "the war released aggressive impulses of which people had been unconscious in calmer times."[39]

In an essay published shortly after the end of World War II entitled "Certain Primary Sources of Aggression in the Social Structure of the

Western World," Talcott Parsons argued that Western child-rearing practices generate insecurity and anxiety at the core of personality structure. This creates an adult who has trouble dealing with aggression and is prone to scapegoating. The problem is exacerbated by an occupational system that places a great deal of emphasis on achievement but has few prizes available. Only a few can win in the corporate race, the rest have to be content with merely having run. And yet those who will not win must cooperate with one another, and with the winners. Inevitably there are lots of aggressive impulses that must be repressed. Ethnic scapegoating is one way to relieve the pressure of this repressed aggression. That, Parsons argued, is why the Western world is replete with nationalistic and ethnic antipathy.[40]

Another symptom of this emotional repression is an excessive interest in and concern about black sexuality, a common theme in psychological accounts of racism from Calvin Hernton and Erik Erikson through Joel Kovel to Elisabeth Young-Bruehl.[41] This obsession also shows up in discussions of lynching[42] and in treatments of white images of blacks.[43] The sexuality that interests these people is, in fact, their own sexuality, which they have repressed and then projected onto blacks.

This obsession affected the reception of jazz. While many people, white as well as black, delighted in jazz's rhythms and took them as an occasion for joyous dance, many others were shocked and horrified. Jazz's sensuality gave these people more anxiety than pleasure.

For a good twenty years between 1920 and 1940, these good folk denounced jazz—music and dance—for its lascivious ways.[44] In the 1920s the *Ladies' Home Journal* observed that jazz was "the accompaniment of the voodoo dancer, stimulating the half-crazed barbarian to the vilest deeds."[45] In the late 1930s Arthur Cremin, a music educator in New York City, did an experiment in which he purported to show that if boys and girls were left alone in a room with classical music, they'd just talk. If left in a room with swing, they started necking. He concluded that swing should be outlawed. New York City actually passed laws designed to curb jazz performance, though the laws were not explicitly framed in that way. They remained in effect until the early 1990s.[46]

To understand jazz's reception, I suggest that we think of a population as a set of expressive gradients where an individual's response to musical memes is a function of her emotional and motor style. Individuals with similar styles will group together, attending the same clubs, dances, and concerts, and listening to the same broadcasts and recordings. When we introduce jazz memes into this population we see that the memes "gravitate" to certain "regions" and are "repulsed" from others. We also find that, by and large, the black population, though considerably smaller than the white, produces more jazz memes than the white population. Hence the net flow of jazz memes is from the black population to the white.

But this expressive gradient is only one aspect of the cultural mechanism. The need for a cultural identity is also part of the mechanism. While the occasions for musicking are transient, the pressures on identity are continual and extend beyond the ritual arenas of musicking.

FRAMEWORKS FOR IDENTITY

African Americans were naturally offended by white America's obsession with their sexuality. Denunciation of such foolishness was one of Malcolm X's themes.[47] But this recognition is older than the Civil Rights era. After the *Titanic* sank in 1912, blacks began reciting a narrative poem in which a mythic black boilerman, Shine, escapes from the sinking ship and swims safely ashore. The ship's captain attempts to keep Shine on board, first offering him money and then offering the sexual favors of white women, including his own daughter. Shine rejects all offers and remains steadfast in his determination to swim ashore. The poem thus rejects white evaluation of black character by depicting a white authority figure as being so depraved as to offer his daughter up to a boilerman for no rational purpose. This obsession, it implies, is a white folks' problem and it's about time they dealt with it.[48]

Thus we have a white obsession born out of emotional repression and the black critique of that obsession. That critique reflects common sense grounded in a black frame of reference, not a white one.

The black rejection of white mythology is grounded in a black sense of cultural and social identity that is different from the identity assigned to black folks by whites. Identity in this sense is about how individuals feel themselves connected to the broader currents of history. Few of us ever become one of the "great men" whose acts get recounted in history books, nor do many of us have personal acquaintance with them. But we identify with nations, and national histories are typically told through stories of the deeds of these great men, both real and legendary. Our national identity is our means of connecting with history.

This realization of identity emerges with striking force in Ken Burns's recent documentary history of jazz. Much of the narration and expert commentary is about how jazz is America's music. Not only did jazz originate in America but, as Wynton Marsalis says at the opening of the first episode, "jazz music objectifies America."[49] With that statement and with countless others that follow we're told that jazz captures some American essence, that it *is* what Americans are as a people. When you listen to jazz, you listen, not only to an American voice, but to *the* voice of America.

This nationalist concern with the nature of America and its people dates back to the early nineteenth century, when American intellectuals began to weave a new mythology about "an individual emancipated from history, happily bereft of ancestry, untouched and undefined by the usual inheritances of family and race; an individual standing alone, self-reliant and self-propelled," an individual who was thereby separated from Europe.[50] As David Stowe has shown, jazz became woven into this fabric during the 1930s, in part as "a musical thumbing of the nose at fascism, whose Nazi theorists regarded swing as a debased creation of Jews and blacks."[51] Once installed in the temple of Americanism, jazz remained there.

But not without considerable tension and, with the publication of Amiri Baraka's *Blues People* in 1963, open conflict and dissension. Baraka, a very angry, militant, and brilliant black poet and playwright, saw African Americans as blues people and jazz as a son of the blues. As

such it was essentially black music, but one "that offered such a profound reflection of America that it could attract white Americans to
want to play it or listen to it for exactly that reason. . . . It made a common cultural ground where black and white America seemed only day
and night in the same city . . ."[52] The ethnic and national character of
jazz has been a matter of open contention ever since.

As I suggested earlier, the question of jazz's "identity" is insoluble
precisely because it is framed in nationalist terms. Long before it became assimilated to the concept of the nation-*state*, *nation* was used in
English to designate a racial group. In some contexts, it still retains
the sense of racial or ethnic identity.[53] The concept of a nation thus
tends to work against the cultural plurality that has been critical in the
origins and development of jazz and its descendants.

There is no doubt, for example, that Ellington thought of himself
as a "race man," to use the term of the times. It was as a race man
that, in 1943, he wrote "Black, Brown, and Beige" as a musical por-
trait of (in the terminology of the day) Negro America. Like many
African Americans, Ellington had little difficulty in thinking of himself as simultaneously a Negro, a race man, and a patriotic American
citizen. In the words of Hannah Nelson, who was interviewed by
John Langston Gwaltney for his study of "core black culture,"

> I think it was Frederick Douglass who said we were a nation within a
> nation. I know that will probably bother your white readers, but it is
> nonetheless true that black people think of themselves as an entity . . . .
> We are a nation primarily because we think we are a nation. This
> ground we have buried our dead in for so long is the only ground most
> of us have ever stood upon. . . . Most of our people are remarkably mer-
> ciful to Africa, when you consider how Africa has used us.[54]

Clifford Yancy, "a prudent grandfather in his later fifties," also
interviewed by Gwaltney, expressed the practical significance of
this separateness:

> White people and black people are both people, so they're alike in
> most ways, but they don't think the same about some things. Your

white man might be a little weaker, but that's just because they generally have easier work. I think they are probably as smart as we are because I have seen them doing any kind of work that any of us can do. Now, some of these young white boys might get a job they can't handle just because they know somebody, but, I mean, an experienced white man can do anything an experienced black man can do. I go by what I see going down out here and that's the way it looks to me.[55]

This statement is perfectly matter of fact in its assumption that black performance is the standard by which all performance is to be judged. Yancy is not worried about what white people think about him. He has his own frame of reference. That is what it means to be a member of a nation within a nation: it means you have your own frame of reference.

That's what the discussion of jazz, black, white, and America is about: What is the framework for discussion, analysis, and judgment? Who says so? The history of jazz is also a history of arguments about the nature of jazz. Is swing real jazz, or is New Orleans the only true jazz? Is bebop jazz or is it just a commercial stunt, as some of its detractors thought? Is Ornette Coleman playing jazz, or is he playing all those wrong notes because he can't play the saxophone? Does jazz-rock fusion qualify as jazz or not? At every point in its history, critics, journalists, fans, and scholars have argued about the nature of true jazz. Blues, rock, and hip hop have occasioned similar arguments. To the extent that these discussions have taken place in trade journals, fan magazines, and the commercial press, they shade into the need to commodify the music so that it can be marketed to the appropriate consumers.

These arguments are rarely merely about separating apples from oranges so you can price them right. They are moral arguments. Jazzers argued that rock was inferior and immoral and rockers countered that jazz is old and dried up. These arguments are passionate because they are about personal and cultural identity.

Such arguments are impossible in the social and culture worlds we looked at in chapter 9. Those societies may have recognized differences between children's and adult music, men's and women's songs, songs belonging to particular clans, and so forth. But all of the songs are in the same tradition, the only one members of these homogeneous societies feel they must answer to. Their identity is not at issue—an innocence that is rapidly vanishing as these societies become absorbed into the political life of larger nation-states. In complex cultural pluralities such as the United States, people have to negotiate a new identity for each arena in which they function: home, church, work, social club, political party, whatever. They have many bodies of music to choose from. Musical preference thus becomes a matter of personal choices that imply specific connections to the larger currents of history.[56]

This is the world in which jazz has sought its way. Not only did it emerge from a diversity of rags, blues, tangos, marches, ballads, Broadway tunes, and so forth, but it feeds into a similar diversity. Beyond this, we must consider the evidence presented by Charlie Keil and his students, who have found that individuals listen to a variety of different kinds of music.[57] Someone who likes jazz may also like country and western and a bit of classical. This variety of musical interests is no doubt abetted by the ready availability of recordings, which didn't happen until the first quarter of the twentieth century. But it is quite clear that the musical ensembles in the nineteenth century—brass bands, string bands, minstrel shows—all played a variety of musical styles.

Frameworks of ethnic and national identity set up social boundaries. Even as memes migrate across these boundaries to serve people's emotional and physical needs, thereby reducing the differences between groups, the need to maintain boundaries asserts itself. It also results in new musical styles as black Americans continue to create music they can think of as specifically theirs. This is the mechanism that Amiri Baraka identified in *Blues People*. It is the mechanism that has been driving American popular culture through the twentieth century and into this one.

FROM JAZZ TO HIP HOP

Why do white folks like black music? For much the same reason blacks do: its memes allow them to couple in pleasurable neurodynamics. The erotic sensuality of "Tight Like That" was unmistakable and particularly attractive to a population just discovering that music need not be made in accordance with the ancient Gregorian contract. More important, that sensuality is routine. It is not a special accomplishment as it was in, for example, Mozart's "Là ci darem" from *Don Giovanni*, the Arietta of Beethoven's *C minor sonata, Op. 111,* the famous Liebestod from Wagner's *Tristan und Isolde*, Ravel's *Bolero*, or Stravinsky's *Le sacre du printemps*. These are sensuous pieces of music, but they are exceptional accomplishments.

Of course, as I noted earlier, it's not just about sex. Whatever dynamo drives jazz, whites found it as attractive as blacks did. Thus, as early as there was jazz, white folks listened to it, danced to it, played it.[58] But just as whites were constantly remaking their musical culture on black models, so blacks seemed to respond by creating new forms of musicking, forms more specifically their own.

While I believe that Baraka is correct in identifying this process, his analysis is flawed. For one thing, he takes as a major example bebop, which he sees primarily as a black reaction to increasing white hegemony in the swing world.[59] I don't think the process was so overt, and a desire to play more complex and difficult music was a more important motivation.[60] Once the techniques of swing improvisation became routine, the music became boring, at least for the most adventurous musicians and their audience. It no longer conjured up the exhilarating flow that makes jazz so pleasurable. So the adventurous musicians sought more sophisticated challenges.

The shift from swing to bop is a complex phenomenon that is being examined by a variety of scholars.[61] This is no place to attempt a summary of that literature beyond simply pointing out that we're dealing with an interrelated network of phenomena, some long-term, but others of more limited duration, such as a union-imposed two-year recording ban in the middle of World War II that gave a nudge to vocal music and World War II itself and its aftermath.

In the mid-1950s, about a decade after swing had receded and bebop had emerged, rock and roll became the dominant force in American popular music and dance. Though pioneered by black performers such as Fats Domino, Chuck Berry, and Little Richard, rock's first superstar was a white truck driver named Elvis Presley. In the mid-1960s the British invaded, Bob Dylan went electric and broadened the scope of rock's lyrics, and Jimi Hendrix reinvented the guitar. Add in a good dose of psychedelic drugs and antiwar protest, and rock expanded far beyond its origins in rhythm and blues and country music. Just like jazz, it was greeted with fear and revulsion by many.[62]

But the racial dynamic had changed. Rock became a music performed by whites for whites. That was never the case with jazz, where most of the major performers have been black and the audience, though mixed, has long been mostly white.[63] The black audience left rock to white folks and embraced soul and funk. Although these musics have their own stories, I want to skip them so that we may briefly consider the major African-American response to rock: hip hop.

In the middle and late seventies disco fever spread throughout the land and crossover pop attracted performers and recording companies as moths to light. According to Nelson George, black performers such as Michael Jackson and Lionel Richie became so successful in modifying their music to cross over to white audiences that a vacuum developed. The expressive needs of the black audience were no longer adequately met, especially as people began coming to terms with the erosion of support for civil rights during the Reagan era. Rap–hip hop emerged to fill that vacuum.[64]

Hip hop has some rhythmic antecedents in the tight rhythms of James Brown and his peers, but otherwise it seems to be a complete departure from the musical styles that had emerged over the previous three quarters of a century. Melody and harmony have been severely reduced—one is reminded of Curt Sachs's horizontal melodies—or even eliminated entirely, yielding a music consisting of narrative lyrics over a highly rhythmic background. That narrative style seems derived from the verbal games and poems of the street corner, such as the Shine narrative I mentioned earlier, which may reflect West African styles of boast and verbal contest.[65]

These *toasts*, as they are called, are boasting and confrontational and are of uncertain origin. Folklorists first began collecting them in the 1930s. But the fact that the Shine toast is about the sinking of the

Titanic suggests that they go back at least to the early twentieth century. There is a large body of toasts about tough and violent characters named variously Stackolee, Dolemite, and Peatie Wheatstraw, who are perhaps precedents for the Gangsta mentality. In the early 1970s, the comedian Rudy Ray Moore performed toasts in clubs across the United States and made recordings of them, including *Shine*, *Dolemite*, and *Signifying Monkey*. These performances and recordings are possible sources for rappers who didn't hear these narratives in their neighborhoods.[66]

Rap's rhythmic background employs a kind of musical collage that depends on an extant library of recordings, which producers sample to create a backdrop for the vocals. This began back in the late 1970s as a technique in which a performer using multiple turntables created a rhythmic background of fragments from various sources by moving the records by hand under a phonograph needle. With the advent of digital recording technology this technique evolved into an elaborate and sophisticated digital collage. In either case, the rapper, the MC (master of ceremonies), weaves his or her rhymes over this background.

Hip hop is thus a significant departure from the main line of black–white musical evolution in twentieth-century America. While rhythm and blues and rock, as well as soul and funk and disco, are all clearly descended from the musical styles that were in place just prior to World War II, hip hop is not. It is a radical attempt to create a new beginning, perhaps the most radical since African-American slaves began to reconstitute their religious practice in Christian doctrinal dress.

Hip hop's words are without precedent in mass-mediated popular culture. It is the most relentlessly and consciously Black musical form African America has produced. Significantly, while hip hop has certainly attracted a white audience,[67] its performers have been overwhelmingly black, unlike either rock or jazz.

Hip hop is also the angriest of these musics. To be sure, avant-garde jazz musicians and heavy-metal rockers created angry music. But avant-garde jazz has never had a large audience, while the heavy-metal musicians and audience are both almost exclusively white. Rap is the first mass-audience black form to give broad expressive scope to anger, giving it an ambivalent relationship to heavy-metal rock, one of the sources of its musical samples.[68] Hip hop can no more be reduced to anger than jazz can be reduced to sex; but just as jazz's fundamental rhythms give easy expression to sexuality, so hip hop's boasting rhymes give a ready home to various forms of anger: misogyny, homophobia, other rappers—musical feuding and critiquing is common— as well as anger at the police and the society they represent.

Independently of the lyrics, anger is in the basic sound of the music—a phenomenon to be approached using Manfred Clynes's work on essentic forms. As jazz drummer Max Roach remarked about LL Cool J, who is adept at boasting but is neither political nor a gansta:

> The rhythm was very militant to me because it was like marching, the sound of an army on the move. We lost Malcolm, we lost King and they thought they had blotted out everybody. But all of a sudden this new art form arises and the militance is there in the music.[69]

It is thus fitting that hip hop is the first mass music openly to confront racism. Jazz was and remains primarily an instrumental music. Nor have blues or, for the most part, rock and roll or soul musicians directly confronted and condemned racism in their lyrics. Even the songbook of the civil rights movement was more inspirational than confrontational. But starting in the late 1980s, with the emergence of performers such as KRS-One and Public Enemy, hip hop developed a strong political edge.[70]

This is, I believe, a development of the first magnitude in American culture. It suggests that the musical contract that was forged during the nineteenth-century rise of minstrelsy has been discarded. Black criticism of white folks and white society is not at all new. But public criticism in popular music is. This parallels the development that Mel Watkins outlined in his recent history of African-American comedy, *On the Real Side*. As far back as we have records, African Americans have told jokes and stories at the expense of whites. But until the 1960s, they did so only among themselves. That changed during the Civil Rights era with a generation of comedians that included Dick

Gregory and, above all, Richard Pryor. With the emergence of hip hop that same critical spirit entered popular music.[71]

The old expressive contract was in force until the Reagan era. All of the secular music of African America was created according to the specifications of this contract, as were the white variations on black music. As hope for further gains in civil rights and social justice began to wither in the face of a conservative national politics, African America began negotiating a new contract. Hip hop has emerged as the vehicle of that negotiation. Pointed commentary on white racism is now an explicit part of America's collective entertainment culture. That changes our public discourse, perhaps irreversibly.

WHAT'S NEXT?

Each of these musics—jazz, rock, and hip hop—has loomed large in American culture. Jazz, like Western classical music, is now largely the province of a college-educated elite and no longer has a mass audience. Rock still has a large following, though not so large as country, the most popular kind of music in America.[72] But rock has lost the cultural urgency it had from the mid-1950s into the early 1970s. Hip hop seems firmly established, but it's not clear where hip hop is going.

What's next?

Roughly half a century passed between the emergence of jazz in the early 1900s and the rise of rock in the 1950s. Rap emerged roughly a quarter century later and has been with us almost that long. If the black–white psychocultural smithy is still functioning it should start forging a new style sometime in the next decade or two. But is it still functioning?

When you consider the black–white mixture in the audience, the characteristic emotional resonances of the music, the nature of the lyrics, and the instrumentation and techniques of construction, it is clear that each of these musics is different. The smithy isn't simply repeating itself. It takes some old memes and some new ones, throws them into a population with shifting requirements for emotional satisfaction and identity construction, and produces new music. But the fact that hip hop does not follow from its immediate predecessors suggests that we are at a signficant turning point in this psychocultural evolution.

I don't see that there is any "deeper" source from which this particular mechanism can get materials for yet another expressive move. With racism upfront and on the table, we can either renew the battle against prejudice and injustice, settle into a thrashing mode that produces change but no difference, or disintegrate in a reactionary bloodbath.

This particular mechanism, however, isn't the only game in town. The spectacular success of the Puerto Rican singer Ricky Martin, and the unexpected sales of Carlos Santana's album *Supernatural*, fueled speculation that Latin music had finally arrived. While that doesn't seem to have happened, it is certainly a serious possibility. The Latin population in the United States is growing; it is now almost as large as the black population and will surpass it in the near future. The two-way black–white cultural conversation may thus become a three-way conversation. As three-way conversations have more complicated dynamics, this might bring about a fundamentally new psychocultural regime.

Still, that particular regime would remain more or less within the family of Europe–Africa hybrids. That family has, of course, traveled all over the world interacting with local traditions in multiple ways, yielding a body of musics marketed under the rubric of "world beat."[73] Perhaps one of these musics will catch on and we will see, for example, a carnatic–hip hop hybrid as the next major transnational style, a possibility suggested by the rhythmic vocal performances of R. A. Ramamani.[74] As long as we continue to have international pop megastars and world-traveling hegemonic styles, it would be a good thing to have a cohort of stylistic catalysts outside the Atlantic interchange zone.

Yet it is by no means obvious how much longer we will live in such a world. It is not clear to me that megastardom is a social necessity. It is certainly convenient for recording companies, who do their best business when they can sell many copies of a relatively small number of recordings. But if recording companies dissolve, megastardom may dissolve with them.

Technological evolution now seems to work against recording and distribution companies. Decent recording and mixing equipment is now so cheap that relatively large numbers of individuals can own and use it, and the Internet makes the distribution of recordings easy. Musicians no longer need recording companies to make and distribute their music. Those living in areas with good computer infrastructure can do it themselves. They may not get paid much, if anything, for recordings distributed over the Internet. But few musicians make much money from recordings.

There is, however, a deeper and more fundamental issue than who makes money from the distribution of recorded music. How many people actively make music?

In 1992 the National Endowment for the Arts surveyed public participation in a variety of arts, including music. People were asked whether or not they had performed music in the past year. The following table presents these results expressed as percentages of the total population:[75]

Public Participation in Music		
Type of Music	*Private*	*Public*
play jazz	1.7%	0.70 %
play classical	4.2	0.90
sing opera	1.1	0.24
sing musical	3.8	0.73
sing choral	NA	6.3

While this hardly covers all musics performed in America, the numbers, such as they are, speak for themselves: they are low.

Until the twentieth century you couldn't hear music unless you heard live performers. Some cultures musicked more than others, but everyone sang and danced regularly. This participation was critical for Western classical music. By the nineteenth century pianos graced the parlors of every middle-class household in Europe and America, and someone in those houses played those pianos.[76] Similarly, the working classes of Europe and America were swept by brass bands in the second quarter of the nineteenth century, and these bands flourished well into the twentieth century. That is the world that gave birth to jazz and nursed it into its cultural hegemony during the swing era.

How long can we continue to live on the cultural energy bequeathed us by traditions of active musicking that have become severely attenuated? Are the Western nations living out the consequences of an unholy alliance between Romantic veneration of artistic genius and recording technology? In proper measure, this technology makes a wide variety of music available to each of us, while an appreciation of genius encourages innovation. But the abject veneration of genius devalues the musical capacities of the rest of us and encourages us to substitute recordings for our own music. That path leads to cultural stagnation.

If we wish to hear marvelous new music twenty years from now, we must prepare the way by making our own music now. That music isn't the responsibility of future geniuses. It is ours.

NOTES

CHAPTER ONE

1. Small 1998, 9.

2. I did not take notes during this performance. This description is based on memory and on two recordings Rahsaan made during this period. One is a studio recording made in New York City in late July 1969, *Volunteered Slavery;* the other is a live recording made in Paris in late February 1970, *Live in Paris, 1970*, Vol. 2. The studio recording uses Rahsaan's working band at the time. Trumpeter Howard McGhee doesn't appear on the Paris date although trombonist Dick Griffen does, but he is not credited on the album. I don't recall whether McGhee was at the live concert.

3. Balliett 1986, 176.

4. Epstein 1987, 10.

5. Balliett 1986, 87.

6. Guralnick 1999, 351.

7. Hays 1992.

8. Epstein 1987, 52.

9. Bernstein 1990.

10. Spitzer 1972, 14.

11. Crafts, Cavicchi, and Keil 1993, 138–39.

12. Benzon 1972, 1975.

13. Gillespie and Fraser 1979, 491.

14. Briggs 1982.

15. Russell 1945; Williams 1967.

16. Gardner 1967; Vico 1970.

CHAPTER TWO

1. It is tempting to think that these magic tones are simply upper partials (overtones) in the spectra of individual bells. While upper partials are certainly involved, there is more to the phenomenon. Though you can train yourself to attend to individual partials in an instrument's sound spectrum, you do not ordinarily hear them as distinct pitches; but all of us heard these tones as distinct pitches. If these are ordinary partials, you should hear them when playing bells individually. That is not

the case. Further, these tones appear only during particularly animated playing by the group. Why should partials be prominent only during a certain playing modality? The tones appear only when the group plays and only when the group is animated. These aspects of the phenomenon require an explanation.

My speculation is that these tones reflect constructive interference between upper partials in the spectra from two or more bells that makes them strong enough to be heard as distinct pitches. This requires extremely precise coordination between the players, coordination mediated by the activation of very precise subcortical affective circuitry. Montreal's Albert Bregman (personal communication) speculates that when the group is in an animated state, individuals develop extremely acute hearing that allows them to attend to components of the sound spectrum ordinarily subsumed in the *Gestalt*. Only experimentation will reveal whether either of us is correct.

2. Rasch and Plomp 1999.

3. Reddy 1993.

4. Condon 1974, 1975, 1986.

5. Condon 1986.

6. Johnson 1997, 35.

7. Passingham 1993; Lecanuet 1996.

8. Hays never published this idea in a form as strong as he expressed it privately. What he did publish can be found in Hays 1992.

9. Williams 1980, 55.

10. Perper 1985, 75–111.

11. McNeill 1995, 27.

12. Freeman 1995, 2000.

13. Sacks 1990, 60.

14. Sacks 1990, 282. It's worth pointing out that music is also useful in treating autism; see Rider and Eagle 1986, 231–32.

15. MacLean 1970, 1978, 1990.

16. For criticism of MaClean's concept see LeDoux 1996, 98–103.

17. Jerison 1976; Allman 1999.

18. Bowsher 1973.

19. Shepherd 1994, 444; Porges 1999.

20. Damasio 1994, 1999b; Benzon 2000.

21. Damasio 1999b, 274. Moruzzi and Magoun 1949, is a classic paper. For more recent views see Vanderwolf and Robinson 1981; Amari and Arbib 1977, 119; Kilmer, McCulloch, and Blum 1969, 279; Panksepp 1999, 21ff.; Benzon and Hays 1988; Deacon 1997, 230ff.

22. Freeman 1995, 1999b; MacLean 1990; Panksepp 1998.

23. Freeman 1999b, 112.

24. For expectation and emotion see Mandler 1975; LeDoux 1996. On expectation and music see Meyer 1956; Jones 1992.

25. Porges 1999.

26. Note that these stages don't quite line up with MacLean's triune model, as reptiles have both a parasympathetic and sympathetic nervous system, thus aligning Porges's first two stages with MacLean's first. In general, one should not push these

models too far. It is best to treat them simply as shorthand ways of dealing with matters that are rather complex.

27. Ekman and Friesen 1971; Izard 1971, 1977.

28. James 1890, 449. For some interesting experiments in this tradition see Valins 1970; Strongman 1973, 76–78; Mandler 1975, 131–33.

29. Baron-Cohen 1995.

30. Wallin 1991, 1. On the notion of an isomorphism between a perceptual system and some aspect of the external world, see also Gallistel 1990; Shepard 1975.

31. Patel and Balaban 2000, 80; cf. Elbert and Keil 2000.

32. There is a good methodological reason why Patel and Balaban did not use performances of real music: we do not have a very good understanding of music's structure; it's too complicated. Depending on just what you are interested in discovering, that may make it very difficult to interpret the results of studies using real music. Thus Patal and Balaban chose to create artificial stimuli whose properties they understand, a practice used in many psychological investigations of music. As we develop a better understanding of the brain's response in these relatively simple studies, we can begin to use more realistic examples, interpreting them against the background provided by our knowledge of simpler examples.

33. Pinker 1994, 263–64.

34. When in 1976 Dawkins proposed the notion of a meme as a cultural replicator, he allowed it to be either something in the environment (like our musical sounds) or a dance step, pieces of pottery, an item of clothing, a tent, and so on, or something in people's minds. What was important is that the thing was replicated. Just exactly what it was, and whether or not it was mental or physical, was secondary. However, in his 1982 discussion in *The Extended Phenotype* Dawkins adopted the view that memes exist only in the head and that the objects and processes in the external environment are the phenotypic effects of memes. This has become the standard view as exemplifed in Susan Blackmore's recent *The Meme Machine*. My view, obviously, is quite different, and I have argued it in some detail in Benzon 1996, 1997a, and 1997b.

35. I have explored cultural evolution in general in Benzon and Hays 1990b; Benzon 1993a, 1993b, 1996, 1997a, and 1997b.

36. Tramo 2001, 55.

CHAPTER THREE

1. Glass and Mackey, 1988; Glass 2001.

2. Strogatz and Stewart 1993.

3. Vertebrate nervous systems are known to contain oscillating circuits; see Selverston 1980; Shepherd 1994; Freeman 1995.

4. Kelso 1995, 46ff., 93–94; Turvey and Carello 1995, 390–93; Saltzman, 1995, 155–56.

5. On the abstractness of the coupling see Saltzman 1995, 155–56.

6. Jones 1976.

7. von Neumann 1958, 3ff.

8. See, for example, Diorio and Rao 2000; Hahnloser, Sarpeshkar et al. 2000.

9. von Neumann 1958, 68.

10. For a brief discussion of my views see Benzon and Hays 1990a; Benzon 1997b.

11. To think about computation in terms of the states of the computer is also typical. In these discussions the computer is typically an abstract device, defined by some appropriate mathematical formalism. Mapping these abstract states onto the states of a physical computer is, however, fairly straightforward.

12. For number of neurons see Mountcastle 1998; for number of chemical, see Hobson 1999a, 159.

13. Hebb quoted in Shepherd 1994, 641.

14. Johnson 1997; Bownds 1999.

15. Freeman 1997.

16. Kelso 1995, 6–7.

17. Heron 1967; La Barre 1972, 42ff.

18. Clynes 1977, 88–90; for more elaborate timing data see Clynes 1986.

19. Leng and Shaw 1991. I want to emphasize that these timing studies reflect overall timing of performances, not the moment-to-moment timing of individual notes. Moment-to-moment timing has also been studied and that work makes it clear, as musicians have known for some time, that well-performed music is not metronomically precise (Seashore 1967; Keil 1995; Gabrielsson 1986, 1999; Collier 1993, 41–88; Repp 1998). These studies have been strictly empirical; the measurements have been made and these are the results. These two results, precise overall timings and variable moment-to-moment timings, are suggestive, though of what is not exactly clear. If we think of overall timings as the cumulative result of moment-to-moment timings, there is no a priori reason to believe that those errors will even out over the long run. There are as yet no widely accepted models for the neural and motor mechanisms underlying these results.

20. Freeman 1995. In personal communication Freeman has confirmed my sense that there is no way to compare the states of one brain with the states of another brain.

21. Chernoff 1979, 52–53.

22. Erikson 1968, 1982.

23. Linton 1971.

24. Bloom 2000; Wright 2000.

25. See Gioscia 1971; Maxwell 1971; Carlstein 1982; McGrath and Kelly 1986 for useful discussions of the temporal structure of social activity.

26. Blackmore 1999, 74–81.

27. Néda, Ravasz et al. 2000.

CHAPTER FOUR

1. Kosslyn and Koenig 1995, 4. Note, however, that their thinking about brain and mind is closer to classical computational models than the views staked out in this chapter.

2. Freeman 1995, 1999b; Fischer 1987.

3. The canard about the butterfly and the storm certainly suggests a clear causal link between some particular butterfly and some particular storm; but that is meaningless. As Walter Freeman (personal communication) asks, "Which butterfly and which storm?" The story completely misses pervasive microscale jitter and the way in which any arbitrary fluctuation that goes just a little "too far" can set off an amplification process that recruits more and more jitter to a single pattern. Freeman goes on to point out that there is latent order in chaos that is missing from mere noise, noting that Ilya Prigogine wrote about the "emergence of order from disorder" in which "most fluctuations are folded back into the boiling pot, and only a privileged excursion toward a fractal boundary carries the day." See Prigogine and Stengers 1984.

4. Lutz 1999; MacLean 1990; Panksepp 1998.

5. Of course what happens to Bernstein in the privacy of his study is a function only of his nervous system, and as such requires a different analysis.

6. Powers 1973; Tononi and Edelman 1998; Tononi, Edelman, and Sporns 1998; Freeman 1999a and 1999b.

7. Wiener 1948, 113.

8. Most of his book, in fact, is about those characteristics. Powers argues that behavior regulates perception through a stack of servomechanisms, a conception both attractive and powerful. I have reluctantly concluded, however, that it is outside our current scope.

9. This brief and informal account of Powers's notion of a reorganizing system makes it seem like the often-banished little man in the head. That is not the case. Powers in fact suggests that the reorganizing system can achieve appropriate results by acting randomly, and he has done simple computer simulations on that basis (1989, 290). He doesn't claim the human brain operates in this way, but the principle is important.

10. Freeman 1995, 2000.

11. Benzon 1981, 1993a; Hays 1992.

12. Pinker 1997, 528.

13. Pribram 1971; Milner 1970; Panksepp 1998, 146ff.

14. Freeman 1997.

15. Jerome 1980.

16. Charles Keil, 1994a. A wide variety of work is relevant to the idea that the motor system plays an active role in hearing music: on the motor theory of speech perception see, e.g., Neisser 1966, 191–92; on the general role of the motor system in perception see Berthoz 2000. On oscillator banks see Large and Kolen 1999; Port, Cummins, and McAuley 1995; Haken 1996.

17. Csikszentmihalyi 1990.

18. Melzack 1973.

19. Bowlby 1973; Hope 1996; LeDoux 1996; Lindsley 1970; MacLean 1990; Panksepp 1998.

20. Posner and Raichle 1997, 190.

21. For a dynamical view of attention see Haken 1996.

22. Gray and McNaughton 1996.

23. Wiener 1948, 150ff. Traffic jams in fact have been analyzed using the mathematics of complexity and nonlinear systems (Ball 1999). One of the seminal analytic studies of information flow on the Internet found it to be fractal in nature: see Leland, Taqqu et al. 1995.

24. Hodges 1996; Shaw 2000.

25. Panksepp 1998, 269–70.

26. See, e.g., Freud's *Civilization and Its Discontents*.

27. See, e.g., Kierkegaard 1954; Becker 1975; Borkeneau 1981.

CHAPTER FIVE

1. Stanislavski 1948.

2. Lakoff and Johnson 1999, 267–89; Lakoff 1987, 380–415.

3. Darwin 1998; Ekman and Friesen 1971; Izzard 1971, 1977.

4. Arbib 1972; Barr 1972.

5. Barr 1972; Williams and Warwick 1975. Similarly, Paul Ekman has noted that spontaneous smiles are different from voluntary ones (reported in Baars 1997, 13). See also Damasio 1994, 140.

6. Based on figure 4 from Clynes 1977, 29.

7. Hodges 1996, 249.

8. Menuhin 1986, 126.

9. Wallin 1991, 485–91.

10. See Clynes 1997, 226–29 for the Bach; Clynes and Nettheim 1982.

11. Clynes 1973.

12. Baars (1997, 141) has made a similar suggestion; see also Damasio 1999b.

13. McClary 1991, 68ff.

14. An idea Clynes explores under the rubric of virtual body images, 1977, 148–51.

15. Knobloch, Postolka, and Srnec 1964; Knobloch 1996.

16. Shaffer 1992; Gabrielsson 1999, 520.

17. Maus 1997.

18. Walter Freeman, personal communication.

19. Bregman (1990) devotes a chapter to the auditory analysis of musical performances.

20. Mowshowitz (1992, 1994, 1997) has examined a number of different cases of virtuality.

21. Virtuality merits comparison to the chapter on semblance in Langer 1953.

22. Hobson 1995, 1999a.

23. Ishai and Sagi 1995; Miyashita 1995; Posner and Raichle 1997; Damasio 1999b. For a theoretical perspective consistent with these observations see Powers 1973, 222ff.

24. In particular see the interview with Gail (Crafts, Cavicchi, and Keil 1993, 94–98).

25. Sloboda 1992.

26. The work of John Bowlby (1969, 1973, 1980) has been seminal. See also Parkes and Stevenson-Hinde 1982; MacLean 1990, 250, 397.

27. Panksepp 1998, 269; see also Panksepp 1995; Blood, Zatorre et al. 1999; Blood and Zatorre 2000.

28. Levinson 1997; see also Davies 1997.

29. Hays 1992.

CHAPTER SIX

1. Friedson 1996, 145–47.

2. Gabrielsson 1999, 520–21; Hazeltine, Helmuth, and Ivry 1997.

3. Sakai, Hikosaka et al. 1999.

4. For analyses and simulations of timing and time perception from a dynamics point of view see Church and Broadbent 1990; Gjerdingen 1992, 234–38; Port, Cummins, and McAuley 1995, 363–64; Haken 1996; Large and Kolen 1999. Pittendrigh 1971 suggests that organisms are coupled oscillators; on synchrony between heartbeat and respiration, see Schäfer et al. 1998; for a recent review of physiological rhythms, see Glass 2001.

5. Selverston 1980; Shepherd 1994, 438ff.

6. Wilson 1986, 122; see also Thatcher and John 1977, 179.

7. Petersen, van Mier et al. 1998; see also Posner and Raichle 1997, 125–29.

8. These reports are the results of an informal survey I conducted on an e-mail list of trumpet players.

9. Passingham 1993.

10. Reck 1996.

11. Clynes 1995; for a more extensive discussion of two streams see Epstein 1995.

12. Clynes 1995; Keil 1994a; Small 1998.

13. Edelman 1992, 102, 204.

14. The term *attractor* is misleading to the extent that it suggests, for example, a magnet attracting iron filings or a star attracting orbiting planets. In complex systems theory attractors are simply points or trajectories in a system's state space toward which the system evolves. The causal mechanisms are those of the system itself, such as molecular movement in the case of boiling water, gravity in the case of the solar system, or electrochemistry in the case of the nervous system. In this sense attractors don't do anything. They are simply aspects of a mathematical model of the dynamics of some physical system. To the extent that the model is verified by empirical evidence, its attractors are assumed to be physically real.

15. Weinberger 1997.

16. Sackheim 1993; Waterman 1990.

17. Lord 1960; see also Propp 1968.

18. Jackson 1974; Rose 1994, 86.

19. Schenker 1973, 4; on the developmental origins of expressive gestures see Trevarthen 1993, 1999–2000.

20. On motifs, riffs, and so on see Piston 1947; Reck 1997, 182–251; Jeffrey 1992; Berliner 1994.

21. Meyer 1956.

22. McClary 1991; Small 1998.

23. Piston 1962;, Schenker 1973; Lerdahl and Jackendoff 1983.

24. Simon 1981.

25. Selverston 1980; Shepherd 1994, 438ff.; Kelso 1995, 239ff.

26. Rosenbaum 1998; Ivry 1996; Hazeltine, Helmuth, and Ivry 1997; Rao, Harrington et al. 1997; Edelman 1992, 104–8.

27. Clynes 1995.

28. Lakoff and Johnson 1980, 1999; Cox 1999. Researchers in Lakoff's laboratory have extended this work to neural models; cf. Lakoff and Johnson 1999, 569–83; Narayanan 1997.

29. In a recent review Jude Mark Tramo (2001) suggests there are no neural structures unique to music.

30. For an excellent discussion of the cognitive processes humans use in dead reckoning see Hutchins 1995.

31. Redish 1999, 215; see also Stern and Portugali 1999, for a computer simulation of decision making in urban navigation.

32. Reck 1996; Bor 1999.

33. Cf. Hodges 1996; Marin and Perry 1999.

CHAPTER SEVEN

1. Kirk 1973; Barkan 1974.

2. Tart 1972.

3. Austin 1998, 20, 454.

4. Erickson 2000, 28.

5. Harrington 1992, 214–15.

6. Weinstein 1992, 168.

7. Siegel and Jarvik 1975.

8. Hart and Stephens 1990, 62.

9. Boyd and George-Warren 1992, 176.

10. For a classic treatment of *Gestalt* ideas see Köhler 1947. For applications to music see Gabrielsson 1986; Deutsch 1999b. Rudolph Arnheim (1972) is the best-known advocate of a *Gestalt* approach to the visual arts.

11. Bregman 1990; Jones 1976.

12. Bregman 1990, 462–64.

13. For overviews see Burns 1999; Pierce 1999.

14. Tramo 2001, 54; see also Burns 1999, 242.

15. A complete account should also consider timbre, the tone quality of musical sounds. For a review see Risset and Wessel 1999; Reck 1997, 252–70. See also Wallin 1991, 428ff.

16. Benzon 1976a, 1978, 2000; see also Lamb 1999, 181–82.

17. Vygotsky 1962; Luria 1959a, 1959b; Sokolov 1972; Zivin 1979; Berk 1994.

18. Lakoff 1996; Lakoff and Johnson 1999, 267–89.

19. Damasio 1994, 1999b; Luria 1973.

20. Schachtel 1959.

21. van Eeden 1972.

22. Pribram 1971, 167–71.

23. Miller, Galanter, and Pribram 1960, 104ff.

24. Rouget 1985, 323.

25. Sperry 1968.

26. Springer and Deutsch 1998, 178ff.

27. Hodges 1996; Marin and Perry 1999; Springer and Deutsch 1998, 220–24; Tramo 2001.

28. Springer and Deutsch 1998, 225–34; Hellig 1993; Hauser 1993.

29. I know of no observations of the relevant biochemistry of musicking. Note that investigating these particular biochemicals is quite difficult; see Hobson 1999a.

30. Panksepp 1998, 135.

31. Heron 1967; La Barre 1972, 53ff.

32. Booth 1999, 195–96.

CHAPTER EIGHT

1. Donald 1991, 206.

2. The material in this and the following paragraph is based on: Geist 1978; Allman 1999, 193ff.; Coppens 1994; Klein 1999, 53–61, 253–54, 364; Balter 2001, 1722–25; Balter and Gibbons 2000, 948–50.

3. Lieberman 1998.

4. Kay, Cartmill, and Balow 1998.

5. Allman 1999; Klein 1999.

6. Wallin 1991, 388ff.; Geist 1978, 250–55, personal communication.

7. See Williams 1980, 43–44.

8. Geist 1978, 341.

9. Geist 1978, 255–56; Bickerton 1995, 55–56.

10. Donald 1991, 168.

11. Oubré 1997, 8.

12. Brown 2000.

13. Bickerton 1995, 58–59.

14. Benzon and Hays 1988, 309. Neisser (1976) has an account of the linguistic sign that is relevant here while Benzon (2000) shows how such a model of the sign could be implemented in a cognitive network.

15. Hockett 1967.

16. For a technical discussion of one fragment of this problem, the use of personal pronouns, see Benzon 2000.

17. Sachs 1965, 49–76.

18. Tomasello and Call 1997; Sachs 1965, 49–76.

19. Sachs 1965; Lomax 1968.

20. See the chapters "Social Stress" and "Psychic Castration" in Wickler 1973.

21. On neural localization of the visual word see Kosslyn and Koenig 1995, 167–210; Posner and Raichle 1997, 76–81, 89–90, 115–16; Baynes, Eliassen et al. 1998.

22. Deacon 1997.

23. Stebbins 1982, 134.

24. My level of skepticism about the value of adaptive accounts of musicking has been increased by a recent book on human neural development. Since I haven't yet had time to think this through I have relegated this bit of skepticism to a footnote. The book is *Rethinking Innateness* by Jeffrey Elman, Elizabeth Bates, Mark Johnson, Annette Karmiloff-Smith, Domenico Parisi, and Kim Plunkett. They point out that we do not yet have any evidence that the regional specialization of the neocortex is under genetic control. There do not seem to be any genes that designate some area for vision, another for hearing, another for touch, and so forth, much less do we have genes that lay down the traces of a universal grammar. If the genes can't regulate it, whatever *it* is, then it cannot be the result of biological adaptation. This suggests that it is the neocortex as a whole that is adaptive, along with the range of capacities that it enables, rather than any specific capacity that is implemented in it. Just how any of these capacities are implemented would seem to be the result of interaction with the environment. And that may in fact be why a neocortex is such a useful thing to have. Its functions can be specified through interaction with the external world, thereby increasing the animal's ability to adapt to local conditions (cf. Boyd and Richerson 1985).

25. Blackmore 1999, 66.

26. Croft 2000, 37–40.

27. Caporael 1997. I should note that Caporael is skeptical about memes and memetics.

CHAPTER NINE

1. Levine 1977, 7.

2. Jackson 1974, 30; Levine 1977, 208–17.

3. Tylor 1972; Durkheim 1972.

4. Chatwin 1987, 13ff.

5. Dehaene 1997.

6. Neisser 1966, 1976; Miller 1967.

7. On the relationship between myth and ritual see Segal 1998.

8. On social types see Diamond 1997, 267–81; Hays 1993, ch. 5, 1997; Service 1975; White 1959; Wright 2000. For a review of the literature on hunter-gatherer bands see Barnard 1999.

9. Caporael 1997; Olson 1971.

10. Service 1975, 55–56; Ehrlich 2000, 249–50.

11. There are exceptions to every generalization about human society. The Nuer of southern Sudan are an exception to the relatively small scale of egalitarian societies. They are a herding people whose population was about 200,000 in the 1930s when Evans-Pritchard (1940) worked among them. They had no permanent leaders,

though there had been a few prophets, suppressed by the colonial administration, who came close to such status.

12. Nelson 1997; Trehub 2000. DeNora 2000, 79–87, has an illuminating discussion of music in neonatal intensive care units.

13. Hobson 1995.

14. Bowlby 1969, 293–94.

15. I am playing, of course, on the old formula from developmental biology, ontogeny recapitulates phylogeny. We now know that is not quite true; see Gould 1977.

16. Trehub 2000, 438–39.

17. Nettl 1983, 342–44; idem 2000, 469–71.

18. Blacking 1995b.

19. While I became aware of Mekranoti musicking through a presentation by David Huron (2000), I am basing my account on Dennis Werner's (1990) ethnography.

20. Werner 1990, 48.

21. Werner 1990, 176.

22. Leach 1972.

23. van Gennup 1960; Turner 1969, 1993.

24. Carlstein 1982.

25. Caporael 1997, 283.

26. Fox 1967; Lévi-Strauss 1969.

27. See Hurston 1938; Simpson 1978; Mulira 1990; Creel 1990; Hall 1990; Brandon 1990.

28. Simpson 1978, 65.

29. Deren 1953, 259–60.

30. The standard review of the anthropological literature on trance and possession is Rouget 1985; see also Holm 1982; Lewis 1989; Winkelman 1992; Friedson 1996.

31. Winkelman 1992. Winkelman used the hologeistic methodology developed by George P. Murdock, Raoul Naroll, and others. In such studies one formulates a hypothesis and tests it against a random sample of cultures drawn from a standard set.

32. I came upon Mary Douglas's *Natural Symbols* (1973) too late to incorporate her ideas into my thinking; see her discussion of the social acceptance of trance and possession on pp. 104–35.

33. Eliade 1964; Rouget 1985; Friedson 1996, 26ff.

34. Pribram 1971.

35. Lomax 1968, 133.

36. Lomax's findings are much richer than my discussion indicates. He discusses issues other than solidarity and social complexity and his discussion of those issues is more complex than my discussion indicates. For our purposes the important point is simply that there are patterns here and we have statistically controlled ways of investigating them. My simplifications and biases can be corrected simply by reading Lomax. His simplifications and biases can be corrected through further research.

37. Lomax 1968, 171.

38. While Lomax's measure of social complexity is of a piece with the various measures developed after World War II, he relies very heavily on subsistence mode in

constructing his scale. In his general review of the literature on cultural complexity Hays (1997, 159) notes that all of the indicators so far used for subsistence can be satisfied by cultures at an intermediate level of complexity, thus blunting its usefulness as the mainstay of a complexity index; see also Levinson 1980. I should also note that, while concluding—with others—that these various measures do indeed measure cultural or social complexity, Hays also felt that all of the measures were rather weak. In particular, all measures assume that cultural complexity has only magnitude, and thus can be indicated by a single number. In developing his own measure, Hays decided to evaluate every culture on each of eleven aspects: population, polity, class, legal, commerce, crafts, religion, settlement, subsistence, cognition, war. As two cultures that score the same on one aspect may score differently on one or more other aspects, one cannot use a single number to indicate complexity. Complexity has pattern as well as magnitude. Using the existing literature, Hays then rated each of 470 cultures on every aspect for which the source studies had adequate data. This implies that studies such as Lomax's and Winkelman's need to be redone in view of Hays's more sophisticated approach.

39. Lomax 1968, 134.

40. I take this point from Mario Vaneechoutte, who has made it repeatedly on the memetics discussion list associated with the *Journal of Memetics*. You can find this list at: http://www.cpm.mmu.ac.uk/jom-emit/memetics/about.html.

41. Caporael 1997, 279–81.

42. Lomax 1968, 133. For a general criticism of the view that art "reflects" society see Martindale 1990, 23–28. Note that Martindale works mostly, though not exclusively, with high-art traditions in literate societies, not the preliterate societies that predominate in Lomax's study. Cf. DeNora 2000, 1–20.

43. For an interesting treatment of coherence in the development of scientific ideas see Thagard 1992, 2000.

44. Crafts, Cavicchi, and Keil 1993; DeNora 2000.

CHAPTER TEN

1. Freeman 1995, 135–40.

2. Piaget 1971, 267–68, 320–21; Piaget and Garcia 1974, 126–29; Piaget 1976, 320ff. For a critical look at Piaget's general views about stages see Brainerd 1978; for some remarks placing Piaget in the context of neurodynamics see Thelen and Smith 1994; Benzon and Hays (1988) provide a neurally based interpretation of Piaget's stages.

3. Jaynes 1967, 262.

4. We are clearly in the realm of cognitive semantics; see the appendix on anger in Lakoff 1987, 380–415.

5. For a photograph of this theater see Baldry 1971, 37.

6. Nietzsche 1967, 33.

7. This and subsequent passages are from Nietzsche 1967, 62–66.

8. Else 1965.

9. Wiora 1965, 11–12; see also Benzon 1993b.

10. For an argument favoring this assumption see Hays 1997, 257–61.

11. Wiora 1965, 12.

12. Benzon and Hays 1987, 64; idem 1988, 306–8.

13. McNeill 1970, 20–25.

14. Unfortunately, we have no direct evidence for or against this hypothesis, primarily because no one has gone looking for it. In any event, it's only in the past decade or so, if that, that we have had the experimental tools we need to do this work. For example, the work by Patel and Balaban (2000) we considered in the second chapter uses a methodology that might be suitable for investigating this hypothesis.

15. Wiora's discussion on rhythm and of the first "age" is on pp. 17–44 of his book. For a particularly rich and sophisticated analysis of a West African polyrhythmic culture see Arom 1991.

16. The idea of cultural rank is not specific to music. Over the course of a decade or so David Hays and I have written a number of articles and books discussing cultural rank with respect to cognition (Benzon and Hays 1990b), music (Benzon 1993b), narrative (Benzon 1978, 1993a), expressive culture (Hays 1992), and technology (Hays 1993).

17. Wiora 1965, 59ff.

18. Small 1998, 64ff.

19. Bake 1957, 212–16; Reck 1996; Bor 1999.

20. On *râga* performance see Reck 1996; Slawek 1998; Viswanathan and Cormack 1998.

21. See Neuman 1990 for an ethnography of the world of the professional musician in Northern India.

22. I learned this from Jon Barlow, a former faculty member at Wesleyan University who has studied this tradition.

23. Serafine 1988, 48.

24. In this context, but not generally, *key* has much the same significance as *scale*, *mode*, or most generally *tonality*—the terms generally used to designate the sets of tones that form the basis of melodic and harmonic structures; see Reti 1958, 8–13, on tonality in general, and on melodic tonality, 15–18. In rank 2 music most performances stay within a single key or mode.

25. Abraham 1979; Griffel 1982.

26. Robert Wright has a brief review of theories of cultural evolution in the first chapter of *Nonzero*. Marvin Opler (1960) also reviews this history while David Hays (1997) has written a thorough review and reanalysis of the technical literature on cultural complexity. See also White 1959; Boyd and Richerson 1985; Martindale 1990; Csikszentmihalyi 1993; Taylor 1996; Croft 2000; and Ehrlich 2000.

27. Campbell 1974, as explicated by Martindale 1990, 34. For other accounts of cultural selection see Hull 1988; Taylor 1996.

28. Population growth plays a role in the process, but it's not clear what role; see, e.g., Benzon 1996; Diamond 1997; Ehrlich 2000; Wright 2000.

29. On the violence in face-to-face meetings between strangers see van Gennup 1960, 26; Diamond 1997, 271, 281, 286. See also Douglas 1973 for a discussion of the "plasticity" of group boundaries.

30. Mead 1934.

31. Turner 1969, 167ff.

32. See Benzon and Hays 1987 for a possible neural mechanism.

33. Evans-Pritchard 1940, 1956.

34. Evans-Pritchard 1956, 308.

35. La Barre 1972.

36. Danielson 1997.

37. There is an extensive literature on writing. See, e.g., Havelock 1982; Hobart and Schiffman 1998, 11–84. See also Donald 1991, and Benzon and Hays 1990b, on the cognitive significance of writing.

38. Crafts, Cavicchi, and Keil 1993; DeNora 2000; Frith 1996; Keil and Feld 1994; Lipsitz 1994.

39. For an excellent ethnographic description of a concert in the Western classical tradition see the early chapters of Small 1998.

40. On the neural correlates of reading see Kosslyn and Koenig 1995; Hellige 1993; Springer and Deutsch 1998; Posner and Raichle 1997, 76–81. We have some evidence that the brain adapts to the music typical of one's culture, though the subjects in this study (Bharucha 2000) were all literate individuals from literate cultures.

41. Bernstein reported this in Epstein 1987, 52.

42. Herbert 1997; United States Army 2000.

43. My observations on the functioning of marching bands are based on my own experience during the 1960s in western Pennsylvania. I have no reason to believe that my experience is atypical.

44. The remarks on chant are based on Wiora 1965, 87ff.; Orbach 1999; Grout and Palisca 1996; Jourdain 1997.

45. On chant notation see Apel 1990; Jeffrey 1992; Wiora 1965, 130–32.

46. Hale 1994, 1–50. On the formation of Christendom see McNeill 1963, 441–56.

47. Dudley and Novak 1972. Mozart's Papageno is an example of this wild man.

48. Ansermet 1962.

49. For a fascinating discussion of how artifacts originally collected as ethnographic artifacts became reconceived as aesthetic objects, and thus were moved from natural history museums to art museums, see Clifford 1988, 215–51.

50. Kelly 2000, 256ff.

CHAPTER ELEVEN

1. I own a collection of transcriptions based on these recordings that was published by Leeds Music, Inc. in 1957. However, if you look at the copyright dates for the individual solos, those dates are the same year or a year after Armstrong recorded the solo.

2. Collier 1983, 193.

3. Eric Johnson and Karen Stober are subscribed to the Trumpet Players International Network at http://trumpet.dana.edu/~trumpet/. I found the "hookie kookie" version on the web at this location: http://www.izzy.com/~patri/quotes/humour.html.

4. Bloom's comment led me first to a web page put up by a woman who teaches and performs as Shira at http://www.shira.net/streets-of-cairo.htm; and that web page led me to Fuld 2000, 276–77.

5. Jeanne Pocius is a professional trumpet player and teacher. She has a page on the web at http://members.delphi.com/jeannepocius/index.html.

6. Wallace 1997, 242.

7. Collier 1983, 36ff.

8. Fuld 2000, 276.

9. I have this observation courtesy of Milo Miles, who posts to *Salon*'s Table Talk discussion forum on the web.

10. Gates 1988.

11. I heard him do this at a show in Buffalo and have heard it on recordings, but cannot provide a specific citation.

12. Morgan n.d.

13. Hobsbawn 1993; Rasula 1995.

14. On jazz improvisation see Berliner 1994.

15. On ecstatic Christianity see Bloom 1992, 48, 238; Philips 1990, 231; Small 1987, 88ff.; Williamson 1984, 38; Taves 1999.

16. On banned drums see Peretti 1992, 62. On Congo Square see Buerkle and Barker 1973; Starr 1995.

17. On minstrelsy see Cockrell 1997; Lhamon 1998; Lott 1993; Southern 1983. On Broadway and vaudeville see Douglas 1995; Watkins 1994.

18. Herbert 1997, 177.

19. Southern 1983. See also Handy 1941.

20. Armstrong 1954, 31–32.

21. Lincoln and Mamiya 1990.

22. Levine 1977, 215–17.

23. Garraty and Gay 1981, 301.

24. On sources of West Africans for the slave trade see Johnson and Campbell 1981; Oliver 1970.

25. So far as I know, there is no comprehensive classification of musical styles and lineages (cf. Nettl 1983, 118–19). Charlie Keil has assembled a useful annotated outline of blues styles; see Keil 1991, 217–24. Comprehensive jazz histories all provide accounts of early jazz and jazz's origins. I have used Collier 1978; Gioia 1997. *Time* (1998) magazine published an interesting map of popular music in a special issue on the 100 most important artists and entertainers of the twentieth century.

26. Redrawn after figure 1.2 in Klein 1999, 10.

27. Actually, treelike phylogeny is most characteristic of animals; Hull 1988. Many plants hybridize quite easily and the single-celled species trade genetic material quite freely.

28. For discussions of these differences see Benzon 1996, 1997a; and Speel 1997.

29. Bayles 1994, 22.

30. For other instances where musics in these hybrid traditions are associated with the West see Baraka 1963, 194, 221, 225; Schuller 1968, 6; and Small 1987, 4.

31. For some recent salvos in this debate see Carruth 1993, 185–94; Collier 1993, 193–224; Craddock-Willis, Marsalis, and Collier 1995; and Lees 1995, 187–246. In another context I have gone so far as to suggest that this problem implies that we should scrap notions like "Western," "Eastern," "African," and "Oriental" culture as being useless for cultural analysis; see Benzon 1996, 355–56.

32. Ellington 1973, 80. Episode Three of Ken Burns's documentary *Jazz* has some archival footage of Cotton Club stage shows.

33. Marshall Stearns quoted from Meltzer 1993, 153. Ann Douglas (1995, 458) reports that a black aviator named Hubert Fauntleroy Julian parachuted into Harlem playing a saxophone in April of 1923. Perhaps the floor show was inspired by this act.

34. Merriam 1964, 133ff.; idem 1973; Ames 1973; Nettl 1983, 339–42; Keil 2000.

35. Clifford 1988; Gendron 1995.

36. Levine 1977, 198. Note that I remember a variant of the white version from my own childhood in western Pennsylvania in the 1950s.

37. Keil 1991, 46–47.

38. Freud 1962.

39. Gay 1993, 516.

40. Parsons 1964, 298–322. I should add that, however sympathetic I am to Parsons's argument, it is by no means clear to me that it applies only to the Western world.

41. Hernton 1965; Erikson 1968; Kovel 1984; Young-Bruehl 1996.

42. Williamson 1984; Brundage 1993.

43. Jordan 1974, 19; Fredrickson 1971, 1988.

44. Merriam 1964, 241ff.

45. Quoted in Meltzer 1993, 123.

46. Chevigny 1991.

47. Young-Bruehl 1996.

48. See Jackson 1974, 36–37, 180ff. I should add that we don't actually know that this narrative dates back to the early twentieth century as folklorists didn't start collecting these poems until later. However, I find it difficult to imagine that people would have waited five or ten or twenty or more years after the *Titanic* went down to base a narrative on it.

49. Burns 2000, Episode One.

50. Lewis 1955, 5.

51. Stowe 1994, 53.

52. Baraka 1963, 159–60.

53. On this complex and subtle matter see Gellner 1983; Williams 1976, 178–80.

54. Gwaltney 1993, 5.

55. Gwaltney 1993, 1958.

56. See Frith 1996.

57. Crafts, Cavicchi, and Keil 1993; DeNora 2000. See also DeVeaux 1995, 33–50.

58. As far as I know, James Lincoln Collier (1993, 219) is the scholar who placed jazz's white audience on the intellectual agenda.

59. Baraka 1963, 181ff.

60. Benzon 1993b.

61. For those interested in studying bop's emergence, Scott DeVeaux (1997) is the place to begin. Other sources include Owens 1995, for an overview of bebop style; Stowe 1994, and Schuller 1989, for accounts of the end of the swing era; and Gitler 1985, for oral testimony by the musicians who made the transition.

62. See Martin and Segrave 1992.

63. On the jazz audience see DeVeaux 1995.

64. George 1988.

65. See the discussion of praise songs in Waterman 1990.

66. On toasts in hip hop see Rose 1994, 55; on toasts in general: Abrahams 1970; Jackson 1974.

67. Samuels 1991.

68. On anger see Costello and Wallace 1990, 67–68; George 1992, 130; Rose 1994, 61.

69. Quoted from Lipsitz 1994, 38.

70. On hip hop and politics see Rose 1994; for a useful chronology see George 1992, 9–40.

71. Watkins 1994.

72. DeVeaux 1995, 36ff.

73. See, e.g., Feld 1994; Lipsitz 1994.

74. Karnataka College of Percussion 1993, 1997.

75. Robinson 1993.

76. Starr 1995, 50–51; Southern 1983, 308–9.

BIBLIOGRAPHY

Abeles, H. F., and J. W. Chung. 1996. Responses to Music. In *Handbook of Music Psychology*, edited by D. A. Hodges (285–342). San Antonio, TX: IMR Press.

Abraham, G. 1979. *The Concise Oxford History of Music*. London: Oxford University Press.

Abrahams, R. D. 1970. *Deep Down in the Jungle*. Chicago: Aldine.

Allman, J. M. 1999. *Evolving Brains*. New York: Scientific American Library.

Amari, S-I., and M. Arbib. 1977. Competition and Cooperation in Neural Nets. In *Systems Neuroscience*, edited by J. Metzler (119–65). New York: Academic Press.

Ames, D. D. 1973. A Sociocultural View of Hausa Musical Activity. In *The Traditional Artist in African Societies*, edited by W. L. d'Azevedo (128–61). Bloomington and Indianapolis: Indiana University Press.

Ansermet, E-A. 1962. Bechet & Jazz Visit Europe, 1919. In *Frontiers of Jazz*, edited by R. de Toledano (115–23). New York: Frederick Ungar.

Apel, W. 1990. *Gregorian Chant*. Bloomington and Indianapolis: Indiana University Press.

Arbib, M. 1972. *The Metaphorical Brain*. New York: John Wiley & Sons.

Armstrong, L. 1928. Tight Like This. In *Louis Armstrong*. Vol. 4. *Louis Armstrong and Earl Hines*. CBS CK 4512.

———. 1954. *Satchmo: My Life in New Orleans*. New York: Da Capo Press.

———. 1957. *Louis Satchmo Armstrong's Dixieland Trumpet Solos (with Piano Accompaniment)*. New York: Leeds Music Corporation.

———. 1999. *Louis Armstrong in His Own Words: Selected Writings*. New York: Oxford University Press.

Arnheim, R. 1972. *Toward a Psychology of Art*. Berkeley: University of California Press.

Arom, S. 1991. *African Polyphony and Polyrhythm*. Cambridge: Cambridge University Press.

———. 2000. Prolegomena to a Biomusicology. In *The Origins of Music*, edited by N. L. Wallin, B. Merker, and S. Brown (27–30). Cambridge, MA: MIT Press.

Ashbrook, J. B., ed. 1993. *Brain, Culture, and the Human Spirit*. Lanham, New York: University Press of America.

Austin, J. H. 1998. *Zen and the Brain*. Cambridge, MA: MIT Press.

Baars, B. J. 1997. *In the Theatre of Consciousness*. New York: Oxford University Press.

Bake, A. 1957. The Music of India. In *The New Oxford History of Music: Ancient and Oriental Music*, edited by E. Wellesz. Vol. 1 (195–227). London: Oxford University Press.

Baldry, H. C. 1971. *The Greek Tragic Theatre*. New York: W. W. Norton.

Ball, P. 1999. Transitions Still to Be Made. *Nature* 402 (Suppl., 6761): C73–76.

Balliett, W. 1986. *American Musicians: 56 Portraits in Jazz*. Oxford: Oxford University Press.

Balter, M. 2001. In Search of the First Europeans. *Science* 291: 1722–25.

Balter, M., and A. Gibbons. 2000. A Glimpse of Humans' First Journey Out of Africa. *Science* 288: 948–50.

Baraka, A. 1963. *Blues People*. New York: William Morrow.

———. 1990. Jazz Criticism and Its Effect on the Art Form. In *New Perspectives on Jazz*, edited by D. Baker (55–70). Washington, DC, and London: Smithsonian Institution Press.

Barinaga, M. 1992. The Brain Remaps Its Own Contours. *Science* 258: 216–18.

Barkan, T. 1974. Rahsaan Speaks His Peace. *Down Beat* 41: 13–14, 42.

Barlow, D. H., B. F. Chorpita, and J. Turovsky. 1996. Fear, Panic, Anxiety, and Disorders of Emotion. *Perspectives on Anxiety, Panic, & Fear*, Vol. 43, edited by D. Hope (251–328). Lincoln: University of Nebraska Press.

Barnard, A. 1999. Modern Hunter-Gatherers and Early Symbolic Culture. In *The Evolution of Culture*, edited by R. Dunbar, C. Knight, and C. Power (50–68). New Brunswick, NJ: Rutgers University Press.

Baron-Cohen, S. 1995. *Mindblindness*. Cambridge, MA: MIT Press.

Barr, M. L. 1972. *The Human Nervous System*. New York: Harper & Row.

Bartlett, D. L. 1996. Physiological Responses to Music and Sound Stimuli. In *Handbook of Music Psychology*, edited by D. A. Hodges. San Antonio, TX: IMR Press.

Bayles, A. 1994. *Hole in Our Soul*. New York: The Free Press.

Baynes, K., J. C. Eliassen et al. 1998. Modular Organization of Cognitive Systems Masked by Interhemispheric Integration. *Science* 280: 902–5.

Bechet, S. 1941. Blues of Bechet. *Master Musician—Sidney Bechet*. RCA AXM2–5516.

———. 1941. The Sheik of Araby. *Master Musician—Sidney Bechet*. RCA AXM2–5516.

Becker, E. 1975. *Escape from Evil*. New York: The Free Press.

Benedict, R. 1934. *Patterns of Culture*. Boston: Houghton Mifflin.

Benzon, W. L. 1972. The Articulated Vision: Coleridge's "Kubla Khan." Thesis, *Humanities* Center. Baltimore: Johns Hopkins University.

———. 1976a. Cognitive Networks and Literary Semantics. *MLN* 91: 952–82.

———. 1976b. Comment on Powers' Letter. *MLN* 91: 1619–24.

———. 1978. Cognitive Science and Literary Theory. Dissertation, Department of English. Buffalo: State University of New York at Buffalo.

———. 1980. System and Observer in Semiotic Modeling: An Essay on Semiotic Realism. *Semiotics 1980, Proceedings of the Fifth Annual Meeting of the Semiotic Society of America*. New York: Plenum Press.

———. 1981. Lust in Action: An Abstraction. *Language and Style* 14: 251–70.

―――. 1991. Visual Thinking. In *Encyclopedia of Computer Science and Technology*, edited by A. Kent and J. G. Williams. Vol. 23, Suppl. 8 (411–27). New York and Basel: Marcel Dekker.

―――. 1993a. The Evolution of Narrative and the Self. *Journal of Social and Evolutionary Systems* 16: 129–55.

―――. 1993b. Stages in the Evolution of Music. *Journal of Social and Evolutionary Systems* 16(3): 283–96.

―――. 1993c. The United States of the Blues: On the Crossing of African and European Cultures in the 20th Century. *Journal of Social and Biological Structures* 16(4): 401–38.

―――. 1996. Culture as an Evolutionary Arena. *Journal of Social and Evolutionary Systems* 19(4): 321–62.

―――. 1997a. Culture's Evolutionary Landscape: A Reply to Hans-Cees Speel. *Journal of Social and Evolutionary Systems* 20(3): 314–22.

―――. 1997b. Pursued by Knowledge in a Fecund Universe. *Journal of Social and Evolutionary Systems* 20(1): 93–100.

―――. 2000. First Person: Neuro-Cognitive Notes on the Self in Life and in Fiction. *PSYART: A Hyperlink Journal for Psychological Study of the Arts.* http://web.clas.ufl.edu/ipsa/journal/articles/psyart2000/benzon01.htm.

Benzon, W. L., and D. G. Hays. 1987. Metaphor, Recognition, and Neural Process. *American Journal of Semiotics* 5: 59–79.

―――. 1988. Principles and Development of Natural Intelligence. *Journal of Social and Biological Structures* 11: 293–322.

―――. 1990a. Why Natural Selection Leads to Complexity. *Journal of Social and Biological Structures* 13: 33–40.

―――. 1990b. The Evolution of Cognition. *Journal of Social and Biological Structures* 13: 297–320.

Berendt, J. 1973. *The Jazz Book*. New York: Lawrence Hill.

Berk, L. E. 1994. Why Children Talk to Themselves. *Scientific American* 271(5): 78–83.

Berliner, P. 1994. *Thinking in Jazz: The Infinite Art of Improvisation*. Chicago: University of Chicago Press.

Bernstein, L. 1990. Notes to Igor Stravinsky: Rite of Spring, Firebird. *Bernstein Edition*. Uni/Deutsche Grammaphon 31045.

―――. 1993. *The Infinite Variety of Music*. New York: Anchor Books/Doubleday.

Bernstein, S. 1981. *With Your Own Two Hands: Self-Discovery Through Music*. New York: Schirmer Books.

Berthoz, A. 2000. *The Brain's Sense of Movement*. Cambridge, MA: Harvard University Press.

Bharucha, J. J. 1992. Tonality and Learnability. In *Cognitive Bases of Musical Communication*, edited by M. R. Jones and S. Holleran (213–24). Washington, DC: American Psychological Association.

―――. 1999. Neural Nets, Temporal Composites, and Tonality. In *The Psychology of Music*, edited by D. Deutsch (413–41). San Diego: Academic Press.

Bickerton, D. 1983. Creole Languages. *Scientific American* 249(1): 116–22.

———. 1984. The Language Bioprogram Hypothesis. *Behavioral and Brain Sciences* 7: 173–88.

———. 1995. *Language and Human Behavior*. Seattle: University of Washington Press.

Blacking, J. 1974. *How Musical Is Man?* Seattle: University of Washington Press.

———. 1995a. *Music, Culture, & Experience*. Chicago: University of Chicago Press.

———. 1995b. *Venda Children's Songs*. Chicago: University of Chicago Press.

Blackmore, S. 1999. *The Meme Machine*. Oxford: Oxford University Press.

Blood, A. J., and R. J. Zatorre. 2000. Intensely Pleasant Emotional Responses to Music Correlate with CBF Modulation in Paralimbic and Other Subcortical Brain Regions. Conference on *The Biological Foundations of Music*. New York: New York Academy of Sciences.

Blood, A. J., R. J. Zatorre et al. 1999. Emotional Responses to Pleasant and Unpleasant Music Correlate with Activity in Paralimbic Brain Regions. *Nature Neuroscience* 2(4): 382–87.

Bloom, H. 1992. *The American Religion: The Emergence of the Post-Christian Nation*. New York: Simon and Schuster.

Bloom, H. K. 2000. *Global Brain: The Evolution of Mass Mind from the Big Bang to the 21st Century*. New York: John Wiley & Sons.

Booth, W. 1999. *For the Love of It: Amateuring and Its Rivals*. Chicago: University of Chicago Press.

Bor, J., ed. 1999. *The Râga Guide: A Survey of 74 Hindustani Râgas*. Four CDs and 1984 page book. Nimbus Communications International.

Borkeneau, F. 1981. *End and Beginning: On the Generations of Cultures and the Origins of the West*. New York: Columbia University Press.

Bowlby, J. 1969. *Attachment and Loss*. Vol. 1. *Attachment*. New York: Basic Books.

———. 1973. *Attachment and Loss*. Vol. 2. *Separation: Anxiety and Anger*. New York: Basic Books.

———. 1980. *Attachment and Loss*. Vol. 3. *Loss: Sadness and Depression*. New York: Basic Books.

Bownds, M. D. 1999. *The Biology of Mind*. Bethesda, MD: Fitzgerald Science Press.

Bowsher, D. 1973. Brain, Behavior and Evolution. *Brain, Behavior and Evolution* 8: 386–96.

Boyd, J., and W. H. George-Warren. 1992. *Musicians in Tune*. New York: Fireside/Simon and Schuster.

Boyd, R., and P. J. Richerson. 1985. *Culture and the Evolutionary Process*. Chicago: University of Chicago Press.

Brainerd, C. J. 1978. The Stage Question in Cognitive-Development Theory. *Behavioral and Brain Sciences* 1: 173–82.

Brandon, G. 1990. Sacrificial Practices in Santeria, an African-Cuban Religion in the United States. In *Africanisms in American Culture*, edited by J. E. Holloway. Bloomington and Indianapolis: Indiana University Press.

Bregman, A. 1990. *Auditory Scene Analysis*. Cambridge, MA: MIT Press.

Briggs, K. A. 1982. The Pope: Using the World as His Pulpit. *The New York Times Magazine*, October 10, 24–26, 85–87, 96–97, 102–5, 112–13.

Brown, S. 2000. The "Musilanguage" Model of Music Evolution. In *The Origins of Music*, edited by N. L. Wallin, B. Merker, and S. Brown (271–300). Cambridge, MA: MIT Press.

Brown, S. E. 1986. *James P. Johnson: A Case of Mistaken Identity*. Metuchen and London: The Scarecrow Press and the Institute of Jazz Studies, Rutgers University.

Brundage, W. F. 1993. *Lynching in the New South: Georgia and Virginia, 1880–1930*. Urbana: University of Illinois Press.

Buerkle, J. V., and D. Barker. 1973. *Bourbon Street Black*. New York: Oxford University Press.

Burns, E. M. 1999. Intervals, Scales, and Tuning. In *The Psychology of Music*, edited by D. Deutsch (215–64). San Diego: Academic Press.

Burns, K. 2000. *Jazz: A Film by Ken Burns*. Florentine Films B8262D. Film.

Campbell, D. T. 1974. Evolutionary Epistemology. In *The Philosophy of Karl R. Popper*, edited by P. A. Schilpp (413–63). LaSalle, IL: Open Court.

Campbell, P. S. 1998. *Songs in Their Heads: Music and Its Meaning in Children's Lives*. New York: Oxford University Press.

Caplow, T., L. Hicks, and B. J. Wattenberg. 2001. *The First Measured Century*. Washington, DC: AEI Press.

Caporael, L. R. 1997. The Evolution of Truly Social Cognition: The Core Configurations Model. *Personality and Social Psychology Review* 1(4): 276–98.

Carlstein, T. 1982. *Time Resources, Society and Ecology*. Lund, Sweden: The Royal University of Lund, Department of Geography.

Carneiro, R. L. 1960. The Culture Process. In *Essays in the Science of Culture*, edited by G. E. Dole and R. L. Carneiro (145–61). New York: Thomas Y. Crowell.

———. 1981. The Chiefdom: Precursor of the State. In *The Transition to Statehood in the New World*, edited by G. D. Jones and R. R. Kautz (37–79). Cambridge: Cambridge University Press.

Carruth, H. 1993. *Sitting In*. Iowa City: University of Iowa Press.

Carter, C. S., I. Lederhendler, and B. Kirkpatrick. 1999. *The Integrative Neurobiology of Affiliation*. Cambridge, MA: MIT Press.

Carterette, E. C., and R. A. Kendall. 1999. Comparative Music Perception and Cognition. In *The Psychology of Music*, edited by D. Deutsch (725–91). San Diego: Academic Press.

Chatwin, B. 1987. *The Songlines*. New York: Viking.

Chernoff, J. M. 1979. *African Rhythm and African Sensibility*. Chicago: University of Chicago Press.

Chevigny, P. 1991. *Gigs: Jazz and the Cabaret Laws in New York City*. New York: Routledge.

Chick, G. 1999. Review of Hays. *Journal of Anthropological Research* 55: 596–97.

Church, R. M., and H. A. Broadbent. 1990. Alternative Representation of Time, Number, and Rate. *Cognition* 37: 55–81.

Clarke, E. F. 1999. Rhythm and Timing in Music. In *The Psychology of Music*, edited by D. Deutsch (473–500). San Diego: Academic Press.

Clifford, J. 1988. *The Predicament of Culture*. Cambridge, MA: Harvard University Press.

Clynes, M. 1973. Sentics: Biocybernetics of Emotion Communication. *Annals of the New York Academy of Sciences* 220: 55–131.

———. 1977. *Sentics: The Touch of Emotions*. Garden City, New York: Anchor Press/Doubleday.

———., ed. 1982. *Music, Mind, and Brain: The Neuropsychology of Music*. New York: Plenum Press.

———. 1986. When Time Is Music. In *Rhythm in Psychological, Linguistic and Musical Processes*, edited by J. R. Evans and M. Clynes (169–224). Springfield, IL: Charles C Thomas.

———. 1995. Microstructural Musical Linguistics: Composers' Pulses Are Liked Best by the Best Musicians. *Cognition* 55: 269–310.

Clynes, M., and N. Nettheim. 1982. The Living Quality of Music: Neurobiologic Basis of Communicating Feeling. In *Music, Mind, and Brain: The Neuropsychology of Music*, edited by M. Clynes (47–82). New York: Plenum Press.

Clynes, M., and J. Walker. 1982. Neurobiologic Functions of Rhythm, Time, and Pulse in Music. In *Music, Mind, and Brain: The Neuropsychology of Music*, edited by M. Clynes (171–216). New York: Plenum Press.

Cockrell, D. 1997. *Demons of Disorder: Early Blackface Minstrels and Their World*. Cambridge: Cambridge University Press.

Collier, J. L. 1978. *The Making of Jazz*. New York: Dell.

———. 1983. *Louis Armstrong: An American Genius*. New York: Oxford University Press.

———. 1987. *Duke Ellington*. New York: Oxford University Press.

———. 1993. *Jazz: The American Theme Song*. New York: Oxford University Press.

Condon, W. S. 1974. Synchrony Demonstrated Between Movements of the Neonate and Adult Speech. *Child Development* 45: 456–62.

———. 1975. Multiple Response to Sound in Dysfunctional Children. *Journal of Autism and Childhood Schizophrenia* 5: 37–56.

———. 1986. Communication: Rhythm and Structure. In *Rhythm in Psychological, Linguistic and Musical Processes*, edited by J. R. Evans and M. Clynes (55–78). Springfield, IL: Charles C Thomas.

Coppens, Y. 1994. East Side Story: The Origin of Humankind. *Scientific American* 270(5): 88–95.

Costello, M., and D. F. Wallace. 1990. *Signifying Rappers: Rap and Race in the Urban Present*. New York: The Ecco Press.

Cox, A. 1999. The Metaphoric Logic of Musical Motion and Space. Dissertation. Eugene: University of Oregon.

Craddock-Willis, A., W. Marsalis, and J. L. Collier. 1995. Jazz People: Wynton Marsalis vs. James Lincoln Collier. *Transition* 65(1): 140–78.

Crafts, S. D., D. Cavicchi, and C. Keil. 1993. *My Music*. Hanover, NH: Wesleyan University Press.

Creel, M. W. 1990. Gullah Attitudes Toward Life and Death. In *Africanisms in American Culture*, edited by J. E. Holloway (69–97). Bloomington and Indianapolis: Indiana University Press.

Croft, W. 2000. *Explaining Language Change*. Harlow, England: Pearson Education.

Crosby, A. W. 1997. *The Measure of Reality: Quantification and Western Society, 1250–1600*. Cambridge: Cambridge University Press.

Csikszentmihalyi, M. 1990. *Flow: The Psychology of Optimal Experience*. New York: Harper & Row.

———. 1993. *The Evolving Self*. New York: HarperCollins.

Damasio, A. 1994. *Descartes' Error: Emotion, Reason, and the Human Brain*. New York: Avon Books.

———. 1999a. Commentary by Damasio. *Neuro-Psychoanalysis* 1: 38–40.

———. 1999b. *The Feeling of What Happens*. New York: Harcourt, Brace.

Danielson, V. 1997. *The Voice of Egypt*. Chicago: University of Chicago Press.

Darwin, C. 1998. *The Expression of the Emotions in Man and Animals*. New York: Oxford University Press.

Davies, S. 1997. Why Listen to Sad Music If It Makes One Feel Sad? In *Music and Meaning*, edited by J. Robinson (242–54). Ithaca: Cornell University Press.

Davis, F. 1996. *Bebop and Nothingness*. New York: Schirmer Books.

Dawkins, R. 1982. *The Extended Phenotype*. Oxford and New York: Oxford University Press.

———. 1989. *The Selfish Gene*. Oxford and New York: Oxford University Press.

Deacon, T. W. 1997. *The Symbolic Species: The Co-evolution of Language and the Brain*. New York: W. W. Norton.

Dehaene, S. 1997. *The Number Sense*. New York: Oxford University Press.

DeNora, T. 2000. *Music in Everyday Life*. Cambridge: Cambridge University Press.

Deren, M. 1953. *Divine Horsemen: The Living Gods of Haiti*. London: Thames and Hudson.

Deutsch, D., ed. 1999a. *The Psychology of Music*. San Diego: Academic Press.

———. 1999b. Grouping Mechanisms in Music. In *The Psychology of Music*, edited by D. Deutsch (299–348). San Diego: Academic Press.

DeVeaux, S. 1995. *Jazz in America: Who's Listening?* Carson, CA: National Endowment for the Arts, Seven Locks Press.

———. 1997. *The Birth of Bebop: A Social and Musical History*. Berkeley: University of California Press.

Diamond, J. 1997. *Guns, Germs, and Steel*. New York: W. W. Norton.

Dickinson, M. H., C. T. Farley et al. 2000. How Animals Move: An Integrative View. *Science* 288(5463): 100–106.

Diorio, C., and R. P. N. Rao. 2000. Neural Circuits in Silicon. *Nature* 405(6789): 891–92.

Donald, M. 1991. *Origins of the Modern Mind: Three Stages in the Evolution of Culture and Cognition*. Cambridge, MA: Harvard University Press.

Douglas, A. 1995. *Terrible Honesty: Mongrel Manhattan in the 1920s*. New York: Farrar, Straus and Giroux.

Douglas, M. 1973. *Natural Symbols*. New York: Random House.

Dudgeon, R. T., P. Easton et al. 1997. Playing, Learning, and Teaching Brass. In *The Cambridge Companion to Brass Instruments*, edited by T. Herbert and J. Wallace (193–206). Cambridge: Cambridge University Press.

Dudley, E., and M. E. Novak 1972. *The Wild Man Within*. Pittsburgh: University of Pittsburgh Press.

Dunbar, R., C. Knight, and C. Power, eds. 1999. *The Evolution of Culture*. New Brunswick, NJ: Rutgers University Press.

Durkheim, É. 1972 (1915). The Elementary Forms of the Religious Life. In *Reader in Comparative Religion*, edited by W. A. Lessa and E. Z. Vogt (28–36). New York: Harper and Row.

Edelman, G. M. 1992. *Bright Air, Brilliant Fire*. New York: Basic Books.

Ehrlich, P. 2000. *Human Natures: Genes, Cultures, and the Human Prospect*. Washington, DC, and Covelo, CA: Island Press.

Ekman, P., and W. V. Friesen. 1971. Constants Across Cultures in the Face and Emotion. *Journal of Personality and Social Psychology* 17: 125–27.

Elbert, T., and A. Keil. 2000. Imaging in the Fourth Dimension. *Nature* 404: 29–31.

Eliade, M. 1964. *Shamanism*. Princeton, NJ: Princeton University Press.

Ellington, E. K. 1973. *Music Is My Mistress*. New York: Da Capo Press.

Elman, J., E. A. Bates et al. 1996. *Rethinking Innateness: A Connectionist Perspective on Development*. Cambridge, MA: MIT Press.

Else, G. 1965. *The Origin and Form of Early Greek Tragedy*. Cambridge, MA: Harvard University Press.

Epstein, D. 1995. *Shaping Time*. New York: Schirmer Books.

Epstein, H. 1987. *Music Talks: Conversations with Musicians*. New York: McGraw-Hill.

Erickson, S. 2000. Neil Young on a Good Day. *The New York Times Magazine*, October 10, 26–29.

Erikson, E. H. 1950. *Childhood and Society*. New York: W. W. Norton.

———. 1968. *Identity, Youth, and Crisis*. New York: W. W. Norton.

———. 1982. *The Life Cycle Completed*. New York: W. W. Norton.

Evans, J. R. 1986. Dysrhythmia and Disorders of Learning and Behavior. In *Rhythm in Psychological, Linguistic and Musical Processes*, edited by J. R. Evans and M. Clynes (249–74). Springfield, IL: Charles C Thomas.

Evans, J. R., and M. Clynes, eds. 1986. *Rhythm in Psychological, Linguistic and Musical Processes*. Springfield, IL: Charles C Thomas.

Evans-Pritchard, E. E. 1940. *The Nuer*. New York: Oxford University Press.

———. 1956. *Nuer Religion*. New York: Oxford University Press.

Falk, D. 2000. Hominid Brain Evolution and the Origins of Music. In *The Origins of Music*, edited by N. L. Wallin, B. Merker, and S. Brown (197–216). Cambridge, MA: MIT Press.

Farmer, H. G. 1957. The Music of Islam. In *The New Oxford History of Music: Ancient and Oriental Music*, edited by E. Wellesz. Vol. 1 (419–77). London: Oxford University Press.

Feld, S. 1994. From Schizophonia to Schismogenesis: On the Discourses and Commodification Practices of "World Music" and "World Beat." In *Music Grooves*, edited by C. Keil and S. Feld (257–89). Chicago: University of Chicago Press.

Feld, S., and C. Keil. 1994. Dialogue 3: Commodified Grooves. In *Music Grooves*, edited by C. Keil and S. Feld (290–330). Chicago: University of Chicago Press.

Fell, J. L., and T. Vinding. 1999. *Stride!* Lanham, MD: Scarecrow Press.

Fischer, R. 1975. The Cartography of Inner Space. In *Hallucinations*, edited by R. K. Siegel and L. J. West (197–240). New York: John Wiley & Sons.

———. 1987. Emergence of Mind from Brain: The Biological Roots of the Hermeneutic Circle. *Diogenes* 138: 1–25.

Fox, R. 1967. *Kinship and Marriage*. Harmondsworth, Middlesex: Penguin Books.

Fredrickson, G. M. 1971. *The Black Image in the White Mind*. New York: Harper and Row.

———. 1988. *The Arrogance of Race*. Middletown, CT: Wesleyan University Press.

Freeman, W. J. 1995. *Societies of Brains: A Study in the Neuroscience of Love and Hate*. Hillsdale, NJ: Lawrence Erlbaum.

———. 1997. Happiness Doesn't Come in Bottles. *Journal of Consciousness Studies* 4: 67–70.

———. 1999a. Consciousness, Intentionality and Causality. In *Reclaiming Cognition*, edited by R. Núñez and W. J. Freeman (143–72). Bowling Green, OH: Imprint Academic.

———. 1999b. *How Brains Make Up Their Minds*. London: Weidenfeld and Nicholson.

———. 2000. A Neurobiological Role of Music in Social Bonding. In *The Origins of Music*, edited by N. L. Wallin, B. Merker, and S. Brown (411–24). Cambridge, MA: MIT Press.

Freud, S. 1962. *Civilization and Its Discontents*. New York: W. W. Norton.

Friedson, S. M. 1996. *Dancing Prophets: Musical Experience in Tumbuka Healing*. Chicago: University of Chicago Press.

Frith, S. 1996. Music and Identity. In *Questions of Cultural Identity*, edited by S. Hall and P. de Gay (108–27). London: Sage Publications.

Fuld, J. J. 2000. *The Book of World-Famous Music: Classical, Popular, and Folk*. New York: Dover Publications.

Furst, P. T., ed. 1972. *Flesh of the Gods*. New York: Praeger.

Gabrielsson, A. 1986. Rhythm in Music. In *Rhythm in Psychological, Linguistic and Musical Processes*, edited by J. R. Evans and M. Clynes (131–68). Springfield, IL: Charles C Thomas.

———. 1999. The Performance of Music. In *The Psychology of Music*, edited by D. Deutsch (501–602). San Diego: Academic Press.

Gabunia, L., A. Vekuna et al. 2000. Earliest Pleistocene Hominid Cranial Remains from Dmanisi, Republik of Georgia: Taxonomy, Setting, and Age. *Science* 288(5468): 1019–26.

Gallese, V., and A. Goldman. 1998. Mirror Neurons and the Simulation Theory of Mind-Reading. *Trends in Cognitive Sciences* 2(12): 493–501.

Gallistel, C. R. 1981. Multiple Book Review of "The Organization of Action": A New Synthesis. *Behavioral and Brain Sciences* 4(4): 609–50.

———. 1990. Representation in Animal Cognition: An Introduction. *Cognition* 37: 1–22.

Gardner, P. 1967. Vico, Giambattista. In *Encyclopedia of Philosophy*, edited by P. Edwards. Vol. 8 (247–51). New York: Collier MacMillan.

Garraty, J. A., and P. Gay, eds. 1981. *The Columbia History of the World*. New York: Harper and Row.

Gates, H. L. J. 1988. *The Signifying Monkey*. New York and Oxford: Oxford University Press.

Gay, P. 1993. *The Cultivation of Hatred*. New York: W. W. Norton.

Geist, V. 1978. *Life Strategies, Human Evolution, Environmental Design: Toward a Biological Theory of Health*. New York: Springer-Verlag.

Gellner, E. 1983. *Nations and Nationalism*. Ithaca: Cornell University Press.

Gendron, B. 1995. "Moldy Figs" and Modernists: Jazz at War (1942–1946). In *Jazz Among the Discourses*, edited by K. Gabbard (31–56). Durham, NC: Duke University Press.

George, N. 1988. *The Death of Rhythm and Blues*. New York: Penguin Books.

———. 1992. *Buppies, B-Boys, Baps & Bohos*. New York: HarperCollins.

Gibbon, J., and R. M. Church. 1990. Representation of Time. *Cognition* 37: 23–54.

Gillespie, D., and A. Fraser. 1979. *To Be or Not to Bop*. New York: Doubleday.

Gioia, T. 1997. *The History of Jazz*. New York: Oxford University Press.

Gioscia, V. 1971. On Social Time. In *The Future of Time*, edited by H. Yaker, H. Osmond, and F. Cheek (73–141). Garden City, NY: Doubleday.

Gitler, I. 1985. *Swing to Bop*. New York: Oxford University Press.

Gjerdingen, R. O. 1992. Revisiting Meyer's "Grammatical Simplicity and Relational Richness." In *Cognitive Bases of Musical Communication*, edited by M. R. Jones and S. Holleran (225–43). Washington, DC: American Psychological Association.

———. 1999. Apparent Motion in Music? In *Musical Networks: Parallel Distributed Perception and Performance*, edited by N. Griffith and P. M. Todd (141–74). Cambridge, MA: MIT Press.

Glass, L. 2001. Synchronization and Rhythmic Processes in Physiology. *Nature* 410: 277–84.

Glass, L., and M. C. Mackey. 1988. *From Clocks to Chaos: The Rhythms of Life*. Princeton, NJ: Princeton University Press.

Golledge, R. G. 1999. Human Wayfinding and Cognitive Maps. In *Wayfinding Behavior: Cognitive Mapping and Other Spatial Processes*, edited by R. G. Golledge (5–45). Baltimore: Johns Hopkins University Press.

Gombrich, E. 1951. *The Story of Art*. New York: Phaidon.

Gould, S. J. 1977. *Ontogeny and Phylogeny*. Cambridge, MA: Harvard University Press.

Graburn, N., ed. 1971. *Readings in Kinship and Social Structure*. New York: Harper and Row.

Gray, J., and N. McNaughton. 1996. The Neuropsychology of Anxiety: Reprise. *Perspectives on Anxiety, Panic, & Fear*, Vol. 43, edited by D. Hope (61–134). Lincoln: University of Nebraska Press.

Griffel, L. M. 1982. The Romantic and Post-Romantic Eras. In *Schirmer History of Music*, edited by L. Rosenstiel. New York: Schirmer Books.

Grout, D. J., and C. V. Palisca. 1996. *A History of Western Music*. New York: W. W. Norton.

Guralnick, P. 1994. *Last Train to Memphis: The Rise of Elvis Presley*. Boston: Little, Brown.

———. 1999. *Careless Love: The Unmaking of Elvis Presley*. Boston: Little, Brown.

Gwaltney, J. L. 1993. *Drylongso*. New York: The New Press.

Hahnloser, R. H. R., R. Sarpeshkar et al. 2000. Digital Selection and Analogue Amplification Coexist in a Cortex-Inspired Silicon Circuit. *Nature* 405(6789): 947–51.

Haken, H. 1996. *Principles of Brain Functioning*. Berlin, Heidelberg, New Haven: Springer-Verlag.

Hale, J. 1994. *The Civilization of Europe in the Renaissance*. New York: Atheneum.

Hall, R. L. 1990. African Religious Retentions in Florida. In *Africanisms in American Culture*, edited by J. E. Holloway (98–118). Bloomington and Indianapolis: Indiana University Press.

Handy, W. C. 1941. *Father of the Blues*. New York: Macmillan.

Harlow, H. F., and M. K. Harlow. 1970. Developmental Aspects of Emotional Behavior. In *Physiological Correlates of Emotion*, edited by P. Black (37–60). New York: Academic Press.

Harmetz, A. 1988. How a Rabbit Was Framed. *New York Times*, June 19, 1, 12.

Harrington, D. L., and K. Y. Haaland. 1998. Sequencing and Timing Operations of the Basal Ganglia. In *Timing of Behavior*, edited by D. A. Rosenbaum and C. E. Collyer (35–62). Cambridge, MA: MIT Press.

Harrington, D. L., K. Y. Haaland, and R. T. Knight. 1998. Cortical Networks Underlying Mechanisms of Time Perception. *Journal of Neuroscience* 18(3): 1085–95.

Harrington, W. 1992. *Crossings: A White Man's Journey into Black America*. New York: HarperCollins.

Harris, M. 1977. *Cannibals and Kings*. New York: Random House.

Hart, M. 1990. *Drumming at the Edge of Magic*. New York: HarperCollins.

Hauser, M. D. 1993. Right Hemisphere Dominance for Production of Facial Expression in a Monkey. *Science* 261: 475–77.

Havelock, E. A. 1982. *The Literate Revolution in Greece and Its Cultural Consequences*. Princeton, NJ: Princeton University Press.

Hays, D. G. 1973. The Meaning of a Term Is a Function of the Theory in Which It Occurs. *SIGLASH Newsletter* 6: 8–11.

———. 1976. On Alienation: An Essay in the Psycholinguistics of Science. In *Theories of Alienation*, edited by R. R. Geyer and D. R. Scheitzer (169–87). Leiden: Martinus Nijhoff.

———. 1992. The Evolution of Expressive Culture. *Journal of Social and Biological Structures* 15: 187–215.

———. 1993. *The Evolution of Technology Through Four Cognitive Ranks*. New York: Metagram Press.

————. 1997. *The Measurement of Cultural Evolution in the Non-Literate World: Homage to Raoul Naroll.* New York: Metagram Press.

Hays, D. G., E. Margolis et al. 1972. Color Term Salience. *American Anthropologist* 24: 1107–21.

Hazeltine, E., L. L. Helmuth, and R. Ivry. 1997. Neural Mechanisms of Timing. *Trends in Cognitive Sciences* 1: 163–69.

Hellige, J. B. 1993. *Hemispheric Asymmetry.* Cambridge, MA: Harvard University Press.

Herbert, T. 1997. Brass Bands and Other Vernacular Brass Traditions. In *The Cambridge Companion to Brass Instruments*, edited by T. Herbert and J. Wallace (177–92). Cambridge: Cambridge University Press.

Hernton, C. C. 1965. *Sex and Racism in America.* New York: Grove Weidenfeld.

Heron, W. 1967. The Pathology of Boredom. In *Psychobiology: The Biological Bases of Behavior*, edited by J. L. McGaugh, N. M. Weinberger, and R. E. Whalen (178–82). San Francisco and London: W. H. Freeman.

Herskovitz, M. J. 1988. *The Myth of the Negro Past.* Boston: Beacon Press.

Hirt, A. 1958. *Al Hirt at Dan's Pier 600.* Audio Fidelity AFLP 1877.

Hobart, M. E., and Z. S. Schiffman. 1998. *Information Ages.* Baltimore: Johns Hopkins University Press.

Hobsbawm, E. J. 1993. *The Jazz Scene.* New York: Pantheon.

————. 1994. *The Age of Extremes: A History of the World, 1914–1991.* New York: Pantheon.

Hobson, J. A. 1995. *Sleep.* New York: Scientific American Library.

————. 1999a. *Consciousness.* New York: Scientific American Library.

————. 1999b. The New Neuropsychology of Sleep: Implications for Psychoanalysis. *Neuro-Psychoanalysis* 1: 157–83.

Hockett, C. 1967. The Origin of Speech. In *Human Variation and Origins*, edited by W. S. Laughlin and R. H. Osborne (183–90). San Francisco and London: W. H. Freeman.

Hodges, D. A. 1996. Neuromusical Research: A Review of the Literature. In *Handbook of Music Psychology*, edited by D. A. Hodges (197–285). San Antonio, TX: IMR Press.

Hodgson, M. 1993. *Rethinking World History.* Cambridge: Cambridge University Press.

Hoffman, R. E. 1992. Attractor Neural Networks and Psychotic Disorders. *Psychiatric Annals* 22: 119–24.

Hoffmann, E. T. A. 1810. Review of the Fifth Symphony. In *Beethoven: Symphony No. 5 in C minor*, edited by E. Forbes (150–63). New York: W. W. Norton.

Holloway, J. E., ed. 1990. *Africanisms in American Culture.* Bloomington and Indianapolis: Indiana University Press.

Holm, N. G. 1982. *Religious Ecstasy.* Stockholm: Almqvist & Wiksell International.

Hope, D., ed. 1996. *Perspectives on Anxiety, Panic, & Fear.* Lincoln: University of Nebraska Press.

Horowitz, H. 1990. The American Jazz Audience. In *New Perspectives on Jazz*, edited by D. Baker (1–8). Washington, DC, and London: Smithsonian Institution Press.

Hull, D. L. 1988. *Science as a Process*. Chicago: University of Chicago Press.

Huron, D. 2000. Is Music an Evolutionary Adaptation? Conference on *The Biological Foundations of Music*. New York: New York Academy of Sciences.

Hurston, Z. N. 1938. Tell My Horse. In *Hurston: Folklore, Memoirs, & Other Writings*, edited by C. A. Wall (269–555). New York: The Library of America.

Hutchins, E. 1995. *Cognition in the Wild*. Cambridge, MA: MIT Press.

Ishai, A., and D. Sagi. 1995. Common Mechanisms of Visual Imagery and Perception. *Science* 268(5218): 1772–75.

Ivry, R. B. 1996. The Representation of Temporal Information in Perception and Motor Control. *Current Opinion in Neurobiology* 6: 851–57.

Izard, C. E. 1971. *The Face of Emotion*. New York: Appleton-Century-Crofts.

———. 1977. *Human Emotions*. New York: Plenum Press.

Izard, C. E., and E. A. Youngstrom. 1996. The Activation and Regulation of Fear and Anxiety. In *Perspectives on Anxiety, Panic, & Fear*, edited by D. Hope. Vol. 43 (1–60). Lincoln: University of Nebraska Press.

Jackson, B. 1974. *Get Your Ass in the Water and Swim Like Me*. Cambridge, MA: Harvard University Press.

James, W. 1890. *The Principles of Psychology*. New York: Henry Holt.

Jaynes, J. 1967. *The Origin of Consciousness in the Breakdown of the Bicameral Mind*. Boston: Houghton Mifflin.

Jeffrey, P. 1992. *Re-Envisioning Past Musical Cultures: Ethnomusicology in the Study of Gregorian Chant*. Chicago: University of Chicago Press.

Jerison, H. J. 1976. Paleoneurology and the Evolution of Mind. *Scientific American* 234(1): 90–101.

Jerome, J. 1980. *The Sweet Spot in Time*. New York: Avon.

Johnson, D. M., and R. R. Campbell. 1981. *Black Migration America*. Durham, NC: Duke University Press.

Johnson, M. H. 1997. *Developmental Cognitive Neuroscience*. Oxford: Blackwell.

Jones, M. R. 1976. "Time, Our Lost Dimension: Toward a New Theory of Perception, Attention, and Memory." *Psychological Review* 83: 323–54.

———. 1992. Attending to Musical Events. In *Cognitive Bases of Musical Communication*, edited by M. R. Jones and S. Holleran (91–110). Washington, DC: American Psychological Association.

Jordan, W. 1974. *The White Man's Burden*. New York: Oxford University Press.

Jourdain, R. 1997. *Music, the Brain, and Ecstasy*. New York: Avon Books.

Karnataka College of Percussion. 1993. *Charlie Mariano and the Karnataka College of Percussion*. New York, Intuition Records, Inc. INT 2034 2.

———. 1997. *River Yamuna*. Chapel Hill, NC, Music of the World. MOW145.

Katz, B. E. 1999. An Ear for Melody. In *Musical Networks: Parallel Distributed Perception and Performance*, edited by N. Griffith and P. M. Todd (199–224). Cambridge, MA: MIT Press.

Kay, R. F., M. Cartmill, and M. Balow. 1998. The Hypoglossal Canal and the Origin of Human Vocal Behavior. *Proceedings of the National Academy of Sciences* 95: 5417–19.

Keil, C. 1991. *Urban Blues*. Chicago and London: University of Chicago Press.

————. 1994a. Motion and Feeling through Music. In *Music Grooves*, edited by C. Keil and S. Feld (53–76). Chicago: University of Chicago Press.

————. 1994b. People's Music Comparatively: Style and Stereotype, Class and Hegemony. In *Music Grooves*, edited by C. Keil and S. Feld (197–217). Chicago: University of Chicago Press.

————. 1995. The Theory of Participatory Discrepancies: A Progress Report. *Ethnomusicology* 39(1): 1–20.

————. 2000. Groovology and the Magic of Other People's Music. Typescript.

Keil, C., and S. Feld. 1994. *Music Grooves*. Chicago: University of Chicago Press.

Kelly, T. F. 2000. *First Nights: Five Musical Premieres*. New Haven and London: Yale University Press.

Kelso, J. A. S. 1995. *Dynamic Patterns: The Self-Organization of Brain and Behavior*. Cambridge, MA: MIT Press.

Kierkegaard, S. 1954. *Fear and Trembling and The Sickness Unto Death*. New York: Anchor Books.

Kilmer, W. L., W. S. McCulloch, and J. Blum. 1969. A Model of the Vertebrate Central Command System. *International Journal of Man-Machine Studies* 1: 279–309.

Kirk, R. R. 1969. *Volunteered Slavery*. Rhino R2 71407.

————. 1970. *Live in Paris, 1970*. Vol. 2. Esoldun–INA FCD 115.

————. 1973. *Bright Moments*. Atlantic SD 2–907.

Klein, R. G. 1999. *The Human Career*. Chicago: University of Chicago Press.

Kluckohn, C. 1972. Myths and Rituals. In *Reader in Comparative Religion*, edited by W. A. Lessa and E. Z. Vogt (93–105). New York: Harper and Row.

Knobloch, F. 1996. Musical Experience as Interpersona Process: Revisited. *Contemporary Music Review* 17(Part 2): 59–72.

Knobloch, F., M. Postolka, and J. Srnec. 1964. Musical Experience as Interpersonal Process. *Psychiatry: Journal for the Study of Interpersonal Processes* 27(4): 259–65.

Köhler, W. 1947. *Gestalt Psychology*. New York: Liverright.

Kosslyn, S. M., and O. Koenig. 1995. *Wet Mind: The New Cognitive Neuroscience*. New York: The Free Press.

Kovel, J. 1984. *White Racism: A Psychohistory*. New York: Columbia University Press.

Krystal, J. H., A. Bennett et al. 1996. Recent Development in the Neurobiology of Dissociation: Implications for Posttraumatic Stress Disorder. In *The Handbook of Dissociation*, edited by L. K. M. W. J. Ray (163–90). New York: Plenum Press.

La Barre, W. 1972. *The Ghost Dance*. New York: Dell.

Lakoff, G. 1987. *Women, Fire, and Dangerous Things*. Chicago: University of Chicago Press.

————. 1996. Sorry, I'm Not Myself Today: The Metaphor System for Conceptualizing the Self. In *Spaces, Worlds, and Grammar*, edited by G. Fauconnier and E. Sweetser (91–123). Chicago: University of Chicago Press.

Lakoff, G., and M. Johnson. 1999. *Philosophy in the Flesh*. New York: Basic Books.

Lamb, S. M. 1999. *Pathways of the Brain*. Amsterdam: John Benjamins B. V.

Langer, S. K. 1953. *Feeling and Form*. New York: Charles Scribner and Sons.

Large, E. W., and J. F. Kolen. 1999. Resonance and the Perception of Meter. In *Musical Networks: Parallel Distributed Perception and Performance*, edited by N. Griffith and P. M. Todd (65–96). Cambridge, MA: MIT Press.

Large, E. W., C. Palmer, and J. Pollack. 1999. Reduced Memory Representation for Music. In *Musical Networks: Parallel Distributed Perception and Performance*, edited by N. Griffith and P. M. Todd (279–312). Cambridge, MA: MIT Press.

Leach, E. R. 1972. Two Essays Concerning the Symbolic Representation of Time. In *Reader in Comparative Religion*, edited by W. A. Lessa and E. Z. Vogt (108–16). New York: Harper and Row.

Lecanuet, J-P. 1996. Prenatal Auditory Experience. In *Musical Beginnings*, edited by I. Deliège and J. Sloboda (3–34). Oxford: Oxford University Press.

LeDoux, J. 1996. *The Emotional Brain*. New York: Simon and Schuster.

Lees, G. 1995. *Jazz, Black and White*. New York: Oxford University Press.

Leland, W. E., M. S. Taqqu et al. 1995. On the Self Similar Nature of Ethernet Traffic. *IEEE/ACM Transactions on Networking* 2(1): 1–15.

Leng, X., and G. L. Shaw. 1991. Toward a Neural Theory of Higher Brain Function Using Music as a Window. *Concepts in Neuroscience* 2(2): 229–58.

Lerdahl, F., and R. Jackendoff. 1983. *A Generative Theory of Tonal Music*. Cambridge, MA: MIT Press.

Lévi-Strauss, C. 1969. *The Elementary Structures of Kinship*. Boston: Beacon Press.

Levine, L. W. 1977. *Black Culture and Black Consciousness*. New York: Oxford University Press.

Levinson, D. 1980. Subsistence Systems as a Measure of Cultural Complexity. *Current Anthropology* 21: 128–29.

Levinson, J. 1997. Music and Negative Emotion. In *Music and Meaning*, edited by J. Robinson (215–41). Ithaca: Cornell University Press.

Lewis, I. M. 1989. *Ecstatic Religion: A Study of Shamanism and Spirit Possession*. London: Routledge.

Lewis, R. W. B. 1955. *The American Adam*. Chicago: University of Chicago Press.

Lhamon, W. T. J. 1998. *Raising Cain: Blackface Performance from Jim Crow to Hip Hop*. Cambridge, MA: Harvard University Press.

Lieberman, P. 1998. *Eve Spoke: Human Language and Human Evolution*. New York: W. W. Norton.

Lincoln, C. E., and L. H. Mamiya. 1990. *The Black Church in the African American Experience*. Durham and London: Duke University Press.

Lindsley, D. B. 1970. The Role of Nonspecific Reticulo-Thalamo-Cortical Systems in Emotion. In *Physiological Correlates of Emotion*, edited by P. Black (147–88). New York: Academic Press.

Linton, R. 1971. Status and Role. In *Readings in Kinship and Social Structure*, edited by N. Graburn (291–96). New York: Harper and Row.

Lipsitz, G. 1994. *Dangerous Crossroads*. London and New York: Verso.

Lomax, A. 1968. *Folk Song Style and Culture*. New Brunswick: Transaction.

———. 1973. *Mister Jelly Roll*. Berkeley: University of California Press.

Lord, A. B. 1960. *The Singer of Tales*. Cambridge, MA: Harvard University Press.

Lott, E. 1993. *Love & Theft: Blackface Minstrelsy and the American Working Class*. New York: Oxford University Press.

Luria, A. R. 1959a. The Directive Function of Speech in Development and Dissolution I. *Word* 15: 341–52.

———. 1959b. The Directive Function of Speech in Development and Dissolution II. *Word* 15: 453–64.

———. 1973. *The Working Brain*. New York: Basic Books.

Lutz, T. 1999. *Crying: The Natural & Cultural History of Tears*. New York: W. W. Norton.

MacLean, P. D. 1970. The Limbic Brain in Relation to the Psychoses. In *Physiological Correlates of Emotion*, edited by P. Black (130–46). New York: Academic Press.

———. 1978. The Evolution of Three Mentalities. In *Human Evolution: Biosocial Perspectives*, edited by S. L. Washburn and E. R. McCown (33–58). Menlo Park, CA: Benjamin/Cummings.

———. 1990. *The Triune Brain in Evolution*. New York: Plenum Press.

Mandler, G. 1975. *Mind and Emotion*. New York: John Wiley & Sons.

Marin, O. S. M., and D. W. Perry. 1999. Neurological Aspects of Music Perception and Performance. In *The Psychology of Music*, edited by D. Deutsch (653–724). San Diego: Academic Press.

Martin, L., and K. Segrave. 1992. *Anti-Rock: The Opposition to Rock 'n' Roll*. New York: Da Capo Press.

Martindale, C. 1990. *The Clockwork Muse: The Predictability of Artistic Change*. New York: Basic Books.

Masterman, M. 1970. The Nature of a Paradigm. In *Criticism and the Growth of Knowledge*, edited by I. Lakatos and A. Musgrave (59–123). Cambridge: Cambridge University Press.

Maultsby, P. K. 1990. Africanisms in African-American Music. In *Africanisms in American Culture*, edited by J. E. Holloway (185–210). Bloomington and Indianapolis: Indiana University Press.

Maus, F. E. 1997. Music as Drama. In *Music and Meaning*, edited by J. Robinson (105–30). Ithaca: Cornell University Press.

Maxwell, R. J. 1971. Anthropological Perspectives. In *The Future of Time*, edited by H. Yaker, H. Osmond, and F. Cheek (36–72). Garden City, NY: Doubleday.

McClary, S. 1991. *Feminine Endings: Music, Gender, and Sexuality*. Minneapolis: University of Minnesota Press.

McGrath, J. E., and J. R. Kelly. 1986. *Time & Human Interaction*. New York: Guilford Press.

McNeill, R. 1970. *The Acquisition of Language*. New York: Harper & Row.

McNeill, W. H. 1963. *The Rise of the West: A History of the Human Community*. Chicago: University of Chicago Press.

———. 1995. *Keeping Together in Time: Dance and Drill in Human History*. Cambridge, MA: Harvard University Press.

———. 2000. A Short History of Humanity. *New York Review of Books*, June 29, 9–11.

Mead, G. H. 1934. *Mind, Self, and Society.* Chicago: University of Chicago Press.

Meltzer, D., ed. 1993. *Reading Jazz.* San Francisco: Mercury House.

Melzack, R. 1973. *The Puzzle of Pain.* New York: Basic Books.

Memetics discussion list. N. d. *Journal of Memetics.* Available at http://www.cpm. mmu.ac.uk/jom-emit/memetics/about.html.

Menuhin, Y. 1986. *The Compleat Violinist.* New York: Summit Books.

Merriam, A. P. 1964. *The Anthropology of Music.* Evanston, IL: Northwestern University Press.

———. 1973. The Bala Musician. In *The Traditional Artist in African Societies,* edited by W. L. d'Azevedo (250–81). Bloomington and Indianapolis: Indiana University Press.

Meyer, L. B. 1956. *Emotion and Meaning in Music.* Chicago: University of Chicago Press.

Miller, G. A. 1967. The Magical Number Seven, Plus or Minus Two: Some Limits on Our Capacity for Processing Information. In *The Psychology of Communication* (14–44). New York: Basic Books.

Miller, G. A., E. Galanter, and K. H. Pribram. 1960. *Plans and the Structure of Behavior.* New York: Holt, Rinehart and Winston.

Milner, P. M. 1970. *Physiological Psychology.* New York: Holt, Rinehart and Winston.

Miyashita, Y. 1995. How the Brain Creates Imagery: Projection to Primary Visual Cortex. *Science* 268(5218): 1719–22.

Morgan, L. N. d. *Caramba!* Blue Note BST 82489.

Moruzzi, G., and H. W. Magoun. 1949. Brain Stem Reticular Formation and Activation of the EEG. *Electroencephalography and Clinical Neurophysiology* 1: 455–73.

Mountcastle, V. B. 1998. *Perceptual Neuroscience: The Cerebral Cortex.* Cambridge, MA: Harvard University Press.

Mowshowitz, A. 1992. Virtual Feudalism: A Vision of Political Organization in the Information Age. *Informatization and the Public Sector* 2: 213–31.

———. 1994. Virtual Organization: A Vision of Management in the Information Age. *The Information Society* 10: 267–88.

———. 1997. Virtual Organization. *Communications of the ACM* 40(9): 30–37.

Mulira, J. G. 1990. The Case of Voodoo in New Orleans. In *Africanisms in American Culture,* edited by J. E. Holloway (34–68). Bloomington and Indianapolis: Indiana University Press.

Narayanan, S. 1997. Embodiment in Language Understanding: Sensor-Motor Representations for Metaphoric Reasoning About Event Descriptions. Dissertation, Department of Computer Science, University of California–Berkeley.

Naroll, R., and R. Cohen, eds. 1970. *A Handbook of Method in Cultural Anthropology.* Garden City, NY: The Natural History Press.

Néda, Z., E. Ravasz et al. 2000. The Sound of Many Hands Clapping. *Nature* 403: 849–50.

Neisser, U. 1966. *Cognitive Psychology.* New York: Appleton-Century-Crofts.

———. 1976. *Cognition and Reality.* San Francisco: W. H. Freeman.

Nelson, J. A. N. 1997. Lullabies as Human Adaptation: A Cross-Cultural Analysis of Children's Bedtime Songs. In *Music in Human Adaptation*, edited by D. J. Schneck and J. K. Schneck (61–78). Blacksburg: Virginia Polytechnic Institute and State University College of Engineering.

Nettl, B. 1983. *The Study of Ethnomusicology*. Urbana and Chicago: University of Illinois Press.

———. 2000. An Ethnomusicologist Contemplates Universals in Musical Sound and Musical Culture. In *The Origins of Music,* edited by N. L. Wallin, B. Merker, and S. Brown (463–472). Cambridge, MA: MIT Press.

Neuman, D. M. 1990. *The Life of Music in North India*. Chicago: University of Chicago Press.

Nietzsche, F. 1967. *The Birth of Tragedy and The Case of Wagner*. New York: Vintage Books.

O'Keefe, J. O., and L. Nadel. 1979. Multiple Book Review of J. O. O'Keefe & L. Nadel: The Hippocampus as a Cognitive Map. *Behavioral and Brain Sciences* 2(4): 487–534.

Oliver, P. 1970. *Savannah Syncopators: African Retentions in the Blues*. New York: Stein and Day.

Olson, M. 1971. *The Logic of Collective Action*. Cambridge, MA: Harvard University Press.

Opler, M. 1960. Cultural Evolution and the Psychology of Peoples. In *Essays in the Science of Culture*, edited by G. E. Dole and R. L. Carneiro (354–79). New York: Thomas Y. Crowell.

Orbach, J. 1999. *Sound and Music*. Lanham, MD: University Press of America.

Oubré, A. Y. 1997. *Instinct and Revelation*. Amsterdam: Gordon and Breach.

Owens, T. 1995. *Bebop: The Music and Its Players*. New York: Oxford University Press.

Panksepp, J. 1995. The Emotional Sources of "Chills" Induced by Music. *Music Perception* 13(2): 171–207.

———. 1998. *Affective Neuroscience*. New York: Oxford University Press.

———. 1999. Emotions as Viewed by Psychoanalysis and Neuroscience: An Exercise in Consilience. *Neuro-Psychoanalysis* 1: 15–38.

Parkes, C. M., and J. Stevenson-Hinde. 1982. *The Place of Attachment in Human Behavior*. New York: Basic Books.

Parsons, T. 1964. *Essays in Sociological Theory*. New York: The Free Press.

Passingham, R. 1993. *The Frontal Lobes and Voluntary Action*. Oxford: Oxford University Press.

Patel, A. D., and E. Balaban. 2000. Temporal Patterns of Human Cortical Activity Reflect Tone Sequence Structure. *Nature* 404: 80–84.

Peretti, B. W. 1992. *The Creation of Jazz: Music, Race, and Culture in Urban America*. Urbana and Chicago: University of Illinois Press.

Perper, T. 1985. *Sex Signals: The Biology of Love*. Philadelphia: ISI Press.

Petersen, S. E., H. van Mier et al. 1998. The Effects of Practice on the Functional Anatomy of Task Performance. *Proceedings of the National Academy of Sciences* 95: 853–60.

Philips, J. E. 1990. The African Heritage of White America. In *Africanisms in American Culture*, edited by M. Halle (225–39). Bloomington and Indianapolis: Indiana University Press.

Piaget, J. 1971. *Biology and Knowledge: An Essay on the Relations Between Organic Regulations and Cognitive Processes*. Chicago: University of Chicago Press.

———. 1976. *The Grasp of Consciousness*. Cambridge, MA: Harvard University Press.

Piaget, J., and R. Garcia. 1974. *Understanding Causality*. New York: W. W. Norton.

Pierce, J. R. 1999. The Nature of Musical Sound. In *The Psychology of Music*, edited by D. Deutsch (1–20). San Diego: Academic Press.

Pinker, S. 1994. *The Language Instinct*. New York: William Morrow.

———. 1997. *How the Mind Works*. New York: W. W. Norton.

Piston, W. 1947. *Counterpoint*. New York: W. W. Norton.

———. 1962. *Harmony*. New York: W. W. Norton.

Pittendrigh, C. 1971. On Temporal Organization in Living Systems. In *The Future of Time*, edited by H. Yaker, H. Osmond, and F. Cheek (179–218). Garden City, NY: Doubleday.

Porges, S. W. 1999. Emotion: An Evolutionary By-Product of the Neural Regulation of the Autonomic Nervous System. In *The Integrative Neurobiology of Affiliation*, edited by C. S. Carter, I. Lederhendler, and B. Kirkpatrick (65–80). Cambridge, MA: MIT Press.

Port, R. F., F. Cummins, and J. D. McAuley 1995. Naive Time, Temporal Patterns, and Human Audition. In *Mind as Motion: Explorations in the Dynamics of Cognition*, edited by R. F. Port and T. van Gelder (339–72). Cambridge, MA: MIT Press.

Posner, M. I., and M. E. Raichle. 1997. *Images of Mind*. New York: Scientific American Library.

Powers, W. T. 1973. *Behavior: The Control of Perception*. Chicago: Aldine de Gruyter.

———. 1989. *Living Control Systems*. Gravel Switch: The Control Systems Group.

Pribram, K. 1971. *Languages of the Brain*. Englewood Cliffs, NJ: Prentice-Hall.

Prigogine, I., and I. Stengers. 1984. *Order Out of Chaos*. New York: Bantam Books.

Prögler, J. A. 1995. Searching for Swing: Participatory Discrepancies in the Jazz Rhythm Section. *Ethnomusicology* 39(1): 21–54.

Propp, V. 1968. *Morphology of the Folktale*. Austin and London: University of Texas Press.

Rao, S. M., D. L. Harrington et al. 1997. Distributed Neural Systems Underlying the Timing of Movements. *Journal of Neuroscience* 17(14): 5528–45.

Rasch, R., and R. Plomp. 1999. The Perception of Musical Tones. In *The Psychology of Music*, edited by D. Deutsch (89–112). San Diego: Academic Press.

Rasula, J. 1995. The Media of Memory: The Seductive Menace of Records in Jazz History. In *Jazz Among the Discourses*, edited by K. Gabbard (134–62). Durham, NC: Duke University Press.

Reck, D. 1996. India/South India. In *Worlds of Music*, edited by J. T. Titon (252–315). New York: Schirmer Books.

———. 1997. *Music of the Whole World*. New York: Da Capo Press.

Reddy, M. J. 1993. The Conduit Metaphor: A Case of Frame Conflict in Our Language About Language. In *Metaphor and Thought*, edited by A. Ortony (164–201). Cambridge: Cambridge University Press.

Redish, D. A. 1999. *Beyond the Cognitive Map*. Cambridge, MA: MIT Press.

Repp, B. 1998. Musical Motion in Perception and Performance. In *Timing of Behavior*, edited by D. A. Rosenbaum and C. E. Collyer (125–44). Cambridge, MA: MIT Press.

Reti, R. 1958. *Tonality, Atonality, Pantonality*. Westport, CT: Greenwood Press.

Rider, M. S., and C. T. Eagle, Jr. 1986. Rhythmic Entrainment as a Mechanism for Learning in Music Therapy. In *Rhythm in Psychological, Linguistic, and Musical Processes,* edited by J. R. Evans and M. Clynes (225–248). Springfield, IL: Charles C Thomas.

Risset, J-C., and D. L. Wessel. 1999. Exploration of Timbre by Analysis by Synthesis. In *The Psychology of Music*, edited by D. Deutsch (113–70). San Diego: Academic Press.

Rizzolatti, G., and M. Arbib. 1998. Language Within Our Grasp. *Trends in Neuroscience* 21: 188–94.

Roberts, J. S. 1999. *The Latin Tinge: The Impact of Latin American Music on the United States*. New York: Oxford University Press.

Robinson, J. P. 1993. *Arts Participation in America: 1982–1991,* Research report no. 27. Washington, DC: Research Division, National Endowment for the Arts.

Rose, T. 1994. *Black Noise: Rap Music and Black Culture in Contemporary America*. Hanover and London: Wesleyan University Press and University Press of New England.

Rosenbaum, D. A. 1998. Broadcast Theory of Timing. In *Timing of Behavior*, edited by D. A. Rosenbaum and C. E. Collyer (215–36). Cambridge, MA: MIT Press.

Rouget, G. 1985. *Music and Trance*. Chicago: University of Chicago Press.

Russell, B. 1945. *A History of Western Philosophy*. New York: Simon and Schuster.

Ryle, G. 1949. *The Concept of Mind*. Chicago: University of Chicago Press.

Sachs, C. 1965. *The Wellsprings of Music*. New York: McGraw-Hill.

Sackheim, E., ed. 1993. *The Blues: A Collection of Blues Lyrics from Leadbelly to Muddy Waters*. Hopewell, NJ: The Ecco Press.

Sacks, O. 1990. *Awakenings*. New York: HarperPerennial.

Sakai, K., O. Hikosaka et al. 1999. Neural Representation of a Rhythm Depends on Its Interval Ratio. *Journal of Neuroscience* 19(2): 10074–81.

Saltzman, E. L. 1995. Dynamics and Coordinate Systems in Skilled Sensorimotor Activity. In *Mind as Motion: Explorations in the Dynamics of Cognition*, edited by R. F. Port and T. van Gelder (149–74). Cambridge, MA: MIT Press.

Samuels, D. 1991. The Rap on Rap. *The New Republic* 205: 24–29.

Sarnthein, J., A. von Stein et al. 1997. Persistent Patterns of Brain Activity: An EEG Coherence Study of the Positive Effect of Music on Spatial-Temporal Reasoning. *Neurological Research* 19(April): 107–16.

Schachtel 1959. *Metamorphosis*. New York: Basic Books.

Schäfer, C., M. G. Rosenblum et al. 1998. Heartbeat Synchronized with Ventilation. *Nature* 392: 239–40.

Schenker, H. 1973. *Harmony*. Cambridge, MA: MIT Press.

Schuller, G. 1968. *Early Jazz*. New York and Oxford: Oxford University Press.

———. 1989. *Swing*. New York: W. W. Norton.

Seashore, C. E. 1967. *Psychology of Music*. New York: Dover Publications.

Segal, R. A., ed. 1998. *The Myth and Ritual Theory*. Oxford: Blackwell.

Selverston, A. I. 1980. Are Central Pattern Generators Understandable? *Behavioral and Brain Sciences* 3(4): 535–72.

Serafine, M. L. 1988. *Music as Cognition*. New York: Columbia University Press.

Service, E. R. 1975. *Origins of the State and Civilization*. New York: W. W. Norton.

Shaffer, L. H. 1992. How to Interpret Music. In *Cognitive Bases of Musical Communication*, edited by M. R. Jones and S. Holleran (263–78). Washington, DC: American Psychological Association.

Shaw, G. L. 2000. *Keeping Mozart in Mind*. San Diego: Academic Press.

Shepard, R. N. 1975. Form, Formation, and Transformation of Internal Representations. In *Information Processing and Cognition*, edited by R. L. Solso (87–122). Hillsdale, NJ: Lawrence Erlbaum.

Shepherd, G. M. 1994. *Neurobiology*. New York: Oxford University Press.

Shira. 2000. That "Snake Charmer" Song. Available at http://www.shira.net/streets-of-cairo.htm.

Shweder, R. A. 1991. *Thinking Through Cultures*. Cambridge, MA: Harvard University Press.

Siegel, R. K., and M. E. Jarvik. 1975. Drug-Induced Hallucinations in Animals and Man. In *Hallucinations*, edited by R. K. Siegel and L. J. West (81–162). New York: John Wiley & Sons.

Simon, H. 1981. *The Sciences of the Artificial*. Cambridge, MA: MIT Press.

Simpson, G. E. 1978. *Black Religions in the New World*. New York: Columbia University Press.

Slawek, S. 1998. Terms, Practices, and Processes of Improvisation in Hindustani Instrumental Music. In *In the Course of Performance: Studies in the World of Musical Improvisation*, edited by B. Nettl and M. Russell (335–68). Chicago: University of Chicago Press.

Sloboda, J. 1985. *The Musical Mind*. Oxford: Oxford University Press.

———. 1992. Empirical Studies of Emotional Response to Music. In *Cognitive Bases of Musical Communication*, edited by M. R. Jones and S. Holleran (33–46). Washington, DC: American Psychological Association.

Small, C. 1987. *Music of the Common Tongue: Survival and Celebration in Afro-American Music*. New York: Riverrun Press.

———. 1998. *Musicking*. Hanover and London: Wesleyan University Press.

Sokolov, A. N. 1972. *Inner Speech and Thought*. New York: Plenum Press.

Southern, E. 1983. *The Music of Black Americans*. New York: W. W. Norton.

Speel, H-C. 1997. A Short Comment from a Biologist. *Journal of Social and Evolutionary Systems* 20(3): 309–14.

Sperry, R. W. 1968. Hemisphere Deconnection and Unity in Conscious Awareness. *American Psychologist* 23(10): 723–33.

Spitzer, D. D. 1972. Ira Sullivan: Living Legend. *Down Beat* 39: 14.

Springer, S. P., and G. Deutsch. 1998. *Left Brain, Right Brain: Perspectives from Cognitive Neuroscience*. New York: W. H. Freeman.

Stanislavski, K. 1948. *An Actor Prepares*. New York: Theatre Arts Books.

Starr, S. F. 1995. *Bamboula! The Life and Times of Louis Moreau Gottschalk*. New York: Oxford University Press.

Stebbins, G. L. 1982. *Darwin to DNA, Molecules to Humanity*. San Francisco: W. H. Freeman.

Stern, E., and J. Portugali. 1999. Environmental Cognition and Decision Making in Urban Navigation. In *Wayfinding Behavior: Cognitive Mapping and Other Spatial Processes*, edited by R. G. Golledge (99–119). Baltimore, MD: Johns Hopkins University Press.

Steward, J. 1955. *Theory of Cultural Change*. Urbana and Chicago: University of Illinois Press.

Stowe, D. 1994. *Swing Changes: Big Band Jazz in New Deal America*. Cambridge, MA: Harvard University Press.

Strogatz, S. H., and I. Stewart. 1993. Coupled Oscillators and Biological Synchronization. *Scientific American* (December): 102–9.

Strongman, K. T. 1973. *The Psychology of Emotion*. London: John Wiley & Sons.

Tart, C., ed. 1972. *Altered States of Consciousness*. New York: Anchor Books.

Taves, A. 1999. *Fits, Trances, & Visions*. Princeton, NJ: Princeton University Press.

Taylor, G. 1996. *Cultural Selection*. New York: Basic Books.

Taylor, G. R. 1970. *Sex in History*. New York: Harper and Row.

Thagard, P. 1992. *Conceptual Revolutions*. Princeton, NJ: Princeton University Press.

———. 2000. *Coherence in Thought and Action*. Cambridge, MA: MIT Press.

Thatcher, R. W., and E. R. John. 1977. *Foundations of Cognitive Processes*. Hillsdale, NJ: Lawrence Erlbaum.

Thelen, E., and L. B. Smith. 1994. *A Dynamic Systems Approach to the Development of Cognition and Action*. Cambridge, MA: MIT Press.

Time. 1998. 100 Years of Pop Music. *Time* 151: 157.

Tomasello, M., and J. Call. 1997. *Primate Cognition*. New York: Oxford University Press.

Tononi, G., and G. M. Edelman. 1998. Consciousness and Complexity. *Science* 282: 1846–51.

Tononi, G., G. M. Edelman, and O. Sporns. 1998. Complexity and Coherency: Integrating Information in the Brain. *Trends in Cognitive Sciences* 2(12):474–84.

Torgovnick, M. 1996. *Primitive Passions*. Chicago: University of Chicago Press.

Tramo, M. J. 2001. Music of the Hemispheres. *Science* 291(5501): 54–56.

Trehub, S. 2000. Human Processing Predispositions and Musical Universals. In *The Origins of Music*, edited by N. L. Wallin, B. Merker, and S. Brown (427–48). Cambridge, MA: MIT Press.

Trevarthen, C. 1993. Brain Science and the Human Spirit. In *Brain, Culture, and the Human Spirit*, edited by J. B. Ashbrook (129–82). Lanham, NY: University Press of America.

———. 1999–2000. Musicality and the Intrinsic Motive Pulse: Evidence from Human Psychobiology and Infant Communication. Special issue, *Musicae Scientiae*.

Turner, V. 1969. *The Ritual Process: Structure and Anti-Structure*. Ithaca: Cornell University Press.

———. 1993. Body, Brain and Culture. In *Brain, Culture, and the Human Spirit*, edited by J. B. Ashbrook (77–108). Lanham, NY: University Press of America.

Turvey, M. T., and C. Carello. 1995. Some Dynamical Themes in Perception and Action. In *Mind as Motion: Explorations in the Dynamics of Cognition*, edited by R. F. Port and T. van Gelder (373–402). Cambridge, MA: MIT Press.

Turvey, M. T., and R. E. Shaw. 1999. Ecological Foundations of Cognition I. Symmetry and Specificity of Animal-Environment Systems. In *Reclaiming Cognition*, edited by R. Núñez and W. J. Freeman (95–110). Bowling Green, OH: Imprint Academic.

Turvey, M. T., and R. E. Shaw. 1999. Ecological Foundations of Cognition II. Degrees of Freedom and Conserved Quantities in Animal-Environment Systems. In *Reclaiming Cognition*, edited by R. Núñez and W. J. Freeman (111–23). Bowling Green, OH: Imprint Academic.

Tylor, E. B. 1972. Animism. In *Reader in Comparative Religion*, edited by W. A. Lessa and E. Z. Vogt (9–19). New York: Harper and Row.

United States Army. 2000. *History of U.S. Army Bands*. Ft. Story, VA: U.S. Army Element School of Music's Directorate of Training and Doctrine. Available at http://bands.army.mil/history/default.asp.

Valins, S. 1970. The Perception and Labeling of Bodily Changes as Determinants of Emotional Behavior. In *Physiological Correlates of Emotion*, edited by P. Black (229–45). New York: Academic Press.

van Eeden, F. 1972. A Study of Dreams. In *Altered States of Consciousness*, edited by C. T. Tart (147–260). New York: Anchor Books.

van Gennup, A. 1960. *The Rites of Passage*. Chicago: University of Chicago Press.

Vanderwolf, C. H., and T. E. Robinson. 1981. Reticulo-cortical Activity and Behavior: A Critique of the Arousal Theory and a New Synthesis. *Behavioral and Brain Sciences* 4: 459–576.

Vaneechoutte, M., and J. R. Skoyles. 1998. The Memetic Origin of Language: Modern Humans as Musical Primates. *Journal of Memetics* 2. Available at http://www.cpm.ac.uk/jomemit/1998/vol2/vaneechoutte_m&skoyles_jr.html.

Vico, G. 1970. *The New Science of Giambattista Vico*. Ithaca: Cornell University Press.

Viswanathan, T., and J. Cormack. 1998. Melodic Improvisation in Karnatak Music. In *In the Course of Performance: Studies in the World of Musical Improvisation*, edited by B. Nettl and M. Russell (219–33). Chicago: University of Chicago Press.

von Neumann, J. 1958. *The Computer and the Brain*. New Haven: Yale University Press.

Vygotsky, L. S. 1962. *Thought and Language*. Cambridge, MA: MIT Press.

Wallace, J. 1997. Brass Solo and Chamber Music from 1800. In *The Cambridge Companion to Brass Instruments*, edited by T. Herbert and J. Wallace (236–54). Cambridge: Cambridge University Press.

Wallin, N. L. 1991. *Biomusicology*. Stuyvesant, NY: Pendragon Press.

Wallin, N. L., B. Merker, and S. Brown. 2000. *The Origins of Music*. Cambridge, MA: MIT Press.

Waterman, C. A. 1990. *Jùjú: A Social History and Ethnography of an African Popular Music*. Chicago: University of Chicago Press.

Watkins, M. 1994. *On the Real Side: Laughing, Lying, and Signifying: The Underground Tradition of African-American Humor*. New York: Simon and Schuster.

Weinberger, N. M. 1997. Threads of Music in the Tapestry of Memory. *MuSICA Research Notes* 4(1). Available at http://www.musica.uci.edu/mrn/V4I1S97.html.

Weinstein, N. C. 1992. *A Night in Tunisia: Imagining of Africa in Jazz*. Metuchen, NJ, and London: Scarecrow Press.

Weiss, H., and R. S. Bradley. 2001. What Drives Societal Collapse. *Science* 291(5504): 609–10.

Werner, D. 1990. *Amazon Journey: An Anthropologist's Year Among Brazil's Mekranoti Indians*. Englewood Cliffs, NJ: Prentice-Hall.

White, L. A. 1959. *The Evolution of Culture*. New York: McGraw-Hill.

Wickler, W. 1973. *The Sexual Code*. Garden City, NY: Anchor Books.

Wiener, N. 1948. *Cybernetics*. Cambridge, MA: MIT Press.

Williams, L. 1980. *The Dancing Chimpanzee*. London: Allison & Busby.

Williams, P. L., and R. Warwick. 1975. *Functional Neuroanatomy of Man*. Philadelphia: W. B. Saunders.

Williams, R. 1976. *Keywords: A Vocabulary of Culture and Society*. New York: Oxford University Press.

Williamson, J. 1984. *The Crucible of Race*. New York and Oxford: Oxford University Press.

Wilson, F. R. 1986. *Tone Deaf & All Thumbs?* New York: Random House.

———. 1998. *The Hand: How Its Use Shapes the Brain, Language, and Human Culture*. New York: Random House.

Winkelman, M. J. 1992. *Shamans, Priests and Witches: A Cross-Cultural Study of Magico-Religious Practitioners*. Tempe: Arizona State University Press.

Wiora, W. 1965. *The Four Ages of Music*. New York: W. W. Norton.

Wright, R. 2000. *Nonzero*. New York: Pantheon Books.

Young-Bruehl, E. 1996. *The Anatomy of Prejudices*. Cambridge, MA: Harvard University Press.

Zivin, G., ed. 1979. *The Development of Self-Regulation Through Private Speech*. New York: John Wiley & Sons.

Index